Maryland's German Heritage

Daniel Wunderlich Nead's History

Edited by
Don Heinrich Tolzmann

HERITAGE BOOKS
2023

HERITAGE BOOKS

AN IMPRINT OF HERITAGE BOOKS, INC.

Books, CDs, and more—Worldwide

For our listing of thousands of titles see our website
at
www.HeritageBooks.com

A Facsimile Reprint
Published 2023 by
HERITAGE BOOKS, INC.
Publishing Division
5810 Ruatan Street
Berwyn Heights, MD 20740

International Standard Book Number
Paperbound: 978-0-7884-0064-3

Editor's Introduction

According to the U.S. Census, German-Americans number 26% of the population of the state of of Maryland, thereby making the German element clearly the state's largest ethnic group. (1) A recent directory of Maryland's German-American organizations indicate that there is a wide variety of activities, programs, and events taking place across the state. Among the state's organizations, there are several noteworthy ones.

The German Society of Maryland, established in 1783 "to assist persons of German origin residing in the State of Maryland," is one of the oldest German-American organizations in the U.S. Also of note is the Society for the History of the Germans in Maryland, the nation's oldest German-American historical society, which was established in 1886, and publishes an excellent historical journal. (2)

The foundations for Maryland's German heritage, of course, are to be found in the colonial era of American history. The purpose of this work is to focus on that early period of Maryland German history by means of this new edition of Nead's work, which originally appeared in 1913. (3)

Nead illuminates the German dimension, focusing specifically on the role the Pennsylvania Germans played in founding the German element of Maryland. This demonstrates how inextricably the German heritage of Pennsylvania and Maryland are interrelated. As Germans in the colonial era came to move southwards, they moved not only into Maryland, but also into Virginia, and then onwards into the Ohio Valley. (4)

As Dieter Cunz notes, the Germans from Pennsylvania "pushed forward into the backwoods, penetrated into the hinterland...Boundaries did not mean very much to them. Soon the overflow drifted into the nearest province south of Pennsylvania, into the colony of the Calverts: Maryland." (5)

Regarding the location of the German element in the eighteenth century Albert Faust notes that there were two centers, Western Maryland and Baltimore. In the latter, German-Americans were involved mainly with business, industry, and commerce, whereas in the west they were mainly involved in agriculture. Here they formed a link of the German farms between Pennsylvania and the Valley of Virginia. This work, as noted, focuses on the western German settlement, which came from Pennsylvania. (6)

In his history of the Maryland Germans, Cunz divided Maryland German history into several periods. First, there was the colonial period, which lasted to 1790. Second, there was the period to the Civil War. And, third, there was the period from the Civil War to the period of the World Wars. As his book was published in the 1940s, a following period needs now to be added. This fourth and most recent period of German-American history has been described as the ethnic revival period. (7) As noted earlier, the purpose of this volume is to illuminate the early colonial period of Maryland German history.

For those interested in further information regarding Maryland's German heritage, references can be found in the standard bibliographies of German-American history. (8)

Notes

1. See Don Heinrich Tolzmann, "1990 Census Statistics," **Society for German-American Studies Newsletter.** 14:1(1993): 6-7.

2. For further information on the German societies of Maryland, see **German-American Organizations in Maryland.** (Baltimore, MD: Deutschamerikanischer Bürgerverein von Maryland, Inc., 1990).

3. This work originally appeared as: "The Pennsylvania German in the Settlement of Maryland," **Pennsylvania German Society Proceedings and Addresses.** 22(1913): 5-304.

4. For further information on the Virginia Germans, see Don Heinrich Tolzmann, ed., **The German Element in Virginia: Herrmann Schuricht's History.** (Bowie, MD: Heritage Books, Inc., 1993). For information regarding the German element in the Ohio Valley, see Emil Klauprecht, **German Chronicle in the History of the Ohio Valley and its Capital City Cincinnati in Particular.** Trans. by Dale V. Lally, Jr., Ed. by Don Heinrich Tolzmann. (Bowie, MD: Heritage Books, Inc., 1992).

5. See Dieter Cunz, **The Maryland Germans: A History.** (Princeton, NJ: Princeton University Pr., 1948), p. 11.

6. See Albert B. Faust, **The German Element in the United States.** (Boston: Houghton Mifflin Co., 1909), Vol. 1, p. 176.

7. For a discussion of the periods of German-American history, see Don Heinrich Tolzmann, ed., **Germany and America, 1450-1700: Julius Friedrich Sachse's History of the German Role in the Discovery, Exploration, and Settlement of the New World.** (Bowie, MD: Heritage Books, Inc., 1991), pp. 16-28.

8. For bibliographical references to sources dealing with Maryland's German heritage, see Don Heinrich Tolzmann, **German-Americana: A Bibliography.** (Metuchen, NJ: Scarecrow Pr., 1975), as well as by the same author: **Catalog of the German-Americana Collection, University of Cincinnati.** (München: K.G. Saur, 1990).

The

Pennsylvania=German

in the

Settlement of Maryland

BY

DANIEL WUNDERLICH NEAD, M.D. (UNIV. OF PA.)

*Member of the Pennsylvania-German Society; the Historical Society of
Pennsylvania; the Historical Society of Berks County; the
Pennsylvania Society of Sons of the Revolution, etc.*

"Forsan et haec olim meminisse juvabit."—VIRGIL

ILLUSTRATED BY JULIUS F. SACHSE, LITT.D.

PART XXV. OF A NARRATIVE AND CRITICAL HISTORY
PREPARED AT THE REQUEST OF
THE PENNSYLVANIA-GERMAN SOCIETY

LANCASTER, PA.
1914

PRESS OF
THE NEW ERA PRINTING COMPANY
LANCASTER, PA.

FOREWORD.

FOR a century and a half the term "Mason and Dixon's Line" has been a more or less familiar expression, and for the greater part of the latter half of that period it was frequently on men's tongues. The lines drawn on the earth's surface by geographers or laid out by the wisdom of statecraft are often taken in too literal a sense; and so, in the course of time, it came to pass that Mason and Dixon's Line came to be regarded almost as a tangible barrier: the line dividing the North from the South. Yet, as a mater of fact, were it not for the monuments set up at stated intervals it would be impossible to tell where the jurisdiction of one commonwealth ends and that of the other begins. The mountains and valleys are continuous, the fertile fields lie side by side, there is no difference to be found in the people, and it not unfrequently happens that a farm will lie partly on one side of the line and partly on the other, and there are even houses through which the line runs, one part of the house being in Maryland and the other part in Pennsylvania.

But outside of the question of contiguity there is a sentimental attachment between the states of Maryland and Pennsylvania. Had the boundary between the two colonies been fixed at the point where the respective charters apparently placed it, the fortieth parallel of north latitude, a considerable portion of the territory now included within the state of Pennsylvania would belong to Maryland. The fortieth parallel runs about on a line with Lehigh Avenue in Philadelphia, so that had that meridian been decided on as the dividing line between the two colonies the greater part of the city of Philadelhia would now be situated in Maryland. So too would be a strip of territory nearly twenty miles in width, extending across the state and taking in such towns as West Chester, York, Chambersburg, and all the fertile country surrounding those towns.

In the following pages an attempt has been made to gather together in brief form what is known concerning the influence of the Pennsylvanians in the settlement of the western part of the colony of Maryland. There is no claim of originality, but use has been freely made of the results of other investigations. It is very unfortunate that there are but few records in existence concerning the period under consideration, so that many points cannot be determined, but what is known has been put together in concise form for convenient reference.

The writer wishes here to express his thanks to Dr. Julius F. Sachse for preparing the illustrations, which add materially to the interest in the work, and also to Dr. Frank R. Diffenderffer for material assistance in searching old records.

Daniel Wunderlich Nead

READING, PENNSYLVANIA,
December, 1913.

CONTENTS.

CHAPTER XVII.

CHAPTER XVIII.

CHAPTER XIX.

1**

BIBLIOGRAPHY.

Archives of Maryland.

Banvard, Joseph. Pioneers of the New World, and the Old French War. Chicago, 1880.

Bozman, John Leeds. The History of Maryland from its first Settlement, in 1633, to the Restoration, in 1660. 2 vols. Baltimore, 1837.

Browne, William Hand. Maryland, the History of a Palatinate. Boston, 1904.

Brumbaugh, Martin Grove. A History of the German Baptist Brethren in Europe and America. Mount Morris, Ill., 1899.

Colonial Records of Pennsylvania.

Doddridge, Joseph. Notes on the Settlements and Indian Wars of the Western Parts of Virginia and Pennsylvania, from the Year 1763 until the Year 1783. Wellsburgh, Va., 1824.

Eddis, William. Letters from America, Historical and Descriptive. London, 1792.

Griffith, Thomas W. Annals of Baltimore. Baltimore, 1824.

Harbaugh, Henry. The Life of Michael Schlatter. Philadelphia, 1857.

James, Bartlett B. The Labadist Colony in Maryland. Baltimore, 1899.

Johnson, John. Old Maryland Manors. Baltimore, 1883.

Kercheval, Samuel. A History of the Valley of Virginia. Woodstock, Va., 1850.

Kuhns, Levi Oscar. The German and Swiss Settlements of Colonial Pennsylvania. New York, 1901.

McCormac, Eugene Irving. White Servitude in Maryland, 1634–1820. Baltimore, 1904.

McMahon, J. V. L. An Historical View of the Government of Maryland, from its Colonization to the Present Day. Baltimore, 1837.

McSherry, James. History of Maryland. Baltimore, 1904.

Mereness, Newton D. Maryland as a Proprietary Province. New York, 1901.

Neill, Edward. The Founders of Maryland as Portrayed in Manuscripts, Provincial Records and Early Documents. Albany, 1876.

Pennsylvania Archives, First and Second Series.

Ridgely, David. Annals of Annapolis. Baltimore, 1841.

Scharf, J. Thomas. The Chronicles of Baltimore. Baltimore, 1874.

—— History of Maryland from the Earliest Period to the Present Day. 3 vols. Baltimore, 1879.

—— History of Western Maryland, being a History of Frederick, Montgomery, Carroll, Washington, Allegany and Garrett Counties. 2 vols. Philadelphia, 1882.

Sioussat, St. George Leakin. Economics and Politics in Maryland, 1720–1750. Baltimore, 1903.

Steiner, Bernard C. Beginnings of Maryland, 1631–1639. Baltimore, 1903.

—— Maryland under the Commonwealth. A Chronicle of the Years 1649–1658. Baltimore, 1911.

—— Maryland during the English Civil Wars. Baltimore, 1906–7.

—— Western Maryland in the Revolution. Baltimore, 1902.

Schultz, Edward T. First Settlements of Germans in Maryland. Frederick, Md., 1896.

Society for the History of Germans in Maryland. 16 annual reports.

Thomas, James Walter. Chronicles of Colonial Maryland. Baltimore, 1900.

CHAPTER I.

THE MARYLAND COLONY.

T HE settlement of Maryland was the culmination of the plan of George, Lord Baltimore, to found a colony where the inhabitants might worship God according to the dictates of their consciences.[1] Sir George Calvert was brought up a Protestant and, enjoying the personal friendship of James I., he obtained rapid advancement in the government service and was finally made

---

[1] "It cannot with evident certainty be stated that Sir George Calvert, in the settlement of either of his provinces, Avalon or Maryland, had in view the formation of an asylum for English Catholics, although it is so stated by several historians; such intention of his being nowhere clearly expressed by himself, unless it be in the before mentioned MS. account of Avalon, by Sir George himself, still remaining in the British Museum, the contents of which we have no opportunity of examining. With regard to Maryland, the fact, ascertained in history, as well in the records of the province, that most of the first colonists of that province were Roman Catholics, leaves a strong inference that it was the original contemplation of Sir George thereby to erect for such Catholics a place of refuge. In respect to Avalon, however, we have not this fact, as a ground for such inference."— Bozman's "History of Maryland," Vol. I., p. 242.

principal Secretary of State. In 1624 he became a Roman Catholic and at once resigned his position as Secretary, but the king kept him as a member of the Privy Council and created him Lord Baltimore, of Baltimore, in Ireland.

At this time the laws of England were very severe against the Roman Catholics and in order to escape persecution Lord Baltimore determined to found a colony where religious liberty would be secured to all the inhabitants. For some years he had been interested in schemes for colonizing America, having been one of the councillors of the New England Company and a member of the Virginia Company until its charter was revoked, when he was appointed one of the council for the government of that colony. He first turned his attention to New Foundland and, securing a grant in that locality, he erected a province which he named Avalon.[2]   After first sending a small party of colonists, he went thither himself with his family, but a residence of two years convinced him that that locality was not suited for the successful planting of a colony, and he sailed for Virginia.

The authorities in the Virginia colony would not allow him to land unless he would take the oath of allegiance and supremacy, and this his religious principles would not allow him to do. He, therefore, sailed north and explored the shores of the Chesapeake above the Virginia settle-

[2] Bozman, Vol. 1, p. 240, quotes Oldmixon's "British Empire in America," as follows: "This gentleman" (Sir George Calvert) "being of the Romish religion was uneasy at home, and had the same reason to leave the kingdom, as those gentlemen had, who went to New England, to enjoy the liberty of his conscience. He therefore resolved to retire to America, and finding the New Foundland company had made no use of their grant, he thought of this place for his retreat; to which end he procured a patent for that part of the island, that lies between the bay of Bulls in the east, and cape St. Mary's in the south, which was erected into a province, and called Avalon."

ment, and finding this territory suitable for his purpose he returned to England and petitioned Charles I., who by that time had succeeded his father, for a grant of land in that locality. Opposition arose from the Virginia authorities and, although the king was favorably disposed toward Lord Baltimore, the matter was delayed, and before the charter was finally granted, on June 20, 1632, Lord Baltimore died, and the charter, when issued, was in the name of his eldest son, Cecilius.

The charter granted to Lord Baltimore was the most liberal ever granted by the English crown. It erected the colony into a palatinate,[3] and created the proprietary but little short of a ruling sovereign. He was made "absolute lord of the land and water within his boundaries, could erect towns, cities, and ports, make war or peace, call the whole fighting population to arms, and declare martial law, levy tolls and duties, establish courts of justice, appoint judges, magistrates, and other civil officers, execute the laws, and pardon offenders; he could erect manors with courts-baron and courts-leet, and confer titles and dignities, so that they differed from those of England; he could make laws with the assent of the freemen of the province, and, in cases of emergency, ordinances not impairing life,

[3] The term *Palatinate* originated with the early Frankish or German rulers who bestowed on an officer known as the "Count of the Palace" (*comes palatii*, or *palatinus*) certain powers nearly equaling those of royalty. Later these powers were bestowed on powerful vassals who, to all intents and purposes, became kings, except that they acknowledged the suzerainty of the appointing sovereign. In England certain counties were made palatinates, and the charter granted to Lord Baltimore gave him all the "rights, jurisdictions, privileges, prerogatives, royalties, liberties, immunities and royal rights, and temporal franchises whatsoever . . . as any bishop of Durham, within the bishopric or county palatine of Durham, in our kingdom of England, ever heretofore hath had, held, used, or enjoyed, or of right could, or ought to have held, use or enjoy."

limb, or property, without their assent; he could found churches and chapels, have them consecrated according to the ecclesiastical laws of England, and appoint the incumbents."

Having received his charter, Lord Baltimore immediately proceeded to organize an expedition to colonize the territory which had been granted to him. He secured two vessels, the *Ark* and the *Dove,* on which his party of colonists embarked and sailed from Cowes on November 22, 1633. There were about two hundred in the party, of whom about twenty were "gentlemen adventurers," as they were called: men of fortune who took part in the enterprise partly in a spirit of adventure, although, no doubt, some of them sought a religious asylum, the balance of the company being made up of servants and craftsmen of various kinds. Lord Baltimore had intended accompanying the expedition, but his presence in England being necessary he placed his brother Leonard in command as governor. Early in the following spring they reached the Chesapeake, and after stopping at an island near the mouth of the Potomac, which they named St. Clement's, where, on March 25, 1634, they celebrated their first mass in the new world, Governor Calvert with a small party started out to seek a suitable location for their settlement. He had secured as guide Henry Fleete, an Englishman who was well acquainted with that part of the country, having spent several years among the Indians. But although Fleete was thoroughly acquainted with the surrounding country he was not the first of his countrymen to visit it.

The first white man to visit the territory now embraced within the state of Maryland was Captain John Smith, of Virginia. Very soon after the foundation of the Jamestown settlement that hardy pioneer turned his attention to exploring the country to the north, and in the summer of 1608 he made two trips in an open boat, with a few companions, and made his way as far north as the mouth of the Susquehanna, exploring the different rivers and marking them on his map with an accuracy that is scarcely exceeded at the present day. He rowed up the Potomac river to a point above the present site of Washington, as far as he could go in his boat, and has given us a comprehensive description of that part of the country. Of this expedition Lossing says:[4] "It was one of the most wonderful of exploring expeditions, considered in all its aspects."

Under the guidance of Fleete the party went a short distance up the Potomac, and at a point where an Indian town already existed a tract of land was purchased from the Indians and a town laid out which was named St. Mary's. During their first year the colonists subsisted largely upon supplies of food, chiefly Indian corn, obtained from the Indians. The policy followed by Governor Calvert in his treatment of the Indians was such as to gain their friendship, and thus were avoided many of the disasters which overtook colonists in other parts of the country. The Maryland settlers, as a rule, were free from attacks by hostile Indians.

It was evidently Lord Baltimore's intention to found an aristocratic state, based on large holdings of land, the land to be kept in the family of the original owner through the law of entail. The first allotment of land to the settlers was made with this end in view. In the proprietary's instructions to his brother Leonard, who represented him, he advises him that he is to

4 Quoted by Scharf, "Chronicles of Baltimore," p. 8.

"make or cause to be made under our great seal of that our said province unto every first adventurer for every five men aged between sixteen and fifty years, which such adventurer did bring into our said province to inhabitt and plant there in the year of our Lord 1633, and unto his heirs forever, a grant of two thousand acres of land of English measure for the yearly rent of 400 lb. of good wheat, . . .

And we do further will and authorize you, that every two thousand acres, and every three thousand acres, and every one thousand acres of land so to be passed or granted as aforesaid unto any adventurer or adventurers, be erected, and created into a manor to be called by such name as the adventurer or adventurers shall desire."[5]

But this plan of Lord Baltimore's did not succeed. While it was possible for a colonist, by bringing over a large number of servants, to obtain a large grant of land, it was unusual to find plantations containing more than one thousand acres. Prior to 1700 there were few towns and these did not grow very rapidly. The character and occupations of the inhabitants militated against the growth of towns. The colony of Maryland had been established by Lord Baltimore as a religious asylum where the inhabitants might worship God according to the dictates of their consciences, and although he was a Roman Catholic, no attempt was made to prevent those who belonged to Protestant denominations from settling in the colony. Indeed, it is probable that of the first colonists the greater number were Protestants. Most, if not all, of the "gentlemen adventurers" were probably Roman Catholics, but of the servants and laborers there is no doubt that a very large proportion were Protestants, although there is no way of accurately determining this, as there is no record of the names of all the colonists. These settlers were planters

[5] Bozman's "History of Maryland," Vol. II., pp. 38-40.

and farmers and the plantations were, as a rule, spread over a rather extended territory. There were no manufactories, and what manufactured goods were required were brought over from England.

Following the example of the Virginia colonists, the newcomers almost immediately began the cultivation of tobacco. Indeed more attention was paid to this than to anything else. The chief aim of the planters was to raise as much tobacco as possible, for, being the currency of the colony, all other commodities were purchasable with it, and a man's possessions were reckoned in accordance with the amount of tobacco he could produce. The natural consequence of this state of affairs was that the quality of the tobacco soon began to deteriorate, while the growing of corn and other necessaries of life almost ceased. As early as 1639 an act was passed compelling every grower of tobacco to plant and cultivate two acres of corn for each member of his family. The next year another act was passed limiting the culture of tobacco to so many plants per head, but even these laws did not improve matters much. The colony did not grow very rapidly, the settlers confined themselves almost entirely to the territory adjacent to tidewater, and it was not until the coming of the German settlers, who by their thrift and industry showed the possibilities of the fertile fields, that the colony began to make rapid strides forward.

CHAPTER II.

THE FIRST GERMAN SETTLERS.

THERE is nothing in the records to show that there were any Germans among the first party sent out by Lord Baltimore to found the colony of Maryland, but it is extremely probable that among that company of two hundred people, consisting chiefly of servants and artisans, there were a number of Germans. The colony had been founded as an English settlement, and it is evident that foreigners were not desired, for while there was no direct prohibition of the settlement of foreigners in the colony, there was no inducement to lead them in that direction. The terms upon which land was to be granted to colonists was such as to lead to the formation of an aristocracy, which was undoubtedly Lord Baltimore's purpose, and naturally this aristocracy would be expected to be made up of wealthy Englishmen who could take advantage of the conditions of plantation. According to the

A PENNSYLVANIA-GERMAN LOOM AND SPINNING-WHEEL.

instructions sent out by Lord Baltimore to his brother, in 1636, any member of the first party of colonists who brought over with him five men was to receive two thousand acres of land subject to an annual quit-rent of four hundred pounds of wheat. The same allotment of land was made to those who came over in the years 1634 and 1635, bringing with them ten men, but the rent was to be six hundred pounds of wheat, and those who came over later, or brought fewer men, were to be granted smaller amounts of land.[6] As Bozman says:[7] " It will be readily perceived, that these instructions, or conditions of plantation, were well calculated to induce men of some property in England, who were able to bear the expense of transporting servants and dependents, to emigrate to this province. It is true, that it was sketching out aristocratic features in the future government of the province, which in other times, might have been supposed to operate in discouragement of emigration."

But it was evidently this class of people that Lord Baltimore wanted, and foreigners were not even allowed to own land nor had they any political rights. It was not until 1648 that foreigners were allowed to take up land. In the commission of William Stone, lieutenant of the province, accompanying the conditions of plantation of 1648, and dated at Bath, August 20, 1648, Lord Baltimore writes:

And we do hereby authorize and Require you till we or our heirs shall signify our of their Pleasure to the Contrary from time to time in our name and under the Great Seal of the said Province of Maryland to Grant Lands within our said Province to all Adventurors or Planters to or within the same upon such terms and

[6] Archives of Maryland, Vol. III, p. 47.
[7] " History of Maryland," Vol. II., p. 38.

Conditions as are expressed in the said last Conditions of Plantation bearing date with these presents and according to the forms of Grants above mentioned and not otherwise without further and special warrant hereafter to be obtain[d] for the same under our or our heirs hand and seal at Arms and whereas we are Given to understand that as well divers Frenchmen as some other People of other Nations who by our former as also by these last Conditions of Plantation are not Capable of having any lands within our said Province and are already seated or may hereafter with our or you our Lieutenants leave there for the time being seat themselves in our said Province we do hereby Authorize you to make any Person or Persons of French Dutch or Italian discent as you shall think fit and who either are already planted or shall hereafter come and Plant in our said Province Capable of our said last Conditions of Plantation and do hereby Give you Power to Grant Lands thereupon within our said Province unto them and every of them accordingly as well for and in respect of themselves as for and in respect of any Person or Persons of British or Irish discent or of any of the other discents aforesaid which they or any of them and also which any other Person of British or Irish discent shall hereafter with our or you our said Lieutenants leave transport into the said province in the same and in as ample manner and upon the same terms and Provisoes as you are hereby or by our Commission to you for the Government of the said Province authorised to Grant any Lands to any Adventuror or Planter of British or Irish discent within the said Province.[8]

The following year the conditions of plantation were abrogated and new ones issued under date of July 2, 1649. The new ones were practically the same as those issued the year before except that they authorized an increase in the size of the manors to be granted. Lord Baltimore gives as his reason for issuing the new ones that those of 1648 "were not like to give sufficient encouragement to many

[8] Archives of Maryland, Vol. III., p. 222.

to adventure and plant there." Bozman seems to think[9] that this action on the part of Lord Baltimore, in allowing foreigners to take up land, was prompted chiefly by his anxiety to increase the population of the province, and that he was undoubtedly indifferent as to what sect of Protestant religion his colonists belonged. Whether this liberality on the part of Lord Baltimore led to any increase in the number of Germans who settled in the colony is not evident, but it is extremely probable that it did have that effect. There is no doubt that from a very early period in the history of Maryland the colony was constantly receiving additions from the neighboring colony on the Delaware, which at the time of the founding of the colony of Maryland was under the control of the Dutch. It is true that these additions were not made up of a very desirable class of people, consisting chiefly, as they did, of runaway servants. The records of the Dutch and Swedish colonies on the Delaware frequently mention occurrences of this kind. In a letter from Director-General Peter Stuyvesant to the directors of the Dutch West India Company, dated September 4, 1659, he says:[10]

The City's affairs on the Southriver are in a very deplorable and low state. It is to be feared, that, if no other and better order is introduced, it will be ruined altogether; it would be too long and tedious, to report all the complaints brought from there, nor can all be received (as true;) but it is certainly true, that the people begin to run away in numbers, as for instance, while I write this, there arrives from there an English ketch, which went there with some provisions from Boston three weeks ago; the skipper of it, a well-known and trustworthy man, says that during his stay of 14 days at the Southriver about 50 persons, among them whole families, run away from there to Virginia and Maryland.

9 "History of Maryland," Vol. II., p. 342.
10 Pennsylvania Archives, Second Series, Vol. VII., p. 611.

Again, on the 17th of the same month Stuyvesant writes :[11]

> We mentioned in our last letter the deplorable and bad state of affairs in the City's Colony on the Southriver, caused by the desertion and removal of the Colonists to Maryland, Virginia and other places, which increases daily in such a manner, that hardly thirty families remain.

It is very probable that the state of affairs was greatly exaggerated by Stuyvesant, as there is no record of such wholesale additions to the population of Maryland, and the few stragglers who did make their way into that colony were not in sufficient numbers to leave any records of their doings. One of the first of the German settlers in Maryland of whom we have any record, and the first who may be called a Pennsylvania-German, was Cornelius Commegys. He had formerly lived in the colony on the Delaware, and after spending some time there had removed to Maryland. The exact date of his arrival in the latter colony is not known, but it was probably about 1661, as he was naturalized on July 22 of that year. In the same year Augustine Herman, writing to Vice-Director Beekman, of the Dutch colony on the Delaware, says: "Nothing could be done with Cornelius Comegys this year, it must be done next year and some other instructions sent from the Manhattans, which upon my return home I shall help your Honor to procure."[12] This would seem to indicate that there was some trouble in connection with Commegys's removal to Maryland. Weishaar[13] says that

---

[11] Ibid., p. 617.

[12] Pennsylvania Archives, Second Series, Vol. VII., p. 697.

[13] Report of the Society for the History of the Germans in Maryland, Vol. XV., p. 19.

on July 30, 1666, Commegys received a patent for 150 acres of land in Cecil county. Later on he obtained a much larger tract of land, for the proceedings of Council show[14] that on December 15, 1669, he was granted a patent for 350 acres of land. There is very little known of the history of Cornelius Commegys. Weishaar says: "When in 1679 the two Labadists, Danker-Schilders and Sluyter-Vorstmann visited Maryland, they found Commegys in possession of a large farm, and his son Cornelius was about to buy a farm for himself. His first wife Wilhemintye, however, had died, and he was married again to an English woman."

It may be interesting to note the manner in which foreigners were naturalized at this time. It must be remembered, however, that at that period there was not the same distinction between the terms Dutch and German that there is to-day. In fact, the term German was rarely used, and the appellation *Dutchman* was indiscriminately applied to the representatives of all the Teutonic races. Under the heading "Denization of Swedes and Dutch," in the Proceedings of Council, appears the following paper:[15]

"Cæcelius Absolute Lord and Proprietary of the Provinces of Maryland and Avalon Lord Barron of Baltemore &c To all persons to whome theis shall come Greeting in our Lord God Everlasting. Whereas Peter Meyor late of New Amstell and Subject of the Crowne of Sweeden hauing transported himselfe his wife and Children into this our Province here to inhabite hath besought us to grante him the said Peter Meyor leaue here to Inhabite and as a free Dennizen freedome land to him and his heires to purchase Knowe yee that we Doe hereby Declare them the said Peter Meyor his wife and Children as well those already borne as those here-

14 Archives of Maryland, Vol. V., p. 59.
15 Ibid., Vol. III., p. 428.

2*

after to be borne to be free Dennizens of this our Province of
Maryland And doe further for vs our heires and Successors
straightly enjoyne Constitute ordeine and Command that the said
Peter Meyer be in all things held treated reputed and esteemed as
one of the faythful people of us our heires and Successors borne
within this our Province of Maryland And likewise and lands tenements Revenues Services and other hereditam⁺ˢ whatsoeuʳ within
our said Province of Maryland may inherrite or otherwise purchase
receive take haue hould buy and possesse and them may occupye and
enjoye Give Sell alyen and bequeathe as likewise all libertyes franchises and priviledges of this our Province of Maryland freely
quietly and peaceably haue and possesse occupye and enjoye as our
faythful people borne or to be borne within our said Province of
Maryland without lett Molestacõn vexacõn trouble or Greivance
of us our heires and Successoʳˢ and Custome to the contrary hereof
in any wise notwithstanding Giuen at Saint Marys vnder the Great
Seale of our said Province of Maryland this two and twentyth day
of July in the thirtyth yeare of our dominion over the said Province
of Maryland Annoq domini One thousand six hundred Sixty one
Wittness our Deare Brother Philip Calvert Esqʳ our Leivetennant
of our said Province of Maryland."

Accompanying this paper is the following list of names
of persons who were to be included in this process of
naturalization:

Axell Stille	Bartholomew Hendrickson
Peter Jacobson	Cornelius Urinson
Marcus Sipherson	John Urinson
Clement Micheelson	Andreu Toreson
Hendrik Hendrickson	Paul Johnson
Andrew Clementson	Gothofrid Harmer
Peter Montson	Jacob Micheelson
Hendrick Mathiason	Cornelius Comages
Mathias Cornelison	Michaell Vandernorte
John Wheeler	

While this naturalization apparently accorded to the persons naturalized all the rights and privileges of natural-born citizens, such was evidently not the case, for at the meeting of the assembly thirteen years later, 1674, a number of these persons along with others, presented a petition asking that

they and every one of them shall from henceforth be adjudged reputed and taken as natureall borne people of this Prouince of Maryland and alsoe that they and every one of them shall and may from henceforth by the same Authority be enabled and adjudged to all intents and Purposes able to demand Challenge aske haue hold and Injoy any Lands Tenements Rents & Hereditaments within this Prouince as Heire or Heires to any of their Ancestors by Reason of any discent in fee simple feetayle Generall or Speciall or Remainder vppon and fee Tayle generall or speciall to come to them or any of them by discent in fee simple feetayle Generall Speciall or Remainder vppon any Estate tayle as aforesaid or by any other Lawfull Conveyance or Conveyances or meanes whatsoever as if they and every of them had been borne within this Prouince or were of Brittish or Irish discent as aforesaid and alsoe that they and every of them from henceforth shall and may be Enabled to prosecute maintaine & avow Justifie and defend all manner of accons suites plaints or other demands whatsoever as Liberally franckly freely Lawfully fully and securely as if all of them had been Natureall borne within the Prouince of Maryland.[16]

The most distinguished German who at that period made his home in Maryland was Augustine Herman. Although he was born at Prague, Bohemia, it is very probable that Herman was a German. He entered the service

---

[16] Archives of Maryland, Vol. II., p. 400. The names in this petition show how rapidly the process of anglicizing the names of foreigners proceeded. For instance, Hendrik Hendrickson had become Henry Henderson; Hendrick Mathiason, Henry Mathews; Andrew Clementson, Andrew Clements.

of the Dutch West India Company and came to New
Amsterdam, where he attained a position of prominence
and married a relative of Peter Stuyvesant. When the
trouble between the Maryland colony and the Dutch
settlers on the Delaware seemed to be reaching an acute
stage on account of the actions of Col. Nathaniel Utie,
who had been sent to the Delaware colony by Governor
Fendall, of Maryland, and notified the settlers there that
the territory in question belonged to Maryland and declared that they must either leave or recognize the authority of Maryland, Augustine Herman was sent by Stuyvesant as one of the commissioners to confer with the
Maryland authorities and try to bring about a settlement
of the difficulty. Their mission was a failure, but Herman
seems to have been very favorably impressed with the
locality and determined to make his home in Maryland.
The various boundary disputes had taught Herman the
importance of having a map of the territory, and he made
a proposition to Lord Baltimore to the effect that he would
make a map of the country if he were granted a certain
amount of land with the privilege of a manor. This proposition was accepted, and in September, 1660, Herman
received a grant of four thousand acres of land, to be
selected where he saw fit. The tract chosen was on the
Elk river, and early in the following year, having bought
the land from the Indians, he settled on Bohemia Manor,
as he named his acquisition. He immediately went to
work on his map, which was completed in 1670. It
covered the whole section of country between North Carolina and the Hudson river. In the acknowledgment of
the receipt of the map Herman was informed

That His Lordship had received no small Satisfaction by the
variety of that mapp, and that the Kings Majesty, His Royall

Highness, and all others commended the exactness of the work, applauding it for the best mapp that ever was drawn of any country.

Herman was naturalized by act of assembly on September 17, 1763, it being the first act of this kind passed by the assembly. It also included Herman's brother-in-law, George Hack, Garrett Ruttzn and Jacob Clauson. The record of this transaction in the "Assembly Proceedings, September–October, 1663," is as follows:[17]

Thursday Sep[t] 17th

Then was read the pet[n] of Augustine Herman for an Act for Naturalizacōn for himselfe Children and his brother in Lawe George Hack

Ordered that An Acte of Naturalizacōn be prepared for the Consideracōn of both howses to naturalize Garrett Ruttzn and his Children and Jacob Clauson ffreemen of this Province

.   .   .   .

Ordered likewise that an Acte of Naturalizacōn be prepared for Augustine Herman, and his Children and his brother in Lawe George Hack and his wife and Children.

Herman attained considerable prominence in the colony and filled various offices. He took an active part in the quarrels arising over the boundary between Maryland and Pennsylvania, and his house was named, in 1682, as the place of meeting for Lord Baltimore and Governor Markham, of Pennsylvania, to discuss the question. It was also on Herman's land that the Labadist colony was established.[18] The Labadists were a pietistic sect founded in Germany about 1669 by Jean de Labadie. Labadie, who

[17] Archives of Maryland, Vol. I., p. 462.

[18] For a full account of the Labadists see "The Labadist Colony in Maryland," by Bartlett B. James.

was born in 1610, had been educated as a Jesuit priest, but his pronounced inclination towards mysticism, as well as his eccentricities, made him objectionable to the Society of Jesus, and he easily secured his release from that order and became a free lance. His attacks on the Roman Catholic church, and more particularly the Jesuits, led to his persecution and he was driven by the authorities, civil and ecclesiastical, from one place to another. About 1650 he adopted the Calvinistic doctrines and was ordained a Protestant minister, but he soon found that, from his viewpoint, the Protestant church also needed reformation, and he attempted this reformation so vigorously that he again antagonized both the civil and ecclesiastical authorities and was finally deposed from the ministry. He then established an independent church to teach the pure principles and practices of the Christian faith, as he conceived them. He attracted followers and located at different places but was compelled to move, until finally, after the death of Labadie, the colony located at Weiward, in Friesland. The needs of the colony required more land for their support than they could procure at Weiward, and in 1679 the Weiward assembly sent Peter Sluyter and Jasper Danckers to America to look for a location for a new colony. These two men traveled under the names of P. Vorstman and J. Schilders. While in New York they made the acquaintance of Augustine Herman's son Ephraim and accompanied him to Maryland, where they met the elder Herman. The two Labadists were much pleased with the locality and Herman was very favorably impressed with them. They were very anxious to secure part of his land for their colony, but while he would not agree to sell them any of it he became so entangled with them that later on he was compelled by legal action to transfer part of his estate to them.[19] The two commissioners returned to Weiward to make their report to the assembly, and in 1683 brought back with them the nucleus for a colony and, through legal action, compelled Herman to transfer to them nearly four thousand acres of land, consisting of four necks of land eastwardly from the first creek that empties into Bohemia river, from the north or northeast to near the old St. Augustine, or Manor church.[20] The colony did not grow very rapidly and never amounted to much more than one hundred persons. It was dominated by Sluyter, who assumed the title of bishop, and who gradually managed to secure title to most of the land. He exacted rigid obedience from every member of the community, to whom was assigned some part of the work. Some of them had to see to the cooking, others to the housework. The fields had to be cultivated by some, while others looked after the stock. "The different families had dwellings according to their needs, though, by partitioning off the larger compartments, strict economy of space was observed. All rooms were at all times open to the pastors and to those who held oversight in their name. Those who joined the community resigned into the common stock all their possessions. Individuality in attire was suppressed. Degrading tasks were assigned to those suspected of pride. Samuel Bownas, a minister of the Society of Friends, in the record of his visit to the community gives a more particular account of their table discipline than can be found elsewhere. He says: 'After we had dined we took our leave, and a friend, my guide, went with me and brought me to a people called Labadists, where we were civilly entertained in their way. When

---

[19] James, "The Labadist Colony in Maryland," p. 35.
[20] Ibid., p. 38.

supper came in, it was placed upon a large table in a large room, where, when all things were ready, came in at a call, twenty men or upwards, but no women. We all sat down, they placing me and my companion near the head of the table, and having passed a short space, one pulled off his hat, but not so the rest till a short space after, and then they, one after another, pulled all their hats off, and in that uncovered posture sat silent uttering no word that we could hear for nearly half a quarter of an hour, and as they did not uncover at once, neither did they cover themselves again at once, but as they put on their hats fell to eating not regarding those who were still uncovered, so that it might be ten minutes time or more between the first and last putting on of their hats. I afterward queried with my companion as to their conduct, and he gave for an answer that they held it unlawful to pray till they felt some inward motion fõr the same, and that secret prayer was more acceptable than to utter words, and that it was most proper for every one to pray as moved thereto by the spirit in their own minds. I likewise queried if they had no women amongst them. He told me they had, but the women ate by themselves and the men by themselves, having all things in common respecting their household affairs, so that none could claim any more right than another to any part of their stock, whether in trade or husbandry.' "[21]

According to the belief of the Labadists the church was a community of holy persons who had been born again from sin, held together by the love of truth as it is in Jesus Christ. They laid great stress on the power of the Holy Ghost, operating not only through the scriptures and the administration of the sacraments, but also by direct communication with the souls of the elect. The presence of the Holy Ghost was indicated by the conduct of the

[21] Ibid., p. 16.

believer. They did not believe in infant baptism because it could not be foretold whether the child would grow up in the fear of God or in sin. To them baptism was the sealing of a new covenant with God and insured the washing away of sins. They held that the believers and unbelievers should be kept apart, and carried this doctrine to such a length that they believed it was the duty of a husband and wife to separate if either were not of the elect. They held themselves as freed from allegiance to any law.

"Labadism," says James,[22] "was essentially a mystical form of faith, teaching supreme reliance upon the inward illumination of the Spirit. And yet the works of the Labadists disclose a high form of Christian faith and aspiration. Whatever its defects, and the opportunities for hypocritical pretence which it offered, Labadism was yet a standard of faith and conduct which no one could conform to without at the same time exemplifying high Christian graces."

The Labadist colony on Bohemia river ceased to exist as such shortly after the year 1720.

According to Weishaar,[23] other Germans who settled in Maryland prior to 1700 were Martin Faulkner, who was granted 150 acres of land in Anne Arundel county, September 23, 1680; Daniel Hast, Somerset county, August 30, 1680; Robert Knapp, September 22, 1681; Christopher Geist, August 10, 1684; William Gross, October 24, 1684; Richard Schippe; John Leniger, October 10, 1683; Rudolph Brandt, June 12, 1686; William Blankenstein, about 1685; John Falkner, 1685; Thomas Faulkner, June 12, 1688; William Gross, May 2, 1689; William Lange, November 10, 1691; Robert Sadler, April 4, 1689.

[22] "The Labadist Colony in Maryland," p. 14.
[23] Report of the Society for the History of the Germans in Maryland, Vol. XV., p. 20.

These are practically all the Germans who had settled in the colony before 1700. Compared with those of other nationalities they were few in number and were not of sufficient importance to make any impression in considering the character of the inhabitants. Maryland was still English in all respects and it remained so until the large influx of Pennsylvania-Germans a third of a century later.

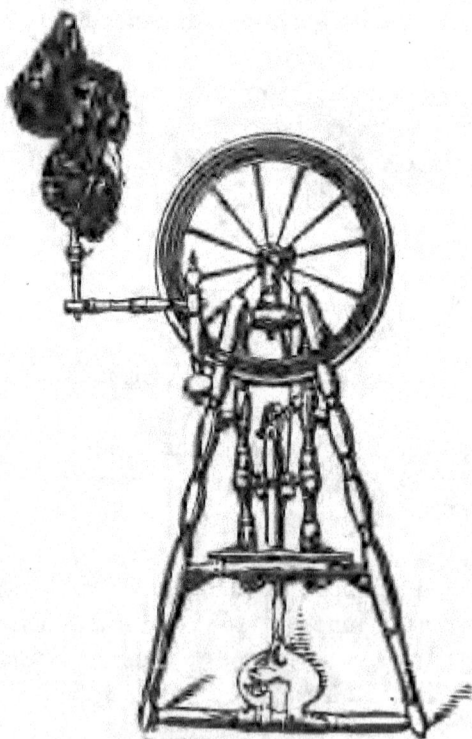

SPINNING WHEEL.

CHAPTER III.

THE GERMANS IN PENNSYLVANIA.

 ROM the time that Moses led the hosts of Israel out of Egypt toward the Promised Land history records no such exodus of a people as that which took place from the Rhenish provinces of Germany in the early years of the eighteenth century. The oppressed and impoverished inhabitants went, not by scores, nor even by hundreds, but literally by thousands. In this day we can scarcely realize the extent of the emigration which took place from Germany at that time, nor the causes which brought it about. These causes were varied, though it was the ruthless devastation of the valley of the Rhine, commonly known as the Palatinate, during the Thirty Years' War and those which followed it, "more than any other cause that started the great and steady stream of German blood, muscle and brains to Pennsylvania's shores."[24]

[24] Julius F. Sachse, Litt.D., in Proceedings and Addresses of the Pennsylvania-German Society, Vol. VII., p. 172.

Almost with the opening of the Thirty Years' War, in
1620, the troops of the Emperor Ferdinand II. of Germany, under Tilly and Maximilian, devastated the Protestant lands and cities of the Palatinate, and began the
ravages which marked that war. The Protestants retali-
ated, with the result that the country was almost depopu-
lated. Before this war the Palatinate was credited with
a population of half a million souls; at the close of the
struggle a census showed less than one third of the original
number.[25] It has been estimated that in the first half of
the seventeenth century two thirds of the people of Germany perished from war, pestilence and famine. One of
the effects of the war was the destruction of almost all
trade and commerce. During the war Alsace, adjoining
the Palatinate, was so terribly devastated by the French
that the German Emperor found himself unable to hold it.
The population was greatly reduced in numbers and much
of the land was left uncultivated.

With the end of the Thirty Years' War the impover-
ished and destitute inhabitants of Germany hoped for a
respite from their troubles and for a chance to rebuild
their homes and rehabilitate their fortunes. But that hope
was in vain. In 1674, during the Dutch War, Turenne
pushed forward into the Palatinate, defeated the imperial-
ists at Sinzheim, and deliberately destroyed the whole
country. After the revocation of the Edict of Nantes, in
1685, large numbers of Huguenots left France and settled
in the Palatinate. The French king becoming angered
because the Palatine Elector gave shelter to these perse-
cuted people, sent Louvois with one hundred thousand
soldiers, with orders to destroy the Palatinate. "How
well this horde of murderers did his bidding," says Dr.

[25] Ibid., p. 125.

Sachse, "is a matter of history. Even to the present day, after the lapse of two centuries, the line of march may be traced from the Drachenfels to Heidelberg. Crumbling walls, ruined battlements and blown-up towers still remain as mementoes of French vandalism."[26]

But even this was not the end of their chapter of horrors, for with the opening of the eighteenth century the War of the Spanish Succession caused the country again to be overrun, and what little the previous marauders had left was destroyed by the flames and battles of another invasion. The few people who were left were in the direst poverty. Even those who a few years before were well-to-do, were now no better off than their poorest neighbors, for with their homes destroyed and their fields uncultivated they had nothing, and no prospects of having anything.

But, as though the trial by the sword and flames was not enough, nature did what she could to still further afflict the stricken inhabitants of the Palatinate. The winter of 1708–9 was unusually severe. The cold was intense and long-continued, and the half-starved and destitute inhabitants were illy-prepared to withstand the rigors of that unusually severe winter, so that many of them perished from the cold. To the little remnant that was left it seemed as though they had been forsaken by God as well as by man, and they were ready to turn in any direction that offered an escape from the terrible situation in which they found themselves.

At this juncture the agents sent out by William Penn, and to a lesser degree by some of the proprietors of some of the other American colonies, made their appearance and distributed broadcast glowing accounts of the new

[26] Proceedings and Addresses of the Pennsylvania-German Society, Vol. VII., p. 170.

homes that might easily be founded in the land across the sea. The poverty-stricken, starving people jumped at the chance that was offered and rose *en masse* and made their way as best they could to the nearest seaports and started for England as the first stage in their journey to the new home beyond the sea. They went literally by the thousand. In May or June, 1709, the Germans began to arrive in London, and by October between 13,000 and 14,000 had come.[27] The coming into England of so large a number of destitute people with no means of sustenance presented to the English people a problem which had to be met promptly. As Dr. Diffenderffer says, "Never before, perhaps, were emigrants seeking new homes so poorly provided with money and the other necessaries of life to support them on their way as were these Palatines. . . . From the day of their arrival in London they required the assistance of the English to keep them from starving. There was little or no work; bread was dear, and the only thing to do was to bridge the crisis by raising money by public subscriptions."

A large amount of money was collected and by direction of Queen Anne one thousand tents were taken from the Tower of London and set up in the country outside of London. In these camps many of the emigrants were sheltered, while others were housed in barns and warehouses, and some in private houses. The government took active steps to get rid of the foreigners as quickly as possible, and eventually they were disposed of. Nearly four thousand of them were sent to Ireland,[28] where their descend-

[27] Frank R. Diffenderffer, Litt.D., in Proceedings and Addresses of the Pennsylvania-German Society, Vol. VII., p. 266.

[28] Dr. Diffenderffer is of the opinion that if these German colonists did not actually establish the linen industry in Ireland they gave it such an impulse as to make it the most important textile industry in that country.

ants live to this day. Many of the Roman Catholics were returned to the places from which they had come, and a large party, numbering over three thousand, was sent to the New York colony, many of whom eventually found their way down into Pennsylvania and settled in the Tulpehocken region.

This was practically the beginning of the German emigration to America, although the Crefeld colony under Pastorius had made a settlement at Germantown in 1683 and Kocherthal, with his fifty-three companions, had founded Newburg on the Hudson at the beginning of 1709. A constant stream of German colonists followed, at first slowly, then in larger numbers, the greater number going to Pennsylvania. By 1717 so many of them had arrived in that colony that alarm was excited in the minds of the authorities. In that year Governor Keith thought the matter of sufficient importance to recommend that the masters of all vessels bringing in foreign passengers be required to furnish lists of all such persons and that the emigrants be required to take the oath of allegiance. Through this recommendation being, at a later period, enacted into a law a fairly accurate record of the number of German emigrants who came into Pennsylvania has been preserved. The exact number is not known, as many came before the records were begun, in 1727, and some of these records appear to have been lost, but Professor Oscar Kuhns has gone over the lists very carefully and has figured out that between 1727 and 1775 the number of Germans who came to Pennsylvania was about 68,872.[29] The authorities of the province did not look kindly upon this influx of German emigrants. Secretary James Logan was particularly outspoken in his opposition to them, and on a

---

[29] " The German and Swiss Settlements of Colonial Pennsylvania," p. 57.

number of occasions wrote unfavorably concerning them. On march 25, 1727, he wrote to John Penn: "We have many thousands of foreigners, mostly Palatines, so-called, already in yᵉ Countrey, of whom near 1500 came in this last summer; many of them are a surly people, divers Papists amongst them, and yᵉ men generally well arm'd. We have from the North of Ireland, great numbers yearly, 8 or 9 Ships this last ffall discharged at Newcastle. Both of these sorts sitt frequently down on any spott of vacant Land they can find, without asking questions; the last Palatines say there will be twice the number next year, & yᵉ Irish say yᵉ same of their People."

The proprietaries were naturally influenced by the unfavorable reports sent to them concerning the German emigrants and in consequence, although they were doubtless actuated by other motives, determined to have them settle on the outlying lands so that they might serve as a bulwark between the inhabitants of the more-thickly settled parts of the province and the hostile Indians. In 1729, John, Thomas and Richard Penn wrote to Secretary Logan: "As to the Palatines, you have often taken notice of to us, wee apprehend have Lately arrived in greater Quantities than may be consistent with the welfare of the Country, and therefore, applied ourself to our Councill to find a proper way to prevent it, the result of which was, that an act of assembly should be got or endeavoured at, and sent us over immediately, when we would take sufficient Care to get it approved by the King. With this resolution we acquainted the Governour, by Capᵗ Stringfellow, to Maryland, the 25ᵗʰ Febʳʸ a Duplicate of which we have since sent by another shipp, both wᶜʰ times we also enclos'd Letters for thee; but as to any other people coming over who are the subjects of the British

TALLOW CANDLE MOULDS.
FLAX HACKLES.

Crown, we can't Conceive it anyways practicable to prohibit it: but supposing they are natives of Ireland & Roman Catholicks, they ought not to settle till they have taken the proper Oaths to the King, & Promis'd Obedience to the Laws of the Country, and, indeed, we Can't Conceive it unreasonable that if they are Inclinable to settle, they should be oblig'd to settle, either Backwards to Sasquehannah or north in yᵉ Country beyond the other settlements, as we had mentioned before in relation to the Palatines; but we must desire Care may be taken that they are not suffered to settle towards Maryland, on any account."[30]

Not only did the provincial authorities feel apprehension concerning the large number of Germans who were coming into the colony, but the same impression prevailed among the English generally, and even as late as 1751 Benjamin Franklin said: "Why should the Palatine boors be suffered to swarm into our settlements, and, by herding together, establish their language and manners, to the exclusion of ours? Why should Pennsylvania, founded by the English, become a colony of aliens, who will shortly be so numerous as to Germanize us, instead of our Anglicifying them, and will never adopt our language or customs any more than they can acquire our complexion?" Franklin later realized that he had made a mistake in speaking so contemptuously of this element which formed so large a proportion of the population of Pennsylvania, and tried to smooth it over by trying to make it appear that he had used the word "boor" in the sense of "farmer."

But in spite of the opposition to them the Germans continued to come in increasing numbers. It is said that in 1719 six thousand German emigrants came to Pennsylvania, but as accurate records were not kept at that time it is

[30] Pennsylvania Archives, Second Series, Vol. VII., p. 140.

3*

probable that this estimate is exaggerated. In 1727, when fairly accurate records were kept, over twelve hundred landed, while in 1732 the number was between two and three thousand. As the eastern section of the country became more thickly settled the Germans spread out to the west and southwest and settled in the more remote parts of the colony, often on land not yet purchased from the Indians, as was the case with the party from Schoharie county, New York, who made their way through the unbroken forests, following the Susquehanna, and settled at Tulpehocken. They were part of the party who settled in Livingston Manor, in 1710, and after spending some years there had gone to Schoharie, whence they were again impelled to move. The Indians naturally resented this encroachment upon their lands and frequently assumed a hostile attitude, making attacks on unprotected settlements. The settlers appealed to the authorities for aid in repelling these attacks, but, in addition to the fact that the Quaker authorities were opposed to furnishing means for warfare and bloodshed, they were almost continually having controversies with the governors and proprietaries, and but little was done in the way of furnishing protection, and the inhabitants of the outlying sections were usually left to their own devices.

The condition of these settlers is well illustrated in a letter[31] written by Casper Wistar from Philadelphia, under date of November 8, 1732:

Being importuned daily by so many of our countrymen to relieve them from the great distress, into which they have come, partially through their own thoughtlessness, and partially by the persuasion of others, and it being absolutely impossible to help all,

[31] Quoted by Rev. Dr. Henry E. Jacobs, in Proceedings and Addresses of the Pennsylvania-German Society, Vol. VIII., p. 142.

sympathy for the poor people still in the Fatherland, and who, before undertaking such a journey, have time to reflect, constrains me to give a true account of the conditions of things in this new land. I make this particular request that these facts may be reported everywhere, that no one may have the excuse for learning them only from his own personal experience.

Some years ago this was a very fruitful country, and, like all new countries, but sparsely inhabited. Since the wilderness required much labor, and the inhabitants were few, ships that arrived with German emigrants were cordially welcomed. They were immediately discharged, and by their labor very easily earned enough to buy some land. Pennsylvania is but a small part of America, and has been open now for some years, so that not only many thousand Germans, but English and Irish have settled there, and filled all parts of the country; so that all who now seek land must go far into the wilderness, and purchase it at a higher price.

Many hardships also are experienced on the voyage. Last year one of the ships was driven about the ocean for twenty-four weeks, and of its one hundred and fifty passengers, more than one hundred starved to death. To satisfy their hunger, they caught mice, and rats; and a mouse brought half a gulden. When the survivors at last reached land, their sufferings were aggravated by their arrest, and the exaction from them of the entire fare for both living and dead. This year ten ships with three thousand souls have arrived.

One of the vessels was seventeen weeks on the way and about sixty of its passengers died at sea. All the survivors are sick and feeble, and what is worst, poor and without means; hence, in a community like this where money is scarce, they are a burden, and every day there are deaths among them. Every person over fourteen years old, must pay six doubloons (about 90 dollars) passage from Rotterdam, and those between four and fourteen must pay half that amount. When one is without the money, his only resource is to sell himself for a term from three to eight years or more, and to serve as a slave. Nothing but a poor suit of clothes is received when his time has expired. Families endure a great trial when they see the father purchased by one master, the mother by another, and each of the children by another. All this for the money only that they owe the Captain. And yet they are only too glad, when after waiting long, they at last find some one willing to buy them; for the money of the country is well nigh exhausted. In view of these circumstances, and the tedious, expensive and perilous voyage, you should not advise any one for whom you wish well to come hither. All I can say is that those who think of coming should weigh well what has been above stated, and should count the cost, and, above all, should go to God for counsel and inquire whether it be His will, lest they may undertake that whereof they will afterward repent. If ready to hazard their lives and to endure patiently all the trials of the voyage, they must further think whether over and above the cost they will have enough to purchase cattle, and to provide for other necessities. No one should rely upon friends whom he may have here; for they have enough to do, and many a one reckons in this without his host. Young and able-bodied persons, who can do efficient work, can, nevertheless, always find some one who will purchase them for two, three or four years; but they must be unmarried. For young married persons, particularly when the wife is with child, no one cares to have. Of mechanics there are a considerable number already here; but a good mechanic who can bring with him sufficient capital to avoid beginning with debt, may do well, although of almost all classes and occupations, there are already more than too many. All this I have, out of sincere love for the interests of my neighbor, deemed it necessary to communicate concerning the present condition in Pennsylvania.

CHAPTER IV.

THE MOVEMENT TO MARYLAND.

DURING the first century of its existence the colony of Maryland did not grow very rapidly and it was, relatively, of minor importance. The territory actually settled consisted chiefly of a narrow strip along Chesapeake Bay, the colonists showing but little inclination to locate very far from tidewater. This was but natural, for everyone was devoting his energies to raising tobacco, and to dispose of this it had to be shipped abroad, and the numerous inlets along the coast afforded ample opportunity for this shipment, without the necessity of a long haul to the port of lading. It is curious to note how every settler devoted all his time and labor to the raising of tobacco, without regard to reason, and to the exclusion of the necessaries of life; but tobacco was the only medium of barter and exchange, and all debts, public and private, were settled in that commodity. Naturally, therefore, everyone wanted to raise as much tobacco as possible, and the result was that but little attention was paid to the quality, and the consequent lowering of value of the product brought the young colony into financial difficulties with all the evils attendant on a depreciated currency. The enactment of laws requiring the settlers to raise a certain amount of corn and other commodities had scarcely any effect, and it was not until 1748, more than a hundred years after the founding of the colony, that an effective law regulating the production of tobacco was enacted. It was this restriction of the settlements to the neighborhood of the coast and the evils arising from the unlimited cultivation of tobacco that undoubtedly limited the growth of the colony, although the feudal system in force in the tenure of land had something to do with it. The colony was practically at a standstill. In 1689, fifty-six years after its foundation, it had a population of but 25,000. In the next twenty-one years, to 1710, the population increased but five thousand, and in 1733 the number of taxable inhabitants, including all males above the age of fifteen, was but 31,470; but about this time the German settlers began to come into Maryland from Pennsylvania, although it was not until some years later that they came in sufficient numbers to materially affect the progress of the colony. When this movement reached its height the effect was decidedly noticeable, and by 1756 the population had increased to 130,000, and by far the greater number of these were Pennsylvania-Germans.[32]

When the Germans began to arrive in Pennsylvania in large numbers in the early part of the eighteenth century, and spread out over that colony to the west and south, it was but natural, in view of the unsettled condition of the boundary between Maryland and Pennsylvania, that some of them should get over the dividing line into Maryland.

[32] Louis P. Hennighausen, in Report of the Society for the History of Germans in Maryland, Vol. VI., p. 14.

As early as 1710 this has been noted, for on October 27 of that year the journal of the Maryland House of Delegates records that

This House being informed several Palatines were come to settle in this Province & being willing and desirous to encourage those poor People in their Industry have resolved that those Palatines with their Servants shall be free this present year from paying any publick, County, or Parish Levy or Charge, to which they pray the Concurrence of the Honble Council.[33]

But there was no marked movement of the Germans from Pennsylvania into Maryland until the latter part of the second decade of the eighteenth century, and then one of the chief causes in bringing about this movement was the indifference of the Quaker authorities of Pennsylvania to the safety of the inhabitants of the back counties. They were well satisfied to have these sturdy Germans on the western frontier to serve as a barrier between themselves and the hostile Indians, but they were very unwilling to go to any expense to provide the settlers with means of protecting themselves. Among the numerous appeals to the Pennsylvania authorities was the following petition from a number of settlers in Colebrook Valley, asking for protection from the attacks of the Indians who had already attacked the settlers near Falckner's Swamp and Goschenhoppen:[34]

To his Excellency Patrick Gordon Esqr Governor Generall In chie(f) Over the Province of pencilvania And the Territoris Belonging Bonbrenors township and the Adjacences Belonging May ye 10th 1728

We think It fit to Address your Excellency for Relief for your Excellency must know That we have Sufered and Is Like to Sufer

[33] Archives of Maryland, Vol. XVII., p. 524.
[34] Pennsylvania Archives, First Series, Vol. I., p. 213.

By the Ingians they have fell upon ye Back Inhabitors about falkners Swamp & New Coshahopin Therefore We the humble Petitionors With our poor Wives And Children Do humbly Beg of your Excellency To Take It into Consideration And Relieve us the Petitionors hereof Whos Lives Lie at Stake With us and our poor Wives & Children that Is more to us than Life Therefore We the humble Petitionors hereof Do Desire An Answer from your Excellency By ye Bearor With Speed So no More at present from your poor Afflicted People Whose names are here Subscribed

John Roberts	Henrich Kolb
Jn Pawling	John fret
Henry Pannebeckers	Paul fret.
Wm Lane	Wm Smith
John Jacobs	Peter Rambo
Isaac Dubois	David young
Israell Morris	Christopher Schmit
Benjamen Fry	Garret Clemens
Jacob op den graef	Johannes Reichardt
Johannes Scholl	Mathias Tyson
Richard Adams	Peter Johnson
George Poger	Jost hyt
Adam Sollom	Christian Alibock
Dirtman Kolb	hans Rife
Martin Kolb	Daniel Stowford
Gabriel Showler	Abraham Schwartz.
Anthony halmon	Johann Vallentin Kratz.
John Isaac Klein	John Johnson
Hans Detweiler	Colly hafilfinger
William Bitts	Nickolas huldiman
Heinrich Rutt	Michal Sigler
Hubburt Castle	Christian Stoner
Henery Fentlinger	Johannes Garber
Christian Weber	John huldiman
Gerhart de hesse	Claus Johnson

To his Excellency Patrick Gorden Esqr Governor Generall In chef Over the Province of pensilvania And the Teritories thereunto Belonging

Bucheanons township and the Adjacencies Belonging may ye 10th 1728

We think It fit to Adress your Excellency for Relief for your Excelency must know That we have Suffered and Is Like to Suffer By the Ingions they have fell upon ye Back Inhabitors about falkners Swamp & New Cossahopin Therefore We the humble Petitioners With our poor Wives And Children Do humbly Beg of your Excelency To Take It into Consideration And Relieve us the Petitioners hereof Whos Lives Lies At Stake With us and our poor Wives & Children that Is more to us then life Therefore We the humble Petitioners hereof Do Desire An Answer from your Excellency By ye Bearer With Speed So no more At present from your poor Afflicted People Whose names are here Subscribed

John Roberts
Jn Pawling
Henry Panacbekers
Wm Lane
John Jacobs
Isaac Dubois
Israell Morris
Benjamen Fry
Jacob op Den graef
Johannes [illegible]
Richard Adams
George Boger
Adam Soliom
Ditman Kolb
Martin Kolb
Gabriel Shouler
Anthony Halmon
John Isaac Klein
Jacob [illegible]
William [illegible]
Heinrich Roth
Hubbart Cassel
Henry Prettlinger
Christian Weber
Gerhard Dekeffe

Lorentz Engerman
Richard Jacob
Hermann Kuster
Peter Rieser
Jacob Engnet
Jacob Zimmerman
Conrad Kuster
Jacob Merrikle
Christian Nyswanger
Conradt Kriest
Jacob Kolb
Hans Wolly Bogg
John Meer
Heinrich Kolb
John Frey
Paul Frey
Wm Smith
Peter Rambo
Daniel Young
Christoffel [illegible]
Garret Clemens
Johannes [illegible]
Mathias Tyson
Peter Johnson
Yost Heyt
Christian Allebach

Hans Rife
Daniel Stoufferd
Abraham [illegible]
Johann Stallenknecht
John Johnson
Colly Hafelfinger
Nicholas Haldeman
Michael Zigler
Christian Stover
Johannes Gerber
John Haldeman
Claus Johnson
Nicholas Hicks
Johannes Lieber
Jacob Shimer
Michael Krebs
Peter Rife
George Rife
George Miri
Gestron Smith
Edward Johnson
Christian Toll
Jacob Conter
Jacob Stofferd
Henry Stoffard
Paul Frey Junior

PETITION FROM THE SETTLERS IN COLEBROOK VALLEY, PA.

Lorentz Bingamon
Richard Jacob
Hermanes Küsters
Peter Bun
Jacob Engners
Hans ————
Conrad Cusson
Jacob Mernke
Christian Nighswanger
Conrad Knight
Jacob Kolb
hons Wolly Bergy
John Mior

Nicholas hicks
Johannes Lisher
Jacob Shimor
Michall Cross
Peter Rife
George Rife
George Mire
Postron Smith
Edward Scherer
Jacob Crontor
Jacob Stoferd
Henrey Stoferd
Paul fret. Junior.

This appeal, like so many others of similar import, brought no response from the authorities. Among the signers of this petition was Jost Hyt, or Jost Hite, as he is generally designated in the Virginia records. Hite, who appears to have been a man imbued with the courage of his convictions, apparently became disgusted with the manner in which the rights of the inhabitants were ignored by the authorities, and determined to seek a home in some other locality where the safety of the settlers would not be a matter of indifference to those in authority. Thus was started a movement which resulted in the peopling of a state.

In 1709 Franz Ludwig Michel and Baron Christopher von Graffenried, from Berne, Switzerland, established a colony in North Carolina, but on account of the Indian massacres, as well as the fact that the settlers were not able to obtain land upon as favorable terms as they had expected, most of the colonists removed into the colony of Virginia. Here they were favorably received by Governor Alexander Spottswood, who established a colony for them at Germanna, where he erected an iron-works in which a number of the foreigners found employment. This settlement, however, did not prosper and soon became extinct, and the inhabitants located in other parts of the colony. The presence of these Germans with their thrift and industry naturally excited a desire to have more of the same kind of people in the colony, and in 1730 Isaac and John Van Meter, two Dutchmen whose father had settled on the Hudson, obtained from the Governor of Virginia a patent for 40,000 acres of land in that colony, on condition that they would settle two hundred German families on the land ceded to them. In looking for a place where he might locate under more favorable conditions than he had found to obtain in Pennsylvania, Jost Hite made an agreement with the Van Meters and became a partner in the plan to found a German colony in Virginia, and in 1732, with his family, his son-in-law, George Bowman, Jacob Chrisman and Paul Froman, with their families, and several others—sixteen families in all—left York, crossed the Potomac, and settled near where Winchester now stands. Although a little before this, as early as 1729, a few Germans had made their way down from Pennsylvania into Maryland and settled near the Monocacy river, this settlement of Hite's may be considered as the entering wedge which started the great movement of the Germans from Pennsylvania into Maryland and Virginia. In pursuance of their plan Hite and Van Meter traveled through the German settlements to the north and extolled the advantages of the territory they were exploiting, and thus started the movement towards the south.

Charles, Lord Baltimore, becoming aware of this movement, and desiring to obtain settlers for the unoccupied

ALEXANDER SPOTSWOOD,
GOVERNOR OF VIRGINIA.   BORN 1676;   DIED 1740.

western portion of his colony, issued the following proclamation:

By the Right Honourable Charles Absolute Lord and Proprietary of the Provinces of Maryland and Avalon Lord Baron of Baltimore &c

Wee being Desireous to Increase the Number of Honest people within our Province of Maryland and willing to give Suitable Encouragement to such to come and Reside therein Do offer the following Terms:

1ˢᵗ That any person haveing a ffamily who shall within three Years come and Actually Settle with his or her Family on any of the back Lands on the Northern or Western Boundarys of our said province not already taken up between the Rivers Potomack and Susquehana (where wee are Informed there are Several large Bodies of Fertile Lands fit for Tillage, Which may be Seen aithout any Expence) Two hundred Acres of the said Lands in ffee Simple Without paying any part of the fforty Shillings Sterling for every hundred Acres payable to Us by the Conditions of Plantations, And without paying any Quit Rents in three Years after the first Settlement, and then paying four Shillings Sterling for Every hundred of Acres to us or our Heirs for every Year after the expiration of the said three Years.

2ᵈ To allow to Each Single person Male or Female above the Age of Thirty & not under Fifteen One hundred Acres of the said Lands upon the same Terms as mentioned in the preceding Article.

3ᵈ That We will Concour in any reasonable Method that shall be proposed for the Ease of such New Comers in the payment of their Taxes for some Years And We doe Assure all such that they shall be as well Secured in their Liberty & property in Maryland as any of his Majesty's Subjects in any part of the British Plantations in America without Exception And to the End all persons Desireous to come into and Reside in Maryland may be Assured that these Terms will be Justly & Punctually performed on our part Wee have hereunto sett our hand and Seal at Arms, at Annapolis this Second day of March Annoq Domini 1732.[35]

This exceedingly liberal offer of land at a rental of about one cent per acre per annum, with no rent to be paid for three years, naturally attracted the attention of the emigrants, and, as Hennighausen says,[36] "the settlers on their way to Spottsylvania, seeing the rich soil of Frederick county offered to them on such liberal terms, did not proceed further, but stuck their spades into the ground right then and there."

A little later another element that had considerable weight in inducing many already settled in Pennsylvania to go farther south was the fact that the winter of 1740-1 was an intensely cold one. Not only were there prolonged periods of intense cold, but an unusual quantity of snow fell, so that there was a great deal of suffering all through the settlements of Pennsylvania.[37] While the severe weather prevailed over the most of America, and was almost as marked in Virginia as it was in Pennsylvania, many of the inhabitants of the latter colony, under the impression that farther south the climate would be less rigorous, removed from the settlements already formed in Pennsylvania, and went to Maryland and Virginia.

[35] Archives of Maryland, Vol. XXVIII., p. 25.

[36] Op. cit., p. 15.

[37] Blodget's "Climatology of the United States," p. 144, says: "It was commonly called 'the cold winter.'"

CHAPTER V.

The Monocacy Road.

BEFORE the coming of the white man the original owners of the American continent had made many paths, or "trails," as they were called, running from one section of the country to another for the use of their war parties, or on their hunting expeditions. At first, before any roads were cut, the settlers found it convenient to continue using these trails, as they were generally the shortest route between any two points. They were suitable for travelers on foot or for pack-horses, but could not be used for wagons, and as the needs of the settlers developed many of the Indian trails were widened into roads, and not a few of the well-known highways of to-day are but the amplification of the by-paths over which the redman found his way through the primeval forest. One of these Indian trails started at a point on the Susquehanna river near where Wrightsville now stands and extended through the territory now forming parts of York and Adams

45

counties, Pennsylvania, to a point on the Monocacy river near the boundary between the provinces of Maryland and Pennsylvania, thence to the Potomac river, crossing the South Mountain through a gap known as Crampton's Gap. It was over this trail that the first Germans went from Pennsylvania to Maryland, in 1710, and later when the movement became more extensive the same route was used. When communication between the settlements in Maryland and Pennsylvania became more frequent the necessity of having better means of travel became urgent and steps were taken to have a road properly laid out. In 1739 application was made to the Lancaster county court for the appointment of viewers for such a road. The record of this proceeding may be of interest. It is found in "Road Docket No. 1, from 1729 to 1742," and is as follows:

"1739. At a Court of General Quarter Sessions, held at Lancaster, the Seventh day of August, in the thirtieth year of His Majesty's reign Anno Dom. before John Wright, Tobias Hendricks, Thomas Edwards, Samuel Jones, Edward Smout, Thomas Lindley, Anthony Shaw, Samuel Boyd, James Armstrong and Emanuel Carpenter, Esqrs. Justices of our Lord the King, the Peace of our said Lord the King, in the said county to keep, as also divers ffelonys, tresspasses &c other misdeeds in the said county committed to hear & determine assigned.

"Upon the Petition of Several of the Inhabitants of the township of Hallem, on the West side of Susquehanah, setting forth the necessity of a road from John Wright's fferry, towards Potomac river, and praying that persons may be appointed to lay out the Same: Ordered by ye Court, that Joshua Minshall, Henry Hendricks, ffrancis Worley Junr, Christian Crowl, Michael Tanner & Woolrick Whistler view and, if they or any four of them se cause that they lay the same by course and distance, ffrom the said fferry to the line dividing the Provinces, and report ye same to ye next Court."

At a Court of General Quarter Sessions held on the 5th and 6th days of February, 1740, the following return of the viewers was handed to the Court:

" The Persons appointed at the August Court last & continued to November Court following do report that, pursuant to order, they have viewed and laid out a road from Susquehanah river South Westerly, towards the Province line, according to the courses & distances following, viz.: Beginning at the said river, in the line between the lands of John Wright Jun. and Samuel Taylor; thence South 80 deg. West 430 per. 71 deg. West. 562 per, to Crawl's run: South 70 deg. West, 430 per. to a marked white oak. West 76 per. to the Canoe run; South 68 deg. West 254 per. to a black oak; South 53 deg. West 540 per. to the West branch of Grist creek; South 66 deg. West 280 per.; South 84 deg. West 264 perches; West 166 per. to Little Codorus creek; South 82 lor; thence South 80 deg. West 430 per. 71 deg. West. 562 per. South 72 deg.: West 260 pr. to Big Codorus creek; continuing the same course 360 per. to Perrin's run, West 246 per. to Springle's field; South 72 deg. West 80 per: South-West 160 per; South 60 deg. West, 126 per. to the point of a steep hill: South 48 deg. West 134 per. South 69 deg. West 200 per. South 58 deg. West 240 per. to Loreman's run: South, 57 deg. West 40 per.: South 71 deg. West, 166 per. to a black oak, by Chrn Oyster's South 55 deg. West, 172 per. South 40 deg. West 330 per, South 52 deg. West 172 per. to Nicholas lougher's run: South 44 deg. West 380 per. South 58 deg. West 376 per.: South 22 deg. West 120 per. to the West branch of the Codorus creek: South 30 deg. West 66 per.: South 36 deg. West, 60 per.: South 26 deg. West 66 per.; South 104 per."

Here the court record of this proceeding concerning the road ends, but from the fact that the road was constructed it is quite probable that the report of the viewers was confirmed.

By an act of the Maryland assembly this road was continued to the Potomac river. It practically followed the old Indian trail and was known as the Monocacy Road. It was over this road that Benjamin Franklin, in 1755, sent the 150 wagons and 200 horses he had secured in Pennsylvania to General Braddock in preparation for the ill-fated campaign against Fort Duquesne. Having learned that Braddock had determined to send officers into Pennsylvania to seize the horses and wagons needed, in order to prevent such a catastrophe Franklin offered to secure the necessary equipment, and, making his headquarters at Lancaster, he sent the horses and wagons he was able to obtain over the Monocacy Road to Braddock's camp at Frederick.

This was the route over which the settlers in Maryland sent their produce and manufactures to Philadelphia, at first by pack-horses and later by wagons. At first the wagons were home-made affairs, the wheels being sawed from the trunks of the gum, or buttonwood tree. Later came the well-known Conestoga wagon,[38] with its blue

---

[38] It is remarkable how much misinformation is frequently crowded into the so-called "Historical Novel"—misinformation which is made to masquerade as fact. For instance, in "The Quest of John Chapman," by Rev. Newell Dwight Hillis, D.D., on page 80, appears the following remarkable explanation of the reason for building the Conestoga wagon in the shape in which it was made:

"Not until they came to the Susquehanna did Dorothy appreciate the meaning of these wagons, with the body built like a boat with prow in front and curved behind. Coming to the edge of the river, the driver drove the team into the stream until the wagon floated like a boat. Then the horses and running gears were driven back to the land, and the wheels and axles were placed in the body of the wagon which had now become a boat. One driver poled or paddled, the other led the swimming horses, until all were conveyed safely to the opposite shore."

body and bright-red running gears, drawn by four, six, or even more horses. When the first wagons made their appearance the owners of the pack-horses bitterly opposed their use, just as, a few generations later, the wagoners opposed the building of the railroads.

During the Revolution, when it was desired to transfer the British prisoners from Reading and Lancaster to some point farther in the interior, they were conducted over the Monocacy Road to the barracks at Frederick, Maryland, and to Winchester, Virginia. It was by this same road that General Wayne, in 1781, led the Pennsylvania troops to Yorktown. The Monocacy Road was macadamized in 1808, and, until the railroads were built, it was the main thoroughfare between Maryland and the South and Philadelphia and the eastern section of the country.

4*

CHAPTER VI.

THE FIRST SETTLEMENTS.

IN studying the early history of Maryland one is at once impressed by the fact that there are but few records. Outside of the Council and Assembly proceedings there is very little on record to show the growth and development of the colony during the first half of the eighteenth century. More particularly is this the case as regards the settlement of the western part of the state, the section in which movement of the Germans from Pennsylvania was most prominent. Whether or not there were such records, it is impossible to say, but it is scarcely likely that this was the case. It is more probable that the Pennsylvania-German settlers, intent on preparing their lands for cultivation and building their homes, wasted no time on such matters; and so it happens that the history of the first settlements in that section are shrouded in uncertainty. While it is known that a few Pennsylvania-Germans came down into Maryland during the first quarter of the eighteenth century, there were not many of them and they were so widely separated that there was no attempt made to found a town or village. It was not until after the year 1730 that any considerable number of them settled in Maryland.

The territory now known as Western Maryland, the part that was settled by the Pennsylvania Germans, was originally part of Charles county, which was formed in 1638. There was very little settlement of the western part of this county for nearly one hundred years, so that there was no change made in the county lines, and it was not until the Germans had come in numbers that a further division was deemed necessary. In 1748 the western part of the colony was erected into a county which was named Frederick. It was in this section that the Pennsylvania-Germans made their first settlements.

The first permanent settlement made by the Pennsylvania-Germans was the village of Monocacy.[39] This village which was the most important settlement in western Maryland until it was outstripped in growth by its younger neighbor, the town of Frederick, has disappeared from the map, and even its site was unknown until the investigations of Schultz definitely fixed its location. It was situated on the west side of the Monocacy river near where the Virginia road crossed that stream, and about ten miles north of where Frederick was afterwards laid out. This, as Schultz says, would locate it a little south of the present town of Creagerstown. It was at Monocacy that the first church was built by the Pennsylvania-Germans, a log structure in which Henry Melchior Muhlenberg and Michael Schlatter afterwards held services, and it may

[39] "First Settlements of Germans in Maryland," by Edward T. Schultz, p. 6.

rightly be regarded as the mother-church of the Lutheran and German Reformed denominations in Maryland.

In his investigation to discover the exact site of the ancient village of Monocacy Schultz enlisted the services of Rev. George A. Whitmore, of Thurmont, Maryland, and Mr. Whitmore's report, as given by Schultz, seems to settle definitely the location. Says Mr. Whitmore:[40] "From the information which I have been able to gather from the oldest and most reliable citizens here, one of whom is now ninety years old, and a man remarkably preserved in mind, Mr. W. L. Grimes, Sr., also Mrs. Michael Zimmerman and Miss Melissa Myers, both of them bordering on eighty years, and others, it seems that the present Creagerstown is the site where the old log church stood. These good people, who are all connected with the oldest and most reliable families, remember quite well the old weather-boarded log meeting-house which preceded the present brick church, in 1834. Mr. Grimes helped to tear down the old building and purchased some of the logs and boarding, which he used in the construction of some houses in the village, and they are there to-day. From what I can learn from them, the church was originally built simply of logs, and that the weather-boarding was supplied many years afterwards. The new brick church was erected a few rods north of the old site on a new lot containing one and a half acres, which, together with the old location, is covered with graves. The first graveyard lay immediately in the rear of the old church, and contains also an acre and a-half, but not a tombstone can be found, only the indenture of graves covered with a mat of broom-sage, under which no doubt much history is hidden.

40 Schultz, p. 21.

"Then, again, I have found traces in two instances, plain and unmistakable, of the old Monocacy Road, passing just below the village, in a southwestern direction and crossing Hunting creek where, according to tradition, there was an old tavern, and where there are now three or four old dwellings. Tradition also says the Monocacy Road crossed the river at Poe's Ford, which has not been used for over a century. The road on both sides of the creek lies in timber land of old sturdy oak."

At this late day it is impossible to determine the cause of the decadence of the town of Monocacy and its passing out of existence, but it is very probable that the laying out of another town a short distance away and on land that had a higher elevation, was one of the chief causes. Schultz says: "John Cramer, a German, or a descendant of a German, between 1760 and 1770 laid out a village on grounds belonging to him, which was named in his honor, Creagerstown. The site selected was a few rods north of the old log church and little less than a mile from the first settlement. The site selected for the new village was on more elevated ground, which fact doubtless caused it to expand to the detriment of the older village." That the existence of Monocacy as a town was well known is shown by the following letter addressed to Benjamin Tasker, esquire:

LONDON, July the 9th 1752.

Sir: By the ship "Patience," Captain Steel, a number of Palatines are embarked for Maryland to settle there, which being notified to me, and a Recommendation to you desired of me, in favour of Messieurs F. & R. Snowdens & D. Wolstenholme, to whose care they are consigned and recommended.

I therefore desire you will give such necessary Assistance to the People on their Arrival, to forward them to Manockesy (which I

understand is in Frederick County) or where else they shall want
to go to settle within the Province, as in your Power, and that
they may be accomodated in a proper manner; But the charges
attending any such service to them must be done in the most moderate manner in respect to the Proprietor and to answer their
requisites necessary to their service. The increase of People being
always welcome, your prudence would have supplied this Letter
in a kind Reception of them; nevertheless as particular occasions
may require your Favour I conclude my recommendation of them,
in giving them all possible satisfaction relating to the manner and
Place they shall choose to settle in Maryland. I am, Sir,

> *Your most obedient servant,*
> CÆCILIUS CALVERT.

Washington in one of his letters also speaks of Monocacy.

Another very early settlement was the village of Conococheague, near the present site of Clearspring. This was
a well-known place and is mentioned by Washington and
other letter writers of that period. Until after the French
and Indian War this was the most westerly settlement in
Maryland. One of the early settlers in that locality was
Jonathan Hager, who afterwards laid out Elizabeth-Town,
now known as Hagerstown. Jonathan Hager was unquestionably a Pennsylvania-German. All writers on the
subject say that it is impossible to find out just when he
came to America, and Scharf says:[41] "Capt. Hager came
from Germany about 1730." Yet the Pennsylvania
Archives[42] and Rupp's "Thirty Thousand Names"[43] both
give the time of his arrival in Pennsylvania as 1736. According to these records among the passengers on the ship

[41] "History of Western Maryland," Vol. II., p. 1059.
[42] Second Series, Vol. XVII., p. 122.
[43] Second Edition, p. 101.

Harle, which arrived at Philadelphia September 1, 1736, was Jonathan Heger, whose age is given as 22. The first record of his being in Maryland was when he obtained a patent for two hundred acres of land near the present site of Hagerstown. This was on December 16, 1739, so that it is probable that he spent about three years in Pennsylvania. According to Scharf, "the earliest information of Jonathan Hager, Sr., is found in the statement that he received a patent of certain land on which a portion of the city of Philadelphia now stands," but, unfortunately, Scharf rarely gives authority for his quotations. After his settlement in Maryland, at various times until 1765, Hager obtained patents to different plats of land until his holdings amounted to almost twenty-five hundred acres. He laid out the town of Elizabeth-Town (Hagerstown) in 1762. This was apparently a very successful undertaking, for ten years later, under date of September 7, 1772, Eddis writes:[44] "About thirty miles west of Frederick-town, I passed through a settlement which is making quick advances to perfection. A German adventurer, whose name is Hagar, purchased a considerable tract of land in this neighborhood, and with much discernment and foresight determined to give encouragement to traders, and to erect proper habitations for the stowage of goods, for the supply of the adjacent country. His plan succeeded: he has lived to behold a multitude of inhabitants on lands, which he remembered unoccupied: and he has seen erected in places, appropriated by him for that purpose, more than a hundred comfortable edifices, to which the name of Hagar's Town is given, in honor of the intelligent founder."[45]

[44] "Letters from America," p. 133.

[45] Jonathan Hager was born in 1714. In 1740 he married Elizabeth Kershner. He died November 6, 1775, from the effects of an injury, a log

The town of Frederick was laid out in 1745. The territory had been settled ten years before by a party of colonists under the leadership of Thomas Schley, who was their schoolmaster. There is nothing on record to show whether Schley and his party came to Maryland by way of Pennsylvania or not, and it has been assumed that they landed at Annapolis. The fact that their names have not been found in the Pennsylvania records does not prove conclusively that they did not come to that colony first, as did most of the emigrants of that period, for those records are admittedly incomplete.

It is a fact that cannot be controverted that of the thousands of Germans who settled in Maryland prior to 1760 and entirely changed the character of that colony, with but very few exceptions they were Pennsylvania-Germans. In fact, although there were some notable exceptions, the number who came directly to Maryland from Germany can be regarded as a negligible quantity. It is unfortunate that there was no record kept of the arrival of emigrants at the ports of Annapolis and Alexandria, such as was kept at Philadelphia; or, if there was such a record kept, that it has disappeared, for owing to the absence of a record of this kind there is no way of telling just what number of Germans came directly to Maryland without first stopping in Pennsylvania. It is true that all writers who have touched upon this subject, and they are not a few, state that, according to the records of the port of Annapolis, from the year 1752 to 1755 German emigrants to the number of 1,060 arrived at that port, but the evidence presented is not sufficient, in my opinion, to prove

rolling on him and crushing him at a saw-mill where he was superintending the preparation of the lumber for the German Reformed church, in the building of which he took a great interest.

BREAD BASKETS, DOUGH TROUGH SCRAPERS AND COFFEE MILL.
TAR BUCKET, TEA KETTLE, CAULDRON, SKELLET AND
"SETAUM LÖFFELL."

conclusively that this is the case. The authority for this statement is a paper read by Francis **B.** Mayer before the Society for the History of the Germans in Maryland, on October 21, 1890.[46] Some years ago Mr. Mayer saved from destruction at a paper mill two parchment-bound volumes entitled "Records of Arrivals and Clearances at the Port of Annapolis," commencing in 1748. According to this record, among the arrivals at that port were the following:

September 18, 1752, Ship "Integrity," Jo. Coward, Master 150 tons, 6 guns and 14 men—the baggage of 150 Palatine passengers from Cowes.

September 19, 1753, Ship "Barclay," J. Brown, Master, 120 tons, 12 men—baggage of 160 Palatines.

November 8, 1753, Ship "Friendship," baggage of 300 Palatine Passengers.

January 16, 1755, Ship "Friendship," baggage of 450 Palatine Passengers.

It is upon this record that Mr. Mayer bases the statement that 1,060 Palatine emigrants arrived at the port of Annapolis. He says: "Of the arrival of Palatine Passengers, as the Germans were all known as Palatines, we have no mention except in connection with their baggage." It seems to me that this is rather significant, and it at once raises a doubt as to whether the assumption that these ships brought the passengers as well as their baggage is correct.

The story of the oppression and suffering undergone by the German emigrants who sought a home in America two hundred years ago is an oft-told tale; and standing out prominently in the story are the accounts of the villainous

[46] Report of the Society for the History of the Germans in Maryland, Vol. V., p. 17.

methods employed by the promoters, as they would be called to-day; the Neulanders, as they were known then; the men who by every means in their power tried to induce as many as possible to take ship for America. It is a well-known fact that these shipping-agents made a practice of so arranging matters that frequently a family of emigrants would find out too late that their baggage—all their household effects, their clothing, and often even all the money they possessed—was not put on board the vessel on which they had taken passage, but had been left behind on the dock. When this fact was discovered the Neulander would promise that the baggage would follow on the next ship; but in very many such cases the owners never saw their baggage again. It was a very common practice to send such baggage to a port other than the one to which the owner had gone, and when the latter was not on hand to claim it when it did arrive it was usually sold and the proceeds of the sale divided between the captain of the ship and the shipping-agent, the Neulander.

Bearing this fact in mind, when we read of certain ships bringing to Annapolis the baggage of over one thousand Palatine passengers, with no mention of the passengers themselves, the information that has come down to us concerning the methods of the Neulanders is at least sufficient to raise a doubt as to whether there were any German emigrants brought by those ships; whether those different lots of baggage were not some of that literally stolen from the unfortunate emigrants, who, without their belongings, and in many cases their money which had been carefully put away in their chests, were not able to pay for their passage and were sold as Redemptioners. This view of the matter seems but the more likely when we consider the fact that at least two of these ships, the *Friendship* and the

Barclay, and probably also the *Integrity*, were commonly engaged in carrying German emigrants to the port of Philadelphia. Considering all the circumstances of the matter, it seems to me that there is more than a reasonable doubt as to whether there were any emigrants landed at the port of Annapolis from the ships specified.

The town of Frederick grew rapidly and soon outstripped the older villages, and three years after it was laid out, when the county of Frederick was organized, it was made the county seat. In an address delivered at the Centennial celebration held at Frederick in 1876, Dr. Lewis H. Steiner said:

Frederick was laid out by an English gentleman, but its lots and the rich farms immediately surrounding it were soon taken up by a host of honest, thrifty, laborious German emigrants, who fled from the oppressive restrictions of their own fatherland to seek a refuge here for themselves and their families, and whose names underwent many a distortion and mutilation at the hands of the English representatives of the Lord Proprietor, as they labored to write them down from sound upon the pages of our early records. The German was spoken one hundred years ago more freely and frequently upon the streets of Frederick than the English, two of their congregations had their service entirely in that language, the children were instructed in both languages in the schools, the style of houses and barns introduced was that of German rather than English origin, and, in various degrees of modification, had so held its place here that strangers who have had the opportunity of European travel invariably notice how much Frederick resembles a continental town. But these emigrants brought with them their mother-tongue and familiar forms of worship and architecture. They brought also German thrift, industry, and honesty, with ardent love of home—wherever it might be, whether native or adopted,—they brought laborious habits, virtuous lives, truthful tongues, unflinching courage, and an intense longing to do their duty to their families, the community, and the State.

Writing of Frederick in 1771, William Eddis says:[47]
"The third place of importance in the province of Maryland, is situated about seventy miles west of Annapolis,
and is the capital of a most extensive, fertile and populous
county. Frederick Town is the name of this settlement.
Within fifty years, the river Monocacy, about three miles
to the eastward, was the extreme boundary of cultivated
establishments; and Mr. Dulany, father of the present
secretary of the province, was much censured for having
procured considerable tracts of lands, in the vicinity of that
river, which it was generally supposed could not even
repay the trifling charge of the purchase, for many succeeding generations. The richness of the soil, and the salu-
brity of the air, operated, however, very powerfully to
promote population; but what chiefly tended to the advancement of settlements in this remote district, was the
arrival of many emigrants from the palatinate, and other
Germanic states. . . . This place exceeds Annapolis in
size, and in the number of inhabitants. It contains one
large and convenient church, for the members of the established religion: and several chapels for the accommodation
of the German and other dissenters. The buildings, though
mostly of wood, have a neat and regular appearance. Provisions are cheap and plentiful, and excellent. In a word,
here are to be found all conveniences, and many super-
fluities."

The town of Baltimore was laid out in 1730 but it did
not at first, at least, attract the Germans from Pennsylvania. They were, as a rule, farmers by occupation, and
they preferred to settle on the fertile lands in the western
part of the colony rather than make their homes on the
seaboard, particularly as the conditions of living in the

[47] "Letters from America," p. 98.

latter locality were very unfavorably influenced by the fact that tobacco culture overshadowed all other occupations and produced a financial stringency that could not be easily overcome. Among the first, if not the first, of the Pennsylvania-Germans to settle in Baltimore were Leonard and Samuel Barnitz, who came from York about the year 1748 and established the first brewery there. Other Lancaster and York county Germans who later followed them were the Diffenderffers, the Leverings, the Steigers, the Strickers, and others, but, at least until after the Revolution, the additions to the population of Baltimore from this source were not of very great importance compared with the number who were filling up the western part of the state.

Shortly after 1745 a number of Germans from Pennsylvania, chiefly Moravians, made a settlement at what is now the village of Graceham, in Frederick county, about twelve miles northwest of Frederick. Of these people Schultz says:[48] "Its earliest settlers were Germans or descendants of Germans, who drifted into Maryland from the Pennsylvania settlements. Among them were the Harbaughs, Boilers, Hens, Ebenhards, Kreigers, Reinekes, Lydricks, Seiss, Schmidts, Utleys, Williards, Zahns, Herzers, Rosens, Renzands, Schaafs and Richters." The district in which Sharpsburg is located was another section settled chiefly by the Pennsylvania-Germans, although there were also a number of English among them. Among the early German settlers were the families of Cruse, Nead, Sahm, Graff, Bartoon and others. There were a number of other small settlements made by the Pennsylvania-Germans but they did not become places of importance before the Revolution, and after that struggle the number

[48] "First Settlements of Germans in Maryland," p. 16.

of Germans who came to Maryland direct from the Fatherland increased rapidly, and there were numerous additions as well from among the Hessians who had come to fight and remained to be citizens, so that the Pennsylvania-German influence was not so predominant as in the pre-Revolutionary period.

The unceasing stream of Germans which flowed through the province of Pennsylvania to the outposts of civilization and formed a bulwark between the savage aborigines and the older settlements, peopled a wilderness from which they carved an empire. They found nothing there except the fertile land. Whatever of material prosperity they had they produced with their own hands and brain. They were not an ignorant people and although mostly farmers, yet following the German custom, every boy was taught some trade, so that in their new homes with no one to depend upon but themselves, after their homes were built and their fields plowed and sowed they turned their hands to whatever was necessary to be done. As Scharf says,[49] "It is a significant fact that nearly all the German immigrants who came into Maryland soon established themselves in permanent homes, and in almost every instance took rank at once as thrifty and enterprising citizens. The greater number were skilled in agriculture, but there was a large percentage of first-rate mechanics, shoemakers, paper-makers, butchers, watch-makers, bakers, smiths, iron-workers, etc. It is a generally recognized fact that the Protestant population of France and Germany supplied the best class of workmen in the various branches of manufacture. Thus we are told by the historian Lecky that 'twenty thousand Frenchmen attracted to Brandenburg by the liberal encouragement of the elector at the time

---

[49] "History of Western Maryland," Vol. I., p. 63.

of the revocation of the Edict of Nantes, laid the foundation of the prosperity of Berlin and of most of the manufactures of Prussia.' The same is true in a greater or less degree of all the Protestant refugees, and it would be difficult to overestimate the industrial value to our own country of the successive immigration of whole communities from the different German states."

Nor did those in authority hesitate to give the Germans credit for what they were doing. As early as 1745, Daniel Dulany writing to Governor Samuel Ogle, says: "You would be surprised to see how much the country is improved beyond the mountains, especially by the Germans, who are the best people that can be to settle a wilderness; and the fertility of the soil makes them ample amends for their industry." In 1773 Governor Eden, in a letter to Lord Dartmouth, says of the Germans who had settled in the western part of the state:[50] "They are generally an industrious laborious people. Many of them have acquired a considerable share of property. Their improvement of a Wilderness into well-stocked plantations, the example and beneficent Effects of their extraordinary industry have raised in no small degree a spirit of emulation among the other inhabitants. That they are a most useful people and merit the public regard is acknowledged by all who are acquainted with them." Even the narrow-minded Eddis whose British prejudice could find but little to praise in the colony, had a good word to say of the Germans. In one of his letters he says:[51] "These people who, from their earliest days, had been disciplined in habits of industry, sobriety, frugality, and patience, were peculiarly fitted

[50] Collections of the Massachusetts Historical Society, Fourth Series, Vol. X., p. 694.

[51] "Letters from America," p. 99.

for the laborious occupations of felling timber, clearing land, and forming the first improvements; and the success which attended their efforts induced multitudes of their enterprising countrymen to abandon their native homes, to enjoy the plenteous harvest which appeared to await their labors in the wild, uncultivated wastes of America.''

Washington in his numerous journeys through western Maryland had a good opportunity to note the manner in which the Germans had developed that section, and he was so favorably impressed with the evidences of their desirability as colonists that when he was planning to develop the lands presented to him by the British government at the close of the French and Indian War, he seriously considered the advisability of bringing over a number of Germans to settle on his property. With this idea in view he wrote the following letter to James Tilghman, of Philadelphia :[52]

Interested as well as political motives render it necessary for me to seat the lands, which I have patented on the Ohio, in the cheapest, most expeditious, and effectual manner. Many expedients have been proposed to accomplish this, but none, in my judgment, so likely to succeed as the importing of Palatines. But how to do this upon the best terms, is a question I wish to have answered. Few of this kind of people ever come to Virginia, whether because it is out of the common course of its trade, or because they object to it, I am unable to determine. I shall take it very kind in you, therefore, to resolve the following questions, which I am persuaded you can do with precision, by inquiring of such gentlemen, as have been engaged in this business. Whether there is any difficulty in procuring these people in Holland? If so, from whence does it proceed? Whether they are to be had at all times, or at particular seasons only, and when? Whether they are engaged

[52] Sparks' "Washington," Vol. II., p. 382.

previously to sending for them, and in what manner? Or do ships take their chance after getting there? Upon what terms are they generally engaged? And how much for each person do they commonly stand the importer landed at Philadelphia? Is it customary to send an intelligent German in the ship, that is to bring them? Do vessels ever go immediately to Holland for them, and, if they do, what cargoes do they carry? Or are they to go round, and where? In short, what plan would be recommended to me, by the knowing ones, as best for importing a full freight, say two or three hundred or more, to Alexandria? In case of full freight, how are the numbers generally proportioned to the tonnage of a vessel?

At the same time he wrote a letter to Henry Riddell, a ship-owner, in which he offered to pay the traveling expenses of the German emigrants to the Ohio river and to provide the settlers with victuals until a first crop had been gathered, and to exempt them from the payment of any rent for a period of four years, if there was no house on the property at the time of taking possession of it.

CANDLE-STICK, SNUFFERS AND HOUR-GLASS.

5*

CHAPTER VII.

HOME-MAKING IN THE WILDERNESS.

A T this day it is difficult to realize the task accomplished by the hardy pioneers who, nearly two centuries ago, left behind them all the advantages of a civilized community and went into the wilderness to build themselves homes; into a wilderness inhabited by wild animals of every description and, still more to be feared, the savage Indians. It required a courageous and indomitable spirit, for every settler literally took his life in his hands and as well the lives of his loved ones. We have heard many tales of the bravery and daring performances of these men, and, now and then, some woman is mentioned as having performed some act which made her memorable; but the silent woman, those unknown thousands of whom we do not hear, are worthy of as much commendation and their memory is as much to be revered as is that of the men. Their part in the building was as important and as strenuous as that of the men, although, perhaps, not so plainly

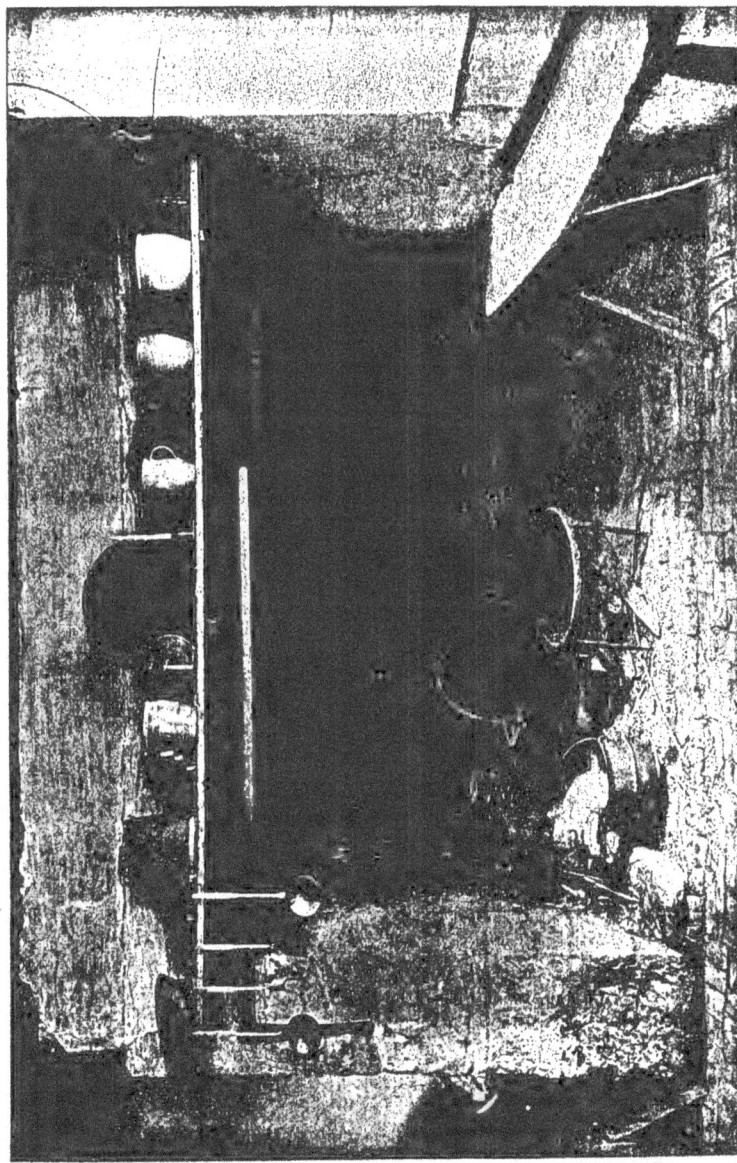

THE PENNSYLVANIA-GERMAN SOCIETY.

PENNSYLVANIA-GERMAN KITCHEN.

discernible. It was no easy matter for them to attend to the ordinary routine of housekeeping with only the rudest utensils to do it with. There was for them no spare time: when there was nothing else to be attended to the spinning-wheel and the loom must be kept busy. They were a hardy race, inured to hard work and the lack of comforts, yet the tombstones which have survived the ravages of time and the church records tell us that even they could not long bear up under the strenuous existence, but were frequently cut off in what we would now consider the prime of life. The advance of civilization and the improvements in the mode of living have materially lengthened the span of life, and on the foundations reared by those venture-some pioneers their descendants to-day live to a far greater age surrounded by comforts and advantages undreamed of in those days.

The first thing the settler had to attend to after deciding upon the place to locate was to provide a shelter. Sometimes natural caves afforded convenient temporary shelter, but, as a rule, it was necessary to erect some sort of a structure. The first dwellings were very simple affairs, the erection of more elaborate cabins and houses being deferred until some of the land had been put under cultivation. The simplest shelter was made by planting two forked poles at the proper distance apart and laying in the forks another pole to serve as a ridge-pole. Against this ridge-pole slabs cut from larger trees were placed, sloping to the ground. One end was closed by other slabs, while the other end was partly closed in the same way, the opening left being covered by a rudely-constructed door or sometimes merely covered by a blanket. Sometimes the hard beaten earth was used as the floor, while at other times the floor would be constructed of the split slabs of wood.

The next dwelling was the cabin built with hewn logs, with a roof of clapboards or plank, and in some cases of shingles, and a plank floor. Until saw-mills were erected all the planks used in building had to be cut from logs with the whip-saw. Kercheval gives the following description of making planks with the whip-saw :[53]

It was about the length of the common mill-saw, with a handle at each end transversely fixed to it. The timber intended to be sawed was first squared with the broadaxe, and then raised on a scaffold six or seven feet high. Two able-bodied men then took hold of the saw, one standing on the top of the log and the other under it, and commenced sawing. The labor was excessively fatiguing, and about one hundred feet of plank or scantling was considered a good day's work for the two hands. The introduction of saw-mills, however, soon superseded the use of the whipsaw, but they were not entirely laid aside until several years after the Revolution.

The building of the log cabin required more extensive preparations. Trees of proper size had to be selected and cut down and hewn into logs with the broadaxe and properly notched, clapboards had to be split for covering the roof and various other purposes, and when shingles were to be used they had to be rived. In the more thickly settled portions of the country a number of neighbors would frequently join with the owner in building his cabin, and in this way a very elaborate structure could be erected in a short time. Dr. Doddridge thus describes the erection of such a structure :[54]

[53] "A History of the Valley of Virginia," p. 134.
[54] "Notes on the Settlements and Indian Wars of the Western Parts of Virginia and Pennsylvania," p. 135 et seq.

The fatigue party consisted of choppers, whose business it was to fell the trees and cut them off at proper lengths. A man with a team for hauling them to the place, and arranging them, properly assorted, at the sides and ends of the building, a carpenter, if such he might be called, whose business it was to search the woods for a proper tree for making clapboards for the roof. The tree for this purpose must be straight grained and from three to four feet in diameter. The boards were split four feet long, with a large frow, and as wide as the timber would allow. They were used without planing or shaving. Another division was employed in getting puncheons for the floor of the cabin; this was done by splitting trees, about eighteen inches in diameter, and hewing the faces of them with a broadaxe. They were half the length of the floor they were intended to make. The materials for the cabin were mostly prepared on the first day and sometimes the foundation laid in the evening. The second day was allotted for the raising.

In the morning of the next day the neighbors collected for the raising. The first thing to be done was the election of four corner men, whose business it was to notch and place the logs. The rest of the company furnished them with the timbers. In the meantime the boards and puncheons were collecting for the floor and roof, so that by the time the cabin was a few rounds high the sleepers and floor began to be laid. The door was made by sawing or cutting the logs in one side so as to make an opening about three feet wide. This opening was secured by upright pieces of timber about three inches thick through which holes were bored into the ends of the logs for the purpose of pinning them fast. A similar opening, but wider, was made at the end for the chimney. This was built of logs and made large to admit of a back and jambs of stone. At the square two end logs projected a foot or eighteen inches beyond the wall to receive the butting poles, as they were called, against which the ends of the first row of clapboards was supported. The roof was formed by making the end logs shorter until a single log formed the comb of the roof; on these logs the clapboards were placed, the ranges of them lapping some distance over those next below them and kept in their places by logs placed at proper distances between them. The roof and sometimes the floor were finished on the same day as the raising.

In the mean time the masons were busy. With the heart pieces of the timber of which the clapboards were made they made billets for chunking up the cracks between the logs of the cabin and chimney. A large bed of mortar was made for daubing up those cracks. A few stones formed the back and jambs of the chimney.

As a rule the furniture used by the early settlers was of the rudest sort, generally home-made. Sometimes there might be a piece or two brought from their old home, and these, of course, were highly prized, and some of them have been handed down to the present day as heirlooms. But the bulky nature of furniture precluded much of it being carried on the journey to the wilderness. The lack of regular furniture was made up by all sorts of make-shifts. A table was usually made from a split slab, the top surface smoothed off and four legs set in auger holes. Three-legged stools were made in the same way, as were also benches on which to sit at the table while eating. Wooden pins driven into the logs and supporting clap-boards served as closets and shelves. Sometimes bed-steads were made in this way: A single fork was placed with its lower end in a hole in the floor and the upper end fastened to a joist. A pole was placed in the fork with one end through a crack between the logs of the wall and this was crossed by a shorter pole within the fork with its outer end through another crack. Sometimes other poles were pinned to the fork a little distance above these for the purpose of supporting the front and foot of the bed, while the walls were the supports of its back and head.

As the settler prospered and his possessions increased, sooner or later, the simple log cabin was replaced by a more pretentious dwelling. This, too, was often built of logs, but in that event the materials were better prepared and the logs joined more evenly, and sometimes the outside was covered with clapboards, and in some instances with plaster, producing the "roughcast" house. In regions where limestone was plentiful the house was often built of stone in a very substantial manner; so much so that some of these houses built by the early settlers are standing to-day. These houses were very much more commodious than the first log cabin, generally being two stories in height, with sometimes a garret, the floors being divided into several rooms, and having a cellar underneath. In many instances the largest room in the house was the kitchen, on one side of which was a large open fire-place, or hearth. These fire-places were quite an institution, in which a great fire of oak or hickory cord-wood was made. During the winter the kitchen was usually the living-room, as in all probability it was the only room in the house in which there was a fire. The family would seat themselves about the fire, with, perhaps, no other light than that made by the burning logs. The only means of producing light was by the use of tallow candles or the fat-lamp, and many a boy who later made his mark in the world learned the letters of the alphabet and to read by the flickering light from the blazing logs in the huge kitchen fireplace.

The cooking utensils were of the simplest kind. There were no stoves and all cooking had to be done over the open wood fire. Iron pots and pans were supported over the coals by an iron tripod, or swung by chains attached to a beam or iron bar set in the chimney. Later the chain was superseded by iron pot-hooks which could be adjusted to different lengths. Baking was accomplished in a Dutch oven, a squat iron pot with an iron cover, over which the hot coals could be heaped. This was succeeded by the large arched oven built of masonry. Sometimes this was detached from the house under a shed, but very often it joined the house, the iron door of the oven opening into the kitchen fireplace. Baking in these ovens was an interesting process, a process rarely seen in private families, at least, nowadays. The oven was large enough to take in cord-wood, with which it was filled and the fire started. When the wood was all consumed the ashes were scraped out, and the floor of the oven swabbed with a wet cloth on a pole, to remove any ashes remaining. The loaves of bread were placed on the floor of the oven with the peel, a broad, flat wooden paddle with a long handle. The baked loaves were removed from the oven in the same way. In preparing the bread for the oven each loaf as it was shaped was set to rise in a bread-basket, made of braided straw, similar to those shown in the illustration.[55]

Until the introduction of stoves the only way of heating a house was by open wood fires, and, as a rule, but few of the rooms were heated. One of the earliest contrivances used was the Franklin stove, named from its inventor, Benjamin Franklin, which was but a modification of the open fireplace. It consisted of iron plates set into the fireplace, a back-piece, with two sides and a top and bottom. The bottom piece, or hearth, extended into the room some distance from the chimney, and the top piece slightly so, the latter forming a shelf upon which articles could be placed to be kept warm. Sometimes instead of iron plates

[55] In the childhood of the writer bread-baskets exactly like those shown in the illustration were used by the juvenile members of the family on Christmas Eve, being set in the chimney-corner, in place of hanging a stocking, in anticipation of the visit of the Kris-kingle.

OLD TIME BAKE OVEN.

slabs of soapstone were used in constructing the Franklin stove. Later came the cast-iron stove, box-like in shape, with its modification, the ten-plate stove, with its oven for baking.

In the absence of refrigerators a spring-house in which to keep milk and butter was almost a necessity, and wherever it was possible such a structure was built. Sometimes the ingenuity of the settler was exercised in constructing a spring-house in the absence of a spring to flow through it. The writer is well acquainted with one good example of a spring-house of this sort, built some time during the eighteenth century. There was no spring on the property, but there was a deep well with an abundant supply of cold water. The spring-house was built near by the well. It was excavated to a depth of about two and a half feet below the surface, and thick stone walls were erected, surmounted by a heavy arch. Along one side a heavy wooden trough was built from which an iron pipe led to the well, where it was inserted into the pumpstock. Every time the pump was used the surplus water remaining in the stock, through siphonage and gravity, flowed into the trough in the spring-house, keeping the latter constantly filled with fresh cold water and answering all the purposes of a spring, in which to set the milk cans and butter pails. This building had a second story, the upper part serving as the smoke-house for curing the meat. At one corner on the outside, about five feet from the ground, an iron fire-box was constructed in the wall, with a flue leading up into the smoke-house. In smoking meat a fire of hickory sawdust and chips was built in the fire-box, the smoke being conducted up into the room where the meat was hung. Being on the outside at the ground level, the fire could be attended to with but little inconvenience. The substantial character of this structure is shown by the fact that although during the Civil War the upper part of the building was destroyed by fire, the arch remained intact and is in as good condition to-day as when it was built a century and a quarter ago.

During the first year or two the matter of providing food for his family was a serious consideration for the settler in a new country, particularly if he were located at a considerable distance from the more thickly settled localities. A family starting off to make a home in the wilderness, even if the cost did not prevent, was not able to carry with them sufficient food to last them until their land could produce what they needed, and at times during their first year there was not much variety in their food. The streams provided them with fish, and the woods with flesh and fowl, but very often their vegetable supply depended upon whether wild tubers and edible roots could be found in their locality. But after the first year, when the land had been cleared and planted with corn and wheat, and vegetable gardens provided, there was usually an abundance of food. Indian corn was one of their staples, and to a less degree wheat, but with both of these the difficulty lay in the grinding, if there was no mill near by. Sometimes a hand-mill was used, and in the absence of this a course meal was made by pounding the grain in a large mortar improvised by burning a deep hole in a wooden block, another block of wood providing the pestle. Hominy was made in much the same way.

Beef was a rarity until a sufficient supply of domestic cattle had been raised, but its lack was supplied by venison and bear meat, of which plenty could be obtained in the forests. They were usually well supplied with pork, as the hogs were allowed to run loose in the woods, where they found plenty upon which to feed. Every family raised a lot of hogs, and about the beginning of winter these were butchered and the meat cured. Butchering day was quite an institution. The hogs were killed and cleaned the day before, and early the next morning the butchers started to work cutting up the carcases. The work called for the assistance of all the members of the family as well as that of what neighbors could be procured, to help to cut up the fat to be rendered into lard. The hams and shoulders were trimmed ready for putting into the brine, to be cured for smoking, many yards of sausage was stuffed, as well as liver-pudding (*Leberwurst*). In preparing the latter the liver and kidneys, with the tenderloin and some of the head-meat, was put into a large iron kettle and boiled until it was thoroughly cooked. It was then transferred to the block and chopped fine and stuffed into skins, like the sausage, or packed in crocks and sealed with a layer of fat. The water in which the meat had been boiled was used to prepare what was commonly called Pon-hoss (*Pfannhase*), that is, Pan-rabbit. A great many fantastic explanations have been given of the derivation of this term, but it is simply one of the humorous names similar to Welsh-rabbit, for a mixture made from cheese, or Leicestershire plover, for a bag-pudding. Pon-hoss was made by using the water in which the pudding-meat had been boiled for making a corn-meal mush. This was put into pans to harden and was then cut into thin slices and fried. Sometimes a mixture of corn-meal and wheat flour, or buckwheat flour was used. A somewhat similar mixture is made nowadays in the larger cities, particularly Philadelphia, and is known as scrapple, but it is not the pon-hoss of the early Germans.[56]

[56] " A University of Pennsylvania professor, whose home is in Vienna, tells me that nowhere on the continent of Europe did he ever eat anything

On Shrove Tuesday every German housewife cooked a great dish of Fastnacht-cakes, or fastnachts (*Anglice* Fosnot) as they were usually called, a cake made of a modified bread-dough and fried in deep fat. These cakes were a very common dish throughout the winter, in some families almost entirely replacing the use of bread. There were a number of dishes peculiar to the Germans, such as " Sauer-Kraut und Speck," " Schnitz und Knöpf," etc., which to those not to the manner born may seem strange, but very often a stranger tasting them for the first time found that they were not to be despised.

Coffee and tea were not for everyday use, nor was there a plentiful supply of dishes and knives and forks for table use. Very often wooden platters, or, in some instances, pewter dishes and spoons, were used, and when individual plates were lacking the members of the family helped themselves from the general dish. Dr. Doddridge gives an interesting account of the first time he saw cups and saucers and tasted coffee:[57]

" I well recollect the first time I ever saw a tea cup and saucer, and tasted coffee. My mother died when I was about six or seven years of age. My father then sent me to Maryland with a brother of my grandfather, Mr. Alexander Wells, to school. At Colonel Brown's in the mountains, at Stony creek glades, I for the first time saw tame geese. . . . The cabin and its furniture were such as I had been accustomed to see in the backwoods, as my country

like scrapple. He is quite certain that it is of American origin. Nor can he, excellent scholar in five languages as he is, and whose mother tongue is German, explain just whence the name ponhaus. I venture to assert that if you said ponhaus to a Philadelphia waiter or possibly to any ordinary market man in this town he wouldn't know what you wanted. I am equally positive that in certain sections of Berks, Lancaster, York and Lehigh counties scrapple is a meaningless jumble of letters."—*Philadelphia Public Ledger,* January 16, 1913.

[57] Op. cit., p. 110.

was called. At Bedford everything was changed. The tavern at which my uncle put up was a stone house, and to make the change still more complete it was plastered in the inside, both as to walls and ceiling. On going into the dining room I was struck with astonishment at the appearance of the house. I had no idea that there was any house in the world which was not built of logs; but here I looked around the house and could see no logs, and above I could see no joists; whether such a thing had been made by the hands of man, or had grown so of itself, I could not conjecture. I had not the courage to inquire anything about it.

"When supper came on ' my confusion was worse confounded.' A little cup stood in a bigger one with some brownish looking stuff in it, which was neither milk, hominy nor broth; what to do with these little cups and the little spoon belonging to them, I could not tell; and I was afraid to ask anything concerning the use of them.

"It was in the time of the war, and the company were giving accounts of catching, whipping and hanging the Tories. The word *jail* frequently occurred: this word I had never heard before; but I soon discovered, and was much terrified at its meaning, and supposed that we were in much danger of the fate of the Tories; for, I thought as we had come from the backwoods, it was altogether likely that we must be Tories too. For fear of being discovered I durst not utter a single word. I therefore watched attentively to see what the big folks would do with their little cups and spoons. I imitated them, and found the taste of the coffee nauseous beyond anything I ever had tasted in my life. I continued to drink, as the rest of the company did, with the tears streaming from my eyes, but when it was to end I was at a loss to know, as the little cups were filled immediately after being emptied. This circumstance distressed me very much, as I durst not say I had enough. Looking attentively at the grown persons, I saw one man turn his little cup bottom upwards and put his spoon across it. I observed that after this his cup was not filled again; I followed his example, and to my great satisfaction, the result as to my cup was the same."

Speaking of the use of table china ware, Dr. Doddridge says: "The introduction of delft ware was considered by many of the backwoods people as a culpable innovation. It was too easily broken, and the plates of that ware dulled their scalping knives; tea ware was too small for men; they might do for women and children. Tea and coffee were only slops, which in the adage of the day 'did not stick by the ribs.' The idea was they were designed only for people of quality, who do not labor, or the sick. A genuine backwoodsman would have thought himself disgraced by showing a fondness for those slops."

The clothing worn by the family was all manufactured in the home from the raw material. The wool or flax was spun and the yarn woven into cloth. A mixture of the two, with flax for the chain and wool for the filling, and known as linsey-woolsey, was the warmest and most substantial cloth that was made, and was quite commonly used for clothing. Some of the women were expert spinners and weavers, and produced linen of the finest weave, and the heavy woolen bed-spreads spun and woven by those pioneer women are much sought after even to-day. One of these in the possession of the writer, spun and woven in the family of an ancestor, still retains its colors as bright as the day it was woven.

The settlers on the frontier were not slow to see the advantage of some parts of the Indian costume, and soon combined it with parts of the European style of dress. The use of the hunting-shirt was almost universal. It was generally made of linsey-woolsey, although some were made of dressed deer skins, but these were very uncomfortable in wet weather. The hunting-shirt was a sort of loose frock, reaching half way down the thighs, with large sleeves, open before, and made so that when belted it would lap over considerably. It usually had a cape, and sometimes was fringed with a piece of cloth of a different color, the edges of which were ravelled. The wide bosom of the shirt was utilized for holding articles of food, or anything else necessary to have convenient. From the belt, which was tied behind, were suspended the tomahawk, the scalping-knife and the bullet bag. The feet were usually covered with moccasins, made of dressed deer skin. These were made of a single piece of skin, with a gathering seam along the top of the foot, and another, without gathers, from the bottom of the heel to a little above the ankle-joint. Flaps were left on each side to reach some distance up the legs. These were adjusted to the ankles and lower part of the leg by thongs of deer skin. In cold weather the moccasins were stuffed with hair from the deer skins or dry leaves.

"In the latter years of the Indian war," says Dr. Doddridge, "our young men became more enamored of the Indian dress throughout, with the exception of the matchcoat. The drawers were laid aside and the leggings made longer, so as to cover the upper part of the thigh. The Indian breech-clout was adopted. This was a piece of linen or cloth nearly a yard long and eight or nine inches broad. This passed under the belt before and behind, leaving the ends for flaps hanging before and behind over the belt. These flaps were sometimes ornamented with some coarse kind of embroidery work. To the same belts which secured the breech-clouts, strings which supported the long leggings were attached. When this belt, as was often the case, passed over the hunting-shirt, the upper .part of the thighs and part of the hips were naked."

CHAPTER VIII.

MECHANICAL ARTS AND INDUSTRIES.

ONE great advantage to be found in a settlement made up of Germans was the fact that every German boy, no matter what his station in life might be, was taught a trade; a custom which prevails in Germany to this day, but which, unfortunately, was to a great extent abandoned by the Germans in this country, about the middle of the nineteenth century. As a result of all the men being trained artisans the German settlers were able to obtain many articles which otherwise they would have had to go without, or else secure them from some of the older settlements at an expenditure of considerable time and money. While they were all skilled in agriculture, there was a large number who were good mechanics, and those who were not able to manufacture for themselves the articles they needed had no difficulty in finding some one to make them for them, and very often there was a trading in this sort of service. One man would make some article for another, who would pay for it by doing in return something in which he was proficient.

At first, until the land was cleared, the fields prepared, and the homes built, there was not much done in the way of starting manufactories, but as the settlements increased and villages and towns sprang up, creating a greater demand for manufactured articles, a larger number of the settlers turned their attention in this direction, leaving the raising of crops to be done by others. There were few trades that were not represented, in a greater or less degree. There were expert cabinet-makers who, besides making the ordinary household furniture, frequently turned out beautiful specimens with lines modeled on the work of Heppelwhite and Chippendale, some of which have come down to this day.

As the only means of conveyance for passengers and freight at that time was by horses, the wagon-makers' trade was an important one. But few wagons were brought from abroad, for without counting the original cost of them, the freight for carrying them across the ocean would have made their cost prohibitive. The first wagons used were made entirely of wood, the wheels being sawed from the trunk of a buttonwood or gum tree. But it was not long before the iron mines were opened and forges set up and after that a better class of wagons were obtainable. There were expert wheelwrights and wagon-builders among them, who turned out large numbers of substantial wagons. The fact that Benjamin Franklin in two weeks was able to obtain from the Germans of Pennsylvania one hundred and fifty wagons for Braddock's expedition shows how well supplied they were in this particular.

Transportation methods of this kind required the use of large quantities of harness and saddles, so that saddlers

6*

and harness-makers were numerous. The manufacture of leather was another very important industry. Leather was needed for making boots and shoes as well as for harness and saddles, and great quantities of it were used. As the leather was all made by the old-fashioned process of tanning, in which the skins were macerated in vats for many months, a great many vats were necessary in order to keep up the supply, so that some of the tanneries were very large establishments. Shortly after 1753 Matthias Nead established a tannery near Clear Spring, Maryland, which was conducted by himself, his son and his grandsons for about three quarters of a century.[58] Fastened with wafers to the wall of this tannery was the following rhyming notice, which has been preserved:

NOTICE.

Ye shoemakers, Cobblers, and others attend,
Just look at this Notice, it is from your friend;
My Purse is so empty, tis light as a feather,
You have worn out your Shoes, and not paid for the Leather.
Now take my Advice and pay off the old score,
Before you get trusted for any skins more;
I have Sheep Skins, & Calf Skins, & Upper, and Soal,
I have all kinds of Leather, from an Ox, to a Foal;
I have leather that's green, and leather that's dry,
But pay down the Rhino if any you'd buy:
A hint to the wise is sufficient tis said,
Pay! and take a Receipt from your good old Friend

NEAD

Nearly every family made the soap they used. Soap-making was an interesting process, a process still in use in

---

[58] It was quite common for a trade or business to descend from father to son for several generations.

Notice

Ye shoe-makers, cobblers, and other artists,
Take took at this Notice, it is from your friend.
My House is not empty, its light as feather.
You have worn out your shoes, and now haus for the Leather.
You take my advice and buy off the Old store,
Before you get trusted for a pair of shining more,
I have Leather items to ... ole Patriots and God.
I have Leather items to ... ole Patriots and Sod.
I have Leather ... Cobler ... your Soul.
I have Leather ... Leather ... that's Very
But you buy down the Price ... if any good buy,
A hint to this wise is sufficient tis said,
Pay's and take a Receipt from your good old Patriot.

Neal

many of the families descended from the early German settlers. The ashes from the hickory wood burned in the open fireplaces or in the cast-iron stoves were carefully saved, and in the early spring the lye for making soap was prepared from them. This was done by means of the ash-hopper, a V-shaped wooden structure raised from the ground, the point downward, with a hole bored at the bottom of one end opening on the trough-like board used for the bottom. The hopper was lined with straw and then filled with hickory ashes, after which a large amount of water was poured in on top of the ashes. The water, percolating through the ashes, extracted all the alkali and came out at the bottom a dark brown liquid, the lye, ready for soap-making. This was boiled in a large iron kettle with the various kinds of fat and grease that had been saved all winter, and the result was soap. Most housewives made both hard and soft soap.

Paper-making was another industry that the Germans early established. With them linen rags was the material used for making paper, but it was a descendant of one of the early German settlers in Maryland who gave to the world straw paper and straw-board, now so universally used. The Shryock family came to Pennsylvania from Germany and later went to Maryland shortly after 1730. They settled in what is now Washington county. A descendant of this family moved over the line to Chambersburg, Pa., in 1790, where he built a mill for the manufacture of banknote paper, with which he supplied the United States government. His son, George A. Shryock, succeeded him, and later discovered the process of making paper from straw, with its allied products straw-board and binders' board. Mr. Shryock has left an account of how he came to engage in the manufacture of straw paper. It appears that Col. William Magaw, who was a relative of Mr. Shryock, was extensively engaged in the manufacture of potash at Meadville, Pa. The potash was made from ashes, the latter being leached just as in preparing lye for making soap. While overseeing the work Colonel Magaw was in the habit of chewing bits of the straw that had been taken from the ash-hoppers when they were emptied. He noticed that when this chewed straw was pressed in the hand the softened fibers matted together, forming a pulp very much like that from which ordinary wrapping paper was made, and it occurred to him that the material might be used for that purpose. He wrote to Mr. Shryock, who was at that time engaged in the manufacture of rag paper at the Hollywell paper mill, just outside of Chambersburg, suggesting to him the advisability of investigating the matter, and later, in the summer of 1829, visited Chambersburg for a test of the idea. "The experiment was, at that time and place, made and proved a decided success," says Mr. Shryock. "I was so well satisfied of its practicability that I bought a large cast iron kettle of John V. Kelly, in Chambersburg, cribbed it with wood staves so that I could boil from seven hundred to one thousand pounds of straw at one filling, and made, for some weeks, from twenty to thirty reams per day. The material used at that time in the preparation of the straw was potash, exclusively. I abandoned the manufacture of rag paper, and devoted my mill exclusively to the manufacture of straw paper for some months. In November, 1829, I visited the east to see a cylinder machine then in operation in Springfield, Massachusetts, by Messrs. Ames. On my way I accidentally met with Mr. Lafflin, of Lee, Massachusetts, at Hays' Pearl Street House, New York, and engaged him to build for me a small cylinder machine, at Hollywell Paper Mill, near Chambersburg, Pennsylvania. This was certainly the first machine that ever operated on that material. Within the first year I introduced the grooved wood roll for the manufacture of binders' and box boards, etc. These two manufactures were (as far as has been ascertained) the very first use of straw paper as a staple article in our world."

In the older settled parts of Maryland it was difficult to induce the settlers to plant anything but tobacco, but the German settlers did not require urging to induce them to turn their attention in other directions. Flax was one of their staple products, and large quantities of it were grown. They used it for the manufacture of their own clothing, they made thread from it for which they found a ready market, and the seed commanded a good price. To raise a good quality of flax required care and attention, but it was needed, for at that period the amount of wool they could raise was not sufficient for them to depend upon it alone for their clothing. The seed was disposed of in Philadelphia and Baltimore, many wagon loads of it finding its way thither.

When the flax was ready to be harvested the stalks were pulled from the ground by the roots and tied in small bunches from which shocks were formed, to allow the seed to dry. When the seed had been beaten out the stalks were ready for the process of retting, or rotting. For this purpose the flax-stalks were spread out in a field and allowed to remain for several weeks, the action of the rain and sun setting up a process of fermentation which loosed the fiber from the woody portion of the stalk.[59] The flax

[59] The best quality of flax was not produced by this process of retting, " dew-retting," as it is called. The plan more generally pursued is to pack the bunches of flax-stalks closely together in pools of water prepared for this

was then dried and was ready to be broken. The simplest sort of a flax-break was made of two pieces of board, hinged together at one end, so that they could be separated and the sharpened edges brought together. Bunches of the flax stalks were passed through the break, the upper part being brought down sharply upon the stalks at many places. In this way the woody portion was broken and loosened from the fiber. When the flax had been well broken it was ready for hackling. The flax hackle was usually made by driving a number of long, sharp-pointed nails through a piece of board so that they projected for several inches. The flax was hackled by the operator grasping a bunch of the straw and drawing it over the hackle. This separated the tow from the flax proper. The oftener the flax was hackled the finer was the quality of the finished product.

The tow was spun and woven into a coarse cloth which was used for making towels, bagging, and coverings of various kinds, while from the flax itself linen of various degrees of fineness was woven, and much of it was disposed of in barter as thread. The spinning of the flax occupied the winter evenings, and in a large family it was no unusual thing to see several spinning-wheels at work by the light from the kitchen fire, operated by a mother and her daughters. Every young woman was taught to spin. A Maryland German writing to his brother and describing his situation says: " I shall now inform you how I am Situated as it Respects the things of this world. I have a small Farm of 100 acres of land and on it a Tan-yard, and By Farming and Tanning a little we are able to Support our selves. Our Soil is well adapted to Clover,

purpose, and allow the fermentation to take place in this way. In Ireland much of the flax is retted in bog-holes.

Wheat, Corn & oats, and Fruit of all sorts. We have 3 sons and 8 daughters—5 are able to turn the Spinning wheel and throw the Shuttle."

There were many metal workers, particularly in iron and copper. At an early date Dirck Pennybacker, a grandson of Heinrich Pannebacker, one of the early settlers at Germantown, Pa., built an iron-works near Sharpsburg, but about 1781 it was destroyed by a freshet and he removed to Virginia. The coppersmiths were skilled workmen who fashioned various utensils, particularly the large copper kettles, which were beaten by hand from one piece of metal, and which were frequently made large enough to hold a barrel of cider. There were many other articles manufactured by the German settlers, and their descendants were not behind those of other nationalities in the products of their inventive genius. According to Scharf it was a Frederick county German, Joseph Weller, of Mechanicstown, who, in 1831, discovered the process and manufactured the first friction matches made in this country.

The Germans in Maryland did not establish any newspapers at a very early date. According to Daniel Miller,[60] the first German newspaper in Maryland was established by Matthias Bartgis at Frederick, in 1785. In 1795 the publication of the *Deutsch Washington Correspondent* was started at Hagerstown by John Gruber. Gruber was born in Strasburg, Lancaster county, Pennsylvania, about 1778. He learned the printing trade in Philadelphia, and in 1793 was in Reading, Pa., a member of the firm of Jungman & Gruber who published *Die Neue Unpartheiische Readinger Zeitung*. He did not remain in Read-

---

[60] "Early German American Newspapers," in Proc. and Add. of the Pennsylvania-German Soc., Vol. XIX., p. 96.

ing very long, as two years later he was located in Hagers-town. In 1796, in addition to his newspaper he began the publication of what has proved to be a monument to his memory which bids fair to last indefinitely: *The Hagers-Town Town and Country Almanack.* This almanac soon attained a very large circulation which it retains to this day, and in most of the homes in western Maryland and southern Pennsylvania it was regarded as a necessity. The farmers planted their crops according to the rules and signs given in it, and it was always consulted before any undertaking was begun. Until 1822 it was printed only in German, but in that year the English edition was begun. In 1836 Mr. Gruber obtained a series of crude wood-cuts appropriate to each month, and from that time to the present the "Almanack" has made its appearance each year exactly as its founder designed it over three quarters of a century ago.

DOOR-LATCH.

Der neue Nord-Americanische

Stadt und Land

Calender,

Auf das Jahr Christi

1797.

Welches ein gemein Jahr ist von 365 Tagen.

Darinnen, nebst richtiger Festrechnung, die Sonn= und Monds=Finsternisse, des Monds Gestalt und Viertel, Monds=Aufgang, Monds=Zeichen, Aspecten der Planeten und Witterung, Sonnen Auf= und Untergang, des Siebengestirns Aufgang, Südpunkt und Untergang, der Venus Auf= und Untergang, Coarten, Fairs, eine Uhr=Tafel und andere zu einem Calender gehörige Sachen zu finden.

Nebst einer kurzen Beschreibung von Kentucky, u. s. w.

Nach dem Märyländischen Horizont und Nordhöhe berechnet; besonders für die westlichen Gegenden in Pennsylvanien, Maryland und Virginien: Jedoch in denen angrenzenden Staaten ohne merklichen Unterschied zu gebrauchen.

Zum Erstenmal herausgegeben.

Hagerstaun, gedruckt und zu haben bey Johann Gruber, nahe beym Courthause. Wie auch bey unterschiedlichen Stohrhaltern und andern zu finden.

TITLE PAGE OF THE FIRST NUMBER OF GRUBER'S HAGERSTOWN ALMANAC.

CHAPTER IX.

THE RELIGIOUS LIFE.

WITH the exception of Virginia, the English colonies planted in America during the seventeenth century were founded for the purpose of escaping religious persecution. The ruling powers having determined that the established church should be paramount, allowed no middle ground, and laws of the greatest severity were put into force against the Roman Catholics, Puritans, Dissenters, etc. The colony of Maryland was founded by Roman Catholics and until the beginning of the eighteenth century the members of that denomination were in the majority, yet a spirit of religious toleration prevailed such as was scarcely to be found in any other colony.[61] This is the more remark-

[61] The excellent character which Cecilius, Lord Baltimore, is said to have always borne, would prompt us to impute this proceeding to the

able considering the attitude of the Roman Catholics in the mother country, particularly during the reign of Queen Mary, and it is a curious side-light on the mutations of human affairs that the only religious persecution that occurred in the colony was directed against the Roman Catholics, following the Puritan Revolution.

At some time previous to 1638 the governor of the province had issued a proclamation prohibiting "all unseasonable disputations in point of religion, tending to the disturbance of public peace and quiet of the colony, and the opening of faction in religion," but when this was issued is not known, for, as Bozman states, the proclamation does not appear in the records. In 1648, in commissioning William Stone as governor, Lord Baltimore included in the oath of office to be taken by the governor a provision that he would not molest or discountenance for his religion any person professing to believe in Jesus Christ and, in particular, no Roman Catholic, if he were neither unfaithful to the Lord Baltimore, nor conspired against the civil government; that he would not make a difference of persons in conferring office or favors, because of religion, but would regard the advancement of Baltimore's interests and the public unity and good of the province

most laudable motives—the liberal indulgence of all men in their religious opinions. But, whoever is acquainted with the history of Europe, during the seventeenth century, must know that no genuine Roman Catholic at that time could entertain these liberal sentiments, or at least openly avow them. All Protestants were deemed by them heretics, and liable to the strong arm of persecution for their impious and presumptuous doctrines. We must, therefore, unavoidably confess that this liberal and tolerant measure of Lord Baltimore wears very much the appearance of that policy of conduct, just herein before alluded to, which the English Catholics are accused of having pursued, that is in joining the two great fanatic sects —the Presbyterians and the Independents, in their united endeavours to effectuate the destruction of the Church of England.—Bozman's "History of Maryland," Vol. II., p. 336.

without partiality; and that if any person in the province should molest any Christian for his religion he would apply his power to protect the person so molested and punish the person troubling him.[62]

In 1649 the assembly enacted a law providing for religious toleration which was in force for nearly half a century. During this time there was no established church; each sect or denomination conducted its affairs as it saw fit, and all support of churches and ministers was voluntary. But in 1692 the assembly passed an act making the Protestant Episcopal church the established church of the province, and imposing an annual tax of forty pounds of tobacco per poll on all taxables for the purpose of building churches and maintaining the clergy. This law was very unpopular and many of the Dissenters, Quakers and Roman Catholics paid their taxes in the poorest quality of tobacco, so that the few ministers who came to the colony under the provisions of the law received very light support. This law remained in force until the Revolution, but there was always more or less opposition to it so that there was great difficulty in obtaining competent ministers.

The German settlers were a pious God-fearing set of people, and their first thought, after settling in a locality, was to provide means for the public worship of God. After securing shelter for themselves the first public improvement was the erection of a building to be used as a church. A history of these churches would be a history of the people, but, unfortunately, in many instances the early records of the churches have been lost or destroyed, so that the history of these congregations has to be constructed from a few fragments, as well as it can be. The settlers were chiefly members of the Lutheran and German

[62] Steiner, "Maryland during the Civil Wars," Part II., p. 106.

Reformed churches, although there were a few Moravians
and other sectarians among them. Their greatest trouble
came from their inability to secure ministers. There were
very few regularly ordained ministers in the country and
those who were sent over from Germany, as a rule, remained at the older settlements, where their services were
more in demand; and for many years the religious wants
of the outlying settlements were looked after by travelling
ministers, or missionaries, who were able to hold services,
baptize the children, and perform the marriage ceremony
at any given point only at long intervals. Then, too, the
people were often imposed upon by dissolute intemperate
men who posed as regularly ordained ministers, who, in
this capacity, secured control of the congregations. Some
of them were indeed such: men who had at one time occupied positions of honor in their churches, and had fallen
from their high estate; but many of them were unprincipled adventurers who, in the dire needs of the different
congregations, saw a means of securing a livelihood with
the least possible expenditure of energy. A great deal of
the trouble which subsequently arose in the various congregations was caused by men of this sort. It was not only
among the German settlers that these pretended ministers
were to be found, sowing their seeds of discord; they were
equally common in the English settlements. In the
absence of regular ministers religious services were usually
conducted by the schoolmaster, who would read sermons.
The church buildings erected were for many years used
jointly by the Lutheran and German Reformed congregations, services usually being held by each congregation
on alternate Sundays.

Dr. Schmauk says[63] that the first Lutheran church in

[63] "A History of the Lutheran Church in Pennsylvania," in Proc. and
Add. of the Pennsylvania-German Society, Vol. XII., p. 381

SUBSCRIPTION LIST, MONOCACY LUTHERAN CHURCH.

Maryland was erected in what is now Cecil county by Swedes from the settlement on the Delaware in 1649, but what may unquestionably be regarded as the mother-church of the Lutheran denomination in Maryland was the little log church erected at the village of Monocacy about 1730. It is unfortunate that nothing is now preserved which shows anything about the organization of this congregation, and it is only in later years that we find anything authentic concerning it. From the records of Rev. John Caspar Stoever we get the names of a number of the early members of the Monocacy congregation, as on his numerous visits to that section of the country he baptized the children of those attached to the congregation. Thus, in 1734, four children of John Jacob Mattheis were baptized. In 1735 we find the names of Heinrich Sinn and Michael Reusner; in 1736, John and Balthasar Fauth, Matthias Roessell, Johannes Mittag, George Lathy, John Jacob Hoof, Adam Baker and Henry Prey; in 1737, John George Geiger and George Henckel; in 1738, Heinrich Fortunee, Joseph Mayhew, Valentine Mueller, Philip Ernst Grueber and George Spengel; in 1739, Wilhelm Dorn and Bernhardt Weinmer; in 1740, John George Beer, Herman Hartman and Michael Schauffle; in 1741, Jacob Verdriess and Jeremias Ellradt, and in 1742 Peter Apfel. Other names of persons connected with the Monocacy congregation at that period are: Traut, Baum, Habach, Berg, Hutzel, Schweinhardt, Schaefer, Schaub, Lein, Teufersbiss, Banckauf, Bruschel, Bronner, Lehnick, Kuntz, Gump, Lutz, Lay, Schreyer, Bischoff, Wetzel, Beyer, Rausch, Boltz, Ort, Kleeman, Geyer, Rudisiel, Mausser and Kauth.

The chief sources of information concerning the early history of the old church at Monocacy are the writings of

Rev. Michael Schlatter and Rev. Henry Melchior Muhlenberg, both of whom paid visits to the congregation. Mr. Schlatter was the first to visit Monocacy. He had been sent to America by the authorities of the German Reformed church in Holland as a missionary to the congregations scattered through Pennsylvania and Maryland. He arrived in Philadelphia in the autumn of 1746 and made numerous journeys to the outlying settlements, organizing congregations where there were none and assisting in whatever way he could those already organized. Early the next spring he started on a visit to the Maryland settlements. "On the 29th of April," he says,[64] "amid earnest prayers that the presence of God might go with me, I undertook a great journey to Monocacy and other places in Maryland, with a view also of visiting the congregations on the borders of the Susquehanna, having before given notice to each congregation of the time when I expected to be with them. On the first day, I got as far as Lancaster, and the following day I reached the Susquehanna, a distance of seventy-three miles. This is the largest stream in the English colonies, which, like all other streams, has received its name from the Indians and until now has retained it. In like manner, also, do the regions of country receive their names from the streams which flow through them. Hence if, in what follows, I shall mention any places not referred to before, it must be remembered that then I have passed over some larger or smaller stream, a matter which is frequently not accomplished without great danger. At least, when I crossed the Susquehanna it was greatly swollen, so that I crossed it with twelve men at the oars of the boat, and

[64] "The Life of Rev. Michael Schlatter," by Rev. H. Harbaugh, A.M., p. 152.

then only reached the opposite shores amid dangers which threatened my life, the river being, at that time, about two miles wide."

He reached York on May 2 and held services there and then went on to Conewago, in Adams county, where he also held services. He then goes on to say: "On the 6th, I journeyed forty miles farther to Monocacy, where, on the following day, I held preparatory service to the Holy Communion, and baptized twenty-six children, and, on the 8th, administered the most excellent Supper of the Lord, with peculiar interest and much edification, to eighty-six members. After divine service was ended, I read my instructions to the people. The congregation, anxious after spiritual food, listened with tears of joy and with gratitude to God, and forty-nine heads of families offered to raise, for the support of a minister, in money and grain, the amount of forty pounds, equal to 266 Dutch guilders. If this congregation were united with another called Connogocheague, lying thirty miles distant, these two would be able to sustain a minister. Farther, I must say of this congregation, that it appears to me to be one of the purest in the whole country, and one in which I have found the most traces of the true fear of God; one that is free from the sects, of which, in other places, the country is filled. For, on 7000 acres of land in that neighborhood there were none but such as are of the German Reformed faith."

Just seven weeks after Mr. Schlatter's visit to Monocacy Mr. Muhlenberg arrived there. He had been met at Conewago (now Hanover) by two men from the Monocacy settlement and the three men starting out in a pouring rain, "were compelled to ride all night through the wilderness with the rain pouring down and the poor horses up to their knees in water and mire." In this manner the journey of thirty-six miles was accomplished and Monocacy was reached in the morning. He found the Lutheran congregation divided into factions, through the efforts of Moravian missionaries and of men who, while posing as Lutheran ministers, were secretly trying to transfer control of the congregation to the Moravians. Mr. Muhlenberg called the congregation together and, as he says:

> Before we began the service I had them give me the church book, and I wrote in it, in the English language, several articles, among others that our German Lutherans confess the holy Word of God in the prophetic and apostolic Scriptures, and besides the Augsburg Confession the other symbolical books; and, where it can be done, they have the sacraments administered to them by regularly called and ordained ministers, and, according to their rules, do not allow open, gross, and persistent offenders against the Ten Commandments and the civil laws to be regarded as members, etc. This I read publicly to the congregation, and explained it in German, and added that he who would be and would remain such a Lutheran should subscribe his name.

This book in which Mr. Muhlenberg wrote the articles for the government of the Lutheran church at Monocacy is now in the possession of the Lutheran church at Frederick. The articles, with the names signed to them are as follows:

> Whereas we the Subscribers, enjoy the inestimable liberty of Conscience under the powerfull Protection of our most Gracious Sovereign King George the Second and His Representatives our gracious Superiour of this Province, and have used this blessed liberty since our first settling Here at Manakasy till this day in Worshipping God Allmighty according to the protestant Lutheran persuasion, grounded in the old and New Testament and in the

PAGE 1.—RULES FOR THE GOVERNMENT OF THE MONOCACY LUTHERAN CHURCH.

WRITTEN BY REV. HENRY MELCHIOR MUHLENBERG.

PAGE 2.—RULES FOR THE GOVERNMENT OF THE MONOCACY LUTHERAN CHURCH.

WRITTEN BY REV. HENRY MELCHIOR MUHLENBERG.

invariata Augustana Confessione ceterisq. libris Symbolicis; We will therefore endeavour to pray for our Most Gracious Sovereign and all that are in Authority, that we may lead a peaceable and quiet life in all Godliness and Honesty.

And whereas we are Several times disturbed by pretended Ministers that Style themselves Lutherans, but can not produce any lawfull Certificate or Credentials of their Vocation Ordination of a lawfull Consistory or Ministry, and cause Strife, Quarrels and Disputations among the Congregations, We the Subscribers, the Church Wardens and members of the protestant Lutheran Congregation, erect and constitute and agree and bind ourselves to the following Articals imprimis

1. The Church we have erected and built at Manakasy and used hitherto shall stand and remain and be for the worship of our protestant Lutheran Religion according to our Confession, and oeconomie as long the blessed acts of Tolerance and of our liberty stand forever. And the Reformed Congregation shall have liberty for their lawfull minister.

2. No Minister shall be admitted and permitted to preach or administer the holy ordinances in our Church without a lawfull Call and Certificate of His lawfull Lutheran ordination and Examination by a Lutheran Consistory or Ministry, and without Consent of the Church Wardens.

3. Every Year shall be chosen four or more blameless Members of our Congregation for Church Wardens, and they shall be chosen *per plurima vota.*

4. The Church Wardens shall hold and preserve the Key of the Church, the Vessels and Ornaments that belong to the Church and Congregation and deliver every piece in time of Worship or when Necessity requireth it.

5. Two of the Church Wardens shall keep an exact account of the alms and be ready to lay at the end of the Year the Reckoning before the rest of the Church Wardens and the Congregation.

6. Whenever a Member or Church Warden of our Congregation should turn to an other persuasion, or lead a notorious sinfull

7*

life against the ten Commendments or against the Constitutions
and laws of our most Gracious Superiours, He or they shall not be
accounted for a Member of our Congregation but be excluded. To
this before mentioned Articals, which only tend to promote peace
and Quietness we set our Hands this 24 day of June 1747, in the
21 year of the Reign of our most Gracious Sovereign King George
the Second, whom the Lord preserve.

Johannes Verdries	Hans Georg Lay
Martin Wetzel	Johannes Kritzman
Michell Reisner	Johan Michal Römer
Heinrich Sechs	Georg Michal Hoffman
Dieder Lehny	Peter Apfel
Johannes Stolmeyer	Henry Sechs
Johan Sechs	Jacob Hoff
Hans Sigfried Guy	Martin Wetzel
Valentine Verdries	Georg Schweinhardt
Hans Georg Soldner	Georg Hützel
Johan Christoph Schmidt	Gabriel Schweinhard
Johannes Vogler	Fillip Küntz
John Davis	Ludwig Weltner
Friedreich Verdries	Johannes Schmidt
Martin Wetzel Junior	
Nicolaus Wetzel	
Friedreich Willhaut	
Georg Honig	
Jerg Kölz	
Johannes Schmidt	

Church Wardens (bracketing Hans Georg Lay, Johannes Kritzman, Johan Michal Römer, Georg Michal Hoffman, Peter Apfel, Henry Sechs)

Accompanying these articles is a subscription list[65] to
which is signed the following additional names:

Fredreich Sinn,	Jacob Bene,
Adam Stoll,	Conradt Künz,
Mateus Kesszele,	Joh. Sattel Meyer,
Adam Spach,	Joh. Georg Götz,
Baltzer Pfaut,	Joh. Georg Gump,
Jacob Mateus,	Jacob Faut.

[65] Nahmen der Persohnen welche zu Erkauftung und Einschreibung
dieses Kirchen buchs mit Noch wermögen beigetragen haben.

But in spite of the efforts of Mr. Muhlenberg there continued to be more or less discord among the members, and the congregation did not prosper, and about the time that Rev. Bernard Michael Hauseal became pastor of the Lutheran church at Frederick, in 1753, the Monocacy congregation was absorbed by the former. This absorption was the final act which led to the decadence and disappearance from the map of the village of Monocacy. The Lutheran congregation at Frederick, which was virtually the successor of the one at Monocacy, was organized about 1735, the exact date not being on record. Among the early members of the congregation were the families of Unsult, Bechtel, Schley, Culler, Angelberger and Metzger. For many years there was no regular pastor, services being conducted at intervals by the ministers stationed at the Lutheran church at Hanover, Pa. In 1753 Rev. Bernard Michael Hauseal became the pastor of the congregation and remained until 1758. From 1763 to 1768 Rev. John William Samuel Schwerdtfeger was pastor, and he was followed by Rev. John Christopher Hartwick. Other ministers connected with the church were Rev. John Andrew Krug, 1771; Rev. John Frederick Wildbahn, 1796; Rev. Frederick Moeller, 1799. The first church was a wooden one, built in 1741–6, which was replaced by a stone one, 1754–60. Among the members of the congregation in 1777 were John George Lay, John Michael Roemer, George Michael Hoffman, Peter Apple and Henry Six, all of whom had been members of the original congregation at Monocacy. The services were conducted in German until 1810.

The German Reformed congregation at Frederick was organized before 1740. When Rev. Michael Schlatter visited the place in 1748 he found a congregation of considerable size, although there was no regular pastor. He preached in a new and unfinished church and administered communion to ninety-seven persons. Rev. Theodore Frankenfeld became the regular minister in 1753. He was succeeded, in 1756, by Rev. John Conrad Steiner. Other pastors of the congregation were: 1760, Rev. Philip William Otterbein; 1766, Rev. Charles Lange; 1768, Rev. Frederick L. Henop; 1784, Rev. John Runkel, who retired in 1801.

One of the historic churches in western Maryland was the old Lutheran church near Sharpsburg. This section was settled about the middle of the eighteenth century. The church was built on ground donated by Col. Joseph Chapline, who laid out the town of Sharpsburg. The deed for this property is recorded in Liber L, Folio 179, of the records of Frederick county, and is as follows:

At the request of Dr. Christopher Cruss the following Deed was recorded the 16th day of March 1768.

THIS INDENTURE made this 5th day of March, One Thousand Seven Hundred and Sixty Eight, between Col. Joseph Chapline of Frederick County and Province of Maryland of the one part, and Dr. Christopher Cruss, Matthias Need, Nicholas Sam and William Hawker, Vestrymen and Church Wardens of the Lutheran Church in the Town of Sharpsburg, in the County aforesaid, of the other part.

Witnesseth that the said Col. Joseph Chapline, for and in consideration of the religious regard which he hath and beareth to the said Lutheran Church as also for the better support and maintenance of the said Church, hath given, granted, aliened, enfeoffed and confirmed, and by these presents doth give, grant, bargain, alien, enfeoff and confirm unto the said Dr. Christopher Cruss, Mathias Need, Nicholas Sam and William Hawker, Vestrymen and Church Wardens and their successors, members of the above

Church, for the use of the Congregation that do resort thereto, One Lot or portion of ground, No. 149, containing One hundred and fifty-four feet in breadth and Two hundred and six feet, more or less, in length, with all profits advantages and appurtenances to the said Lot or portion of ground belonging or appertaining. To have and to hold to them the said Dr. Christopher Cruss, Mathias Need, Nicholas Sam and William Hawker, Vestrymen and Church Wardens, and to their successors forever, to them and their own use, and to no other use, intent or purpose whatsoever forever yielding and paying unto the said Col. Joseph Chapline, his heirs and assigns, *One Pepper Corn,* if demanded, on the ninth day of July One Thousand Seven Hundred and Sixty Eight, and yearly hereafter, and the said Col. Joseph Chapline for himself and his heirs doth covenant and agree to and with them the said Dr. Christopher Cruss, Matthias Need, Nicholas Sam and William Hawker, Vestrymen and Church Wardens and their successors, that them and they shall and may have, hold, and peaceably enjoy and possess the said Lot or portion of ground and other the premises, yielding and paying the rent aforesaid hereinbefore reserved and any rent that may grow due to the Lord Proprietary freely and absolutely, but with this reserve, that if the above named Dr. Christopher Cruss, Matthias Need, Nicholas Sam and William Hawker, Vestrymen and Church Wardens, do not build or cause to be built on said Lot in the term of seven years then the above lot to revert to Col. Joseph Chapline his heirs and assigns.

A log church was erected, thirty-three by thirty-eight feet in size. A bell, which was said to be a very old one, was swung from a pole on the outside. Later a cupola was built on the church and the bell was placed in it. The interior of the church was arranged, as nearly all of the old churches were, with a very high pulpit, reached by nearly a dozen steps. Over the pulpit was an umbrella-shaped sounding-board. There was an elevated platform for the elders and deacons, while the congregation sat in

pews with very high backs. In 1849 the outside of the
building was rough-casted. During the battle of Antietam,
in September, 1862, the church was used as a hospital, but
as it was in the line of fire from the cannon it was so much
damaged as to be unfit for further use, and shortly after
the war it was torn down. The early records of the
church are all lost: probably destroyed during the war,
so that nothing is known of its early history. Among the
families connected with this church at an early date were
those of Roullett, Hovermale, Funk, Nead, Rohrback,
Gardenour, Sheeler and Harman.

The Germans did not settle in Baltimore in any considerable number at a very early date, the greater number
of that nationality going to the rich farming lands in the
western part of the colony, yet it is evident that shortly
after the middle of the eighteenth century there was quite
a number of them there, sufficient to organize two congregations: one Lutheran and the other German Reformed. The exact date when these congregations were
organized is not known, but it could not have been very
long after 1750. In the early records of the first Lutheran
congregation in the city is found the statement that "up
to the year 1758 both Lutherans and German Reformed
worshipped together, and great friendship and harmony
prevailed. In that year they resolved to erect a house of
worship in common, as each party was too weak to build
one alone; and it was at the same time determined that a
pastor should be called by either church, as might best
suit."[66] At first there was no regular minister attached to
the congregation, services being held at intervals as the
presence of a minister would permit. According to
Scharf, Rev. J. S. Gerock was the regular minister in

[66] Scharf's " Chronicles of Baltimore," p. 40.

RG, ON ANTIETAM CREEK, WASHINGTON CO., MARYLAND.

BUILT IN 1768.

1758, but this is evidently a mistake, as at that time Mr. Gerock was pastor of the Lutheran church at Lancaster, Pa., where he continued until 1767, when he removed to New York city.[67] It is probable that he occasionally visited the church in Baltimore. In 1773 among those connected with this church were the families of Lindenberger, Wershler, Hartwig, Hoecke, Rock, Grasmuck, Levely, Barnitz and Dr. Wiesenthall. In 1758 a lottery was conducted to raise funds, with which the new church was erected.

The first German Reformed congregation in Baltimore was organized about the same time as the first Lutheran one. According to a record in one of the books of this congregation, dated January 25, 1769, "the first minister of this congregation was John Christian Faber, born in Mosback on the Neckar, in the Pfaltz, in Europe. His father was a preacher at Gimmeldingen on the river Haardt. May the blessing of God attend this enterprise, and may the church increase and flourish." Mr. Faber was pastor of this congregation for about fourteen years, but his pastorate was far from being a harmonious one. Concerning Mr. Faber, Dr. Ruetenik says:[68] "He proved cold and tedious in the pulpit, and his conversation under the pulpit was devoid of salt—entertaining rather than elevating." For this reason some of the members of the congregation wanted a younger and more warm-hearted minister, and advocated the claims of Rev. Benedict Schwob, or Swope. This resulted in a division in the congregation and a second one was formed in 1770 under the leadership of Mr. Swope. Dissensions continued between

[67] Schmauk. "The Lutheran Church in Pennsylvania," in Proc. and Add. of the Pennsylvania-German Society, Vol. XI., p. 329.

[68] "The Pioneers of the Reformed Church in the United States," p. 97.

the two congregations, and in 1774 Mr. Swope retired and
was succeeded by Rev. Philip William Otterbein, who
remained in charge of the congregation until his death
in 1813.

In the first church Mr. Faber was succeeded by Rev.
George Frederick Wallauer, and he by Rev. Charles
Louis Boehme.   One of the old books of the church
records that "after some time Mr. Boehme got into
trouble and at a meeting of the Rev. Synod held at Reading, Pa., in 1782, he was dismissed from the ministry.
At the same time liberty was given to call another minister,
and they called Rev. Nicholas Pomp, who delivered his
first sermon on the first Sunday in September, 1783.   At
this period Jacob Coberts, Frederick Meyer, Jacob Meyer
and Henry Zorah were the elders of the church; and
Philip Crusius, Andrew Granget, and Philip Miller, the
deacons."[69]

One of the early congregations established by the
Lutherans was the one at Middletown, where a church
was erected about 1755.   Among the pastors of this congregation were Rev. Frederick Gerresheim, in 1779; Rev.
John Andrew Krug, Rev. Jacob Goering, Rev. John
George Schmucker, and Rev. Johan George Graeber, who
was pastor in 1796.

The Rocky Hill church, near Woodsborough, was built
in 1768.   It was a two-story log building and was occupied by the Lutherans, German Reformed and Presbyterians.   Until 1830 preaching was in the German language.   "Apple's Church" was built near Mechanicstown
about 1765 by the Lutherans and German Reformed.
Among the first Reformed ministers of this church were
Rev. Jonathan Rahauser and Rev. Mr. Bassler.   At a

[69] Scharf, "Chronicles of Baltimore," p. 42.

much later period the congregation was served by Revs. S. R. Fisher and E. E. Higbee. One of the Lutheran ministers who was pastor of this congregation was Rev. Reuben Weiser.

St. John's Lutheran church in Hagerstown was organized in 1770. Its constitution was signed by sixty members. Its first pastor was Rev. J. F. Wildbahn. From 1773 to 1793 Rev. John George Young was the pastor, and he was succeeded by Rev. Dr. J. G. Schmucker. In 1791 a lottery was held to raise money for the church. The trustees and managers for the lottery were Peter Hoeflich, Henry Shryock, Peter Woltz, Baltzer Woltz, David Harry, Jacob Harry, William Lee, John Lee, Rezin Davis, Alexander Clagett, Nathaniel Rochester, Henry Schnebly, William Reynolds, Melchior Beltzhoover, John Geiger, John Protzman, Adam Ott, Michael Kapp, George Woltz, John Ragan, Abraham Leider, Robert Hughes, Henry Schroder, Henry Eckert, William Van Lear, Jacob Miller, Frederick Stempel, Peter Whitesides, Andrew Kleinsmith, Philip Entlen and John Ney.

Rev. Jacob Weyman became the pastor of the German Reformed church in Hagerstown in 1770 and remained in charge until 1790. Among the members of the first congregation were William Baker, William Heyser, Philip Osten, Peter Wagner, Jacob Hauser, Jonathan Hager, Ernst Baker, Yost Weygand, Esau Gnadig, Johannes Karr, Frantz Greilich, Herman Greilich, Andreas Link, Eustagines Jung, Wilhelm Conrath, Heinrich Doutweiler, Jacob Fischer, Johannes Steincyfer, Frantz Wagner, Ernst Dietz, Rudolph Bly, Johannes Oster, Michael Eberhart, Matthias Saylor, George Herdic, George Campert, Johannes Nicholas Schister, Johannes Frey, Peter Diller, George Frey, Conrad Eichelberger, Philip Klein, and Ernst Kremer. In 1774 the congregation erected a substantial church building, and it was during the erection of this structure that Jonathan Hager, the founder of Hagerstown, was killed by a heavy timber falling on him.

One of the first Lutheran Churches in what is now Washington county, Maryland, was the Antietam church, situated on Antietam creek, about four miles from Hagerstown. Rev. John G. Young, writing in 1786, says that this church was built in 1756, but the will of Robert Downing, who owned the land on which it was built, speaks of the church as being in existence at the time the will was made, in 1754. Mr. Young says: "About thirteen families of our church united, purchased ten acres of land, and built a sort of church, as their circumstances allowed." Rev. Bernard Michael Hauseal, of the Frederick congregation, was the first minister to hold services at this church. For a short time Rev. J. W. S. Schwerdtfeger conducted services there, and when Rev. J. G. Young became pastor of the Hagerstown church, in 1773, he held services at the Antietam church every four weeks. This he continued to do until 1785. At that time the congregation consisted of from fifty-five to sixty families.

There were a number of Brethren located in that section at an early date. Dr. Martin G. Brumbaugh says: "The Antietam church was organized in 1752. William Stover was the first elder. His parents were not members. He was born about 1725 and died in 1795. He was assisted in the ministry for some time by George Adam Martin and was succeeded by his son Daniel Stover, who died October, 1822. This church extended over a large territory and was a midway point for emigration from eastern Pennsylvania to Virginia and the west. This church was located in the famous Conococheague country. It was the scene of many Indian depredations during the French and Indian Wars and during the Revolution. The early members suffered greatly, and some were ruthlessly murdered. There was no meeting-house for the congregation until 1798, when Price's Church was erected."[70]

[70] " History of the Brethren," p. 512.

DUTCH OVEN.

CHAPTER X.

EDUCATION, REDEMPTIONERS, SERVITUDE.

WHEN the German emigrants began to arrive in this country, and more particularly in Pennsylvania, in large numbers and it became apparent that unless the influx was checked the German settlers would soon outnumber the English, the latter in no uncertain terms voiced their objection to allowing the Germans to come in unlimited numbers, and found all sorts of reasons for this objection. One of the chief reasons advanced on all sides was the statement that the Germans were a rude, ignorant and uneducated class of people. This objection was frequently urged, and from that day to this it has been the custom for those who should know better to speak of the Pennsylvania-German settlers as illiterate and uneducated. No doubt this was, in some degree, due to the fact that the settlers did not, as a rule, learn to speak the English language, but adhered to the use of their own language as well as to their manners and customs. But in point of education, as that term is generally understood, it is very probable that among the German settlers there was as large a percentage of educated people as among those speaking the English language, if, indeed, the percentage was not greater.

At the period when the colony of Maryland was founded it was not considered necessary for everyone to be educated and a very large proportion of the population, even among the well-to-do, were not able to write. This is plainly shown by the number of people who were compelled to make their marks in signing legal papers. Among the "gentlemen adventurers" who came over in Lord Baltimore's first colony were many who came within this category, and it was no unusual thing to find that some of the servants brought over had considerably more of an education than their principals. Indeed, it was quite customary to bring over among the servants some who were able to act as scrivener and letter-writer. The matter of securing an education was considered of minor importance, and if it was thought necessary with some of the younger generation, they were sent back to England for the purpose of securing it; but what they considered an education to be obtained in this way, was not so much a knowledge of the liberal arts as it was of the manners and customs of polite society, to be gained through visiting in the families of their English relatives.

This being the case, there was little interest taken in the matter of establishing schools, and it was many years before there were any schools. There were a number of causes which militated against the establishment of schools, but outside of the lack of interest and the absence of a feeling of necessity for an education, the chief cause was the

scattered condition of the population. The raising of
tobacco was the chief occupation, and of necessity the
settlers were scattered over a wide extent of territory.
There was, in the early history of the colony, little to fear
from the Indians, owing to the founder's pacific treatment
of them, so that there was no occasion for the settlers to
gather together in groups for protection, and towns and
villages were unknown. So much so was this the case that,
as one writer has pointed out,[71] if Maryland had had a
law similar to the Massachusetts law of 1647, which provided that every township of fifty householders should
appoint some one " to teach all such children as shall resort
to him to write and read," it would not have required the
establishment of a single school, as there was no portion
of the province thickly enough settled to have fifty householders in an area equal to a New England township.

The earliest effort to establish an educational institution
was made in 1671, but the bill was amended by the lower
house of the assembly, which had a Protestant majority,
in such a manner as to render it distasteful to the Roman
Catholic upper house, and further consideration of it was
dropped. At frequent intervals other attempts were made
to found a system of schools, but they were generally un-
successful. There were a number of reasons for this lack
of success. In the first place, the country was so sparsely
settled that there was no locality in which a central point
could be selected for a school which would be convenient
of access for the children of the settlers. Then, too, as a
rule, the schools, if they were established, would be chiefly
for the children of the poorer class of settlers, for those of
means usually had their children taught by private teachers, although it must be said that there was not much inter-

[71] Sollers, " History of Education in Maryland," p. 16.

est taken in the matter of education and very many of the wealthier class of settlers had very little education, even some of the judges being unable to write their names. But the chief difficulty in the matter of providing schools was the impossibility of finding suitable teachers. As a rule the men who were secured as teachers were dissolute and intemperate individuals who were unable or unwilling to attempt to make a living in any other occupation. Large landowners who brought over servants frequently secured one who was competent to act as teacher for the younger members of the family. In this way the questions of education and servitude are, in a measure, related to each other. Sometimes a ne'er-do-well son of a wealthy English family was sent to the colony to get rid of him, rather than with an expectation of his bettering himself, and such an one frequently acted as teacher. There were instances, too, where convicts who had been transported to the colony were employed as teachers. In 1745 the officers of the school in Talbot county offered a reward of £5 currency for the capture of their Irish schoolmaster, who had run away with two geldings and a negro slave.

In 1696 a law was passed providing for the erection of a school in each county, but by 1717 but one had been erected, at Annapolis. Every few years a new law was passed providing for the erection of schools, but from one cause or another they proved abortive, and as late as March 21, 1754, a writer in the *Maryland Gazette* complained of the amount of money that was every year being sent to the neighboring province of Pennsylvania for educational purposes. "On inquiry," he says, "it has been found that there are at least 100 Marylanders in the academy at Philadelphia, and it is experimentally known that the annual charges for clothes, schooling, board, etc., amount (at least) to £75 Maryland currency, £50 sterling, for each youth sent thither—that is, to be genteelly and liberally educated. Hence it is evident that if this practice continues but twenty years (at the moderate computation of £5,000 sterling per annum) there must be remitted from Maryland for the benefit of the Pennsylvanians the round plumb or sum of £100,000 sterling. Besides this, 'tis well known that vast sums are every year transmitted to France, etc., for the education of our young gentlemen of the popish persuasion, etc. Though perhaps superior politics, interest and influence may render the saving the money in the latter case (entirely lost to the province) impracticable, yet certainly our Protestant patriots might contrive ways and means for keeping within Maryland the cash advanced (as aforesaid for the use of Pennsylvania), by establishing a college on each shore, or one at Annapolis, at which (if duly endowed and regulated by proper statutes) our Protestant youth might be educated much better, cheaper, and more conveniently accommodated, and at the same time the cost expended would still circulate within the province."

In 1763 Governor Sharpe wrote: "It is really to be lamented that while such great things are being done for the support of Colleges and Accademies in the Neighbouring Colonies, there is not in this even one good Grammar School. I should be glad if either by Donations or some other Method the Fund or annual Income of our School in this City could be augmented so as to enable us to give such a Salary to a Master & Usher as would encourage good & able Men to act in those Capacities."[72]

The matter of education was treated in a very different manner by the German settlers. It was the usual custom

[72] Archives of Maryland, Vol. XIV., p. 115.

THE PENNSYLVANIA-GERMAN SOCIETY.

REWARD OF MERIT.

DRAWN BY A PENNSYLVANIA-GERMAN SCHOOLMASTER.

for a party of German emigrants starting out to form a settlement to take with them a schoolmaster. One of the first buildings erected was a schoolhouse, very often before a church, and until the church building was provided the schoolhouse was used for religious services. It was many years before the different settlements and villages were able to have a regular minister, and in the absence of a pastor the religious services were usually conducted by the schoolmaster. The latter was very often the most important person in the settlement. He was usually well educated and generally he was the one to whom nearly everyone went for advice on almost any matter. He was the scrivener for drawing up legal papers or writing letters for those who were unable to write, and generally being an expert penman he was frequently called upon to draw up marriage certificates or certificates of baptism, which very often were executed in a very artistic manner. This facility in using the pen was put to use in making Rewards of Merit for the children in the school, usually comprising pictures of flowers and birds, an example of which is shown in one of the illustrations. These pen drawings were colored with inks made from various vegetables. In the original of the one illustrated the roses are colored different shades of pink, the ribbon with which they are tied is blue, and the eagle yellow. As a rule, though not always, the schoolmaster was an elderly man and not unfrequently, like Goldsmith's schoolmaster,

> "A man severe he was, and stern to view;
> I knew him well, and every truant knew:
> Well had the boding tremblers learned to trace
> The day's disasters in his morning face."

Sometimes in employing a schoolmaster the German

8*

settlers were deceived by an adventurer, for there was a considerable number of unprincipled dissolute individuals travelling about through the colonies seeking employment wherever they could, sometimes even posing as ministers and securing control of the churches; and as these men were usually well educated they sometimes found employment as schoolmaster, though there were not very many instances of this sort.

If the schoolmaster was unmarried and had no family of his own he generally lived with the families whose children came to his school. "Children were not merely sent to school and their entire mental training left to the schoolmaster. Parents assisted their children in learning their lessons at home, and when schools and schoolmasters were wanting parents were the teachers of their children. . . . The German A B C Book and Spelling Book were frequently printed in this country, also Arithmetics, Readers, including the New Testament, Psalter and other books. The Catechism and Hymn-Book were also used in teaching the young to read. In many homes children would gather in the long winter evenings at the table at which meals were served during the day, that parents might assist them in learning their lessons."[73]

The best known of the early German schoolmasters of Maryland was Thomas Schley, the progenitor of Admiral Winfield Scott Schley, who, in 1735, settled in the locality where ten years later the town of Frederick was laid out. Mr. Schley is said to have built the first house in Frederick. From all accounts of him he appears to have been a man of considerable education, but his abilities were not

[73] Rev. Dr. F. J. F. Schantz, "The Domestic Life and Characteristics of the Pennsylvania-German Pioneer," in Proc. and Add. of the Pennsylvania-German Society, Vol. X., p. 54.

confined to the teaching of the children, for he took an active part in all the affairs of the settlement. Speaking of him, Rev. Michael Schlatter says:[74] "It is a great advantage to this congregation Frederick that they have the best schoolmaster that I have met in America. He spares neither labor nor pains in instructing and edifying the congregation according to his ability, and by means of singing, and reading the word of God and printed sermons on every Lord's day."

Another Pennsylvania-German schoolmaster who settled in Maryland and took an active part in affairs was Benjamin Spyker, Jr., a son of Peter Spyker, president judge of the courts of Berks county, Pennsylvania. He was born in Berks county in 1747 and was given an unusually good education for those times. Shortly after reaching his majority he went to Sharpsburg, Maryland, which had been laid out about five years before, to become the schoolmaster of the German Reformed congregation of that place. Steps were immediately taken to build a schoolhouse, and in 1769, by means of a lottery, the sum of six hundred dollars was raised for this purpose and for completing the church. The managers for this lottery were George Strecher, Christian Orndorff, Joseph Smith, William Good, Abraham Lingenfelder, John Stull, Michael Fockler, George Dyson, and Benjamin Spyker.[75] At the outbreak of the Revolution Spyker raised a company and served as captain in the Flying Camp and later in the Maryland Line.

---

[74] Harbaugh's "Life of Michael Schlatter," p. 177.
[75] *Maryland Gazette,* June 8, 1769.

The first settlers of Maryland brought with them a large number of servants, as according to the different "Conditions of Plantation," the amount of land which a settler was entitled to take up was determined by the number of servants he brought in. It has been estimated that among the original emigrants the ratio of servants to freemen was six to one.[76]

Later there were large numbers of Redemptioners, as they were called, who came to the colony. These were people whose services were sold to the settlers for a term of years, in order to pay for their passage to the colony. Some of the Redemptioners became so voluntarily in order to obtain passage to the colony, but many were forced into this involuntary servitude through misfortune or, as was often the case, through the criminality of the captains and owners of the ships which brought them to this country. While the condition in which these people found themselves was one of servitude, they were, as a rule, not treated badly, and many of them, when their term of service was ended, became landowners themselves. For many years, however, there were few Germans among the Redemptioners who came to Maryland, for the reason that very few German emigrants landed at Maryland ports; but as the German settlers increased in numbers and prospered and required additional help, it was no unusual thing for them to obtain Redemptioners from Philadelphia. This was only natural, for it was at that port that most of the Germans landed, and as the settlers naturally desired those of their own nationality as servants, it was necessary for them to go to that port to obtain them. That there were a great many servants obtained in this way is evident from the fact that in a record of Redemp-

[76] Johnson, "Foundations of Maryland," p. 173.

A SPINSTER OF THE OLDEN TIME.

tioners bound out on their arrival at Philadelphia, covering a period of only two years,[77] twenty-two were sold to residents of Maryland. This record is interesting as showing the length of time these Redemptioners were to serve, as well as the amount paid for their services. Their names and the persons who secured their services are as follows:

October 8, 1771, William Harry, of "Hagars twp., Conecocheig, Md.," secured the services of Jacob Kremewald for 3 years and 6 months for £22.8.7.

October 12, 1771, George Burkhart, of Frederick, Maryland, secured Johan Michael Smith and his wife for 3 years and 9 months at £39.9.1, and Rosina Trubb for 4 years and 6 months at £19.10.7.

October 16, 1771, Baltzer Gole, of Hagar's-Town, Frederick county, secured the services of Peter Drislaan and his wife Elizabeth Barbara, for 5 years for £43.4.6. According to the terms of the indenture they were to be found all necessaries, and at the expiration were to have one new suit of apparel, besides their old clothes.

The same day Nicholas Houer, of Frederick, obtained the services of Johannes Kast and his wife, Rachel Barbara, for 5 years, as servants, for £42.0.6.

October 29, 1771, Michael Fockler, of Frederick, secured Felix Meyer for 3 years for £16.11.6.

November 11, 1771, Joseph Neide, of Bohemia Manor, Cecil county, secured Christiana and Johannes Sappor, the former for 5 years at £22, and the latter for 14 years, 1

---

[77] "Record of Indentures of Individuals bound out as Apprentices, Servants, etc., and of German and other Redemptioners, in the office of the Mayor of the City of Philadelphia, October 3, 1771, to October 5, 1773," in Proc. and Add. of the Pennsylvania-German Society, Vol. XV., p. 9 et seq.

month and 21 days at £23.10.10.   It was also agreed that
Johannes should be taught to read in the Bible and write
a legible hand.

December 4, 1771, Michael Waggoner, of Pipe Creek
Hundred, Frederick county, obtained the services of
Michael Piltz and Barbara, his wife, for 3 years for £25;
Casper Piltz for 13 years for £10, and Rosina Barbara
Piltz for 7 years for £18.

December 11, 1771, Martin Rohrer, of Conecocheague,
Frederick county, obtained Peter Schleitz for 3 years and
6 months for £16.13, and Daniel Volks for 6 years for
£17.5.3.   At the expiration of their terms of services each
was to receive, besides the usual two suits of wearing
apparel, an ax, a grubbing hoe, and a maul and wedges,
or 40 shillings in money.

December 17, 1771, John Innis, "near Conecocheig,
Frederick Town, Frederick co., Md.," obtained Johannes
Koch and Maria Eliza, his wife, for 4 years each, for
£40.16.6.

July 22, 1772, Jacob Kimberlin, Jr., of Elizabeth township, Frederick county, obtained Mary Matthews for 2
years at £10.0.0.

October 24, 1772, Jacob Bear, of Conecocheague,
Frederick county, obtained George Frederick Pindle for
11 years for £14.0.0.

May 31, 1773, Benjamin Esteurn, of Kitochin Hundred, Frederick county, obtained Catherine Manipenny as
a servant, for 5 shillings.   No term was specified in this
case.

Negro slaves were owned in Maryland from a very
early period.   The culture of tobacco required the services
of a large number of servants and this need was most
readily supplied through this source.   As the German

settlers became more numerous and required more assistance they naturally adopted the customs of their neighbors and acquired negro slaves. Some of them had religious scruples against slavery, but, as a rule, they followed the custom of the country and continued owning slaves until, at least, the early years of the nineteenth century, as shown by the following advertisement in the Hagerstown *Herald* of Friday, February 28, 1806, by the son of a Pennsylvania-German who settled in Maryland at a very early date:

TEN DOLLARS REWARD.

Ran away from the subscriber, living near the Big Spring, about 12 miles from Hagerstown, in Washington county, Maryland, on Sunday, the 16th inst. a Negro Woman named Dinah, about 5 feet 3 or 4 inches high, 23 or 24 years of age, squints with the left eye; had on and took with her one light calico gown, one blue and one dark; two jackets, one blue and one light; a white petticoat, two linsey jackets & two petticoats; two home made shifts, one bonnet of lead colour trimmed with black, and a new pair of shoes. Whoever takes up and secures said runaway in any jail, shall have, if taken up within 15 miles of home Five Dollars, and if a greater distance the above reward, to which will be added all reasonable charges if brought back.

Daniel Nead.

February 21, 1806.

It was not at all unusual for the Germans to free a slave by giving him manumission papers, and much more frequently they were freed by will, as was the case with

Peter Hoeflich, one of the first settlers in Hagerstown, whose will directed that "In relation to my negro man Arnold, it is my will that he be emancipated in three years from the 1st day of May, A. D. eighteen hundred and twenty-five, but he must make up all lost time during the three years that is lost from my death until he becomes free."

CHAPTER XI.

THE BORDER TROUBLES.

THE unfortunate controversy between William Penn and his heirs and the Lords Baltimore over the boundary between the colonies of Maryland and Pennsylvania had its foundation in the fact that at the time the respective charters were granted there was no accurate map of the country in existence. At the time the charter was issued to Lord Baltimore the territory it embraced was an unknown and unexplored wilderness. At that time it was not, relatively, of much importance to have the northern boundary of the colony strictly defined, the question becoming a serious one only after William Penn had received his charter, half a century later.

The map used in defining the boundary between the two colonies was the one made by Captain John Smith, in 1606, and while this map was remarkably accurate, considering the difficulties under which it was made, yet it was not absolutely so, particularly in the marking of the

various parallels of latitude; and it was this variation
which was the chief cause of trouble later on. The
charter granted to Lord Baltimore fixed the northern
boundary of his colony at the fortieth parallel of north
latitude, and the charter granted to Penn, fifty years later,
defined the same point as the southern boundary of his
demesne. Had this fortieth parallel been where it was
supposed to be, and where the maps of the period showed
it to be, there probably would have been no trouble. At
the same time, the wording of the Maryland charter is
very far from being clear. According to it Maryland was
to extend "unto that part of the bay of Delaware on the
north, which lieth under the fortieth degree of north latitude from the equinoctial." It will be noted that the
charter does not say that the province was to extend to
the fortieth parallel of north latitude, which was Lord
Baltimore's contention, but to the territory on Delaware
Bay "which lieth under the 40th degree." Now the
fortieth degree begins where the thirty-ninth ends: at the
thirty-ninth parallel of north latitude, so that a strict construction of the letter of the charter would fix the northern
boundary of Maryland at the thirty-ninth parallel of north
latitude.

A great deal has been written on this controversy, most
of which is so strongly tinctured with the partisan bias of
the writer, that it is difficult to arrive at a correct under-
standing of the subject. It is no doubt a fact that both
Penn and Baltimore honestly believed in the correctness
and justice of their respective claims; at the same time,
neither one can be absolved from the charge of indulging
in sharp practices in their efforts to fortify those claims.

From the first settlement of the colony of Maryland
Lord Baltimore was more or less active in looking after

his rights on the northern boundary of his colony, but the question did not become acute until about the close of the first quarter of the eighteenth century. Shortly after the Dutch had captured the Swedish colony on the Delaware, in 1659, the Maryland authorities sent Col. Nathaniel Utie to notify Governor Alrichs, at New Amstel, that the settlers on the Delaware must either acknowledge the jurisdiction of Maryland over that colony or abandon the settlement, threatening dire consequences in the event of failure to comply with the notice. Col. Utie is said even to have taken the trouble to serve similar notices on the individual settlers. However, the Dutch authorities, after threatening to arrest Utie, paid little attention to the notice and nothing came of it.

William Penn was hardly settled in the possession of his colony when the same question came up. At a meeting of the Provincial Council, on April 3, 1684, a letter was received from Samuel Landis, High Sheriff of the County of Newcastle. As the old record has it, "Samuel Lands' Letter was read, Concerning Coll. Geo: Talbot's goeing with three Musqueters to y⁸ houses of Widdow Ogle, Jonas Erskin & Andreis Tille, and tould them that if they would not forthwith yield Obedience to y⁸ Lord Baltemore, & Own him to be their Propor, and pay rent to him, he would Tourne them out of their houses and take their Land from them."[78] This information caused considerable excitement, particularly as Sheriff Landis reported that Jonas Askins had heard Col. Talbot say that if William Penn himself should come into Maryland on his way to Susquehanna Fort, he would seize him, and retain him, and Penn himself wrote out a commission to William

[78] Colonial Records of Pennsylvania, Vol. I., p. 113.

Welch, John Simcock and James Harrison to investigate the matter and report.[79]   But outside of writing some letters back and forth between the Pennsylvania and Maryland authorities nothing was done.

Two years later, at a meeting of the Provincial Council, on June 5, 1686, the record states that

" John White Informes this board that y⁰ Marylanders have Lately Reinforced their fort at Christina and yᵗ they would not suffer him to Cutt hay, but thrittend those he Imployed to do it wᵗʰ their gunns presented against them, and yᵗ what hay they had Cutt y⁰ Mary Landers would not suffer them to Carry it away, and if they did Cutt any more y⁰ Marylanders sayd they would throw it in to y⁰ River.   And further Informs that Majr English a few Days past came in to y⁰ County of New Castle with about fourty armed horse men; Left them at John Darby's whilst Majr Inglish and a Mary Land Capt Came to New Castle, where John White meeting him made Complaint to him of the abuses don him by y⁰ Mary Landers at y⁰ fort.   Majr English tould him that if Thou wilt say you Drunken Dogg, ned Inglish lett me Cutt hay, I will give you Leave: Whereupon y⁰ sd John White Requested y⁰ Councill's advice how he should behave himselfe in this affaire.   The Councill advised him to use no Violence, but bear with patience, not Doubting but y⁰ King will soon put an End to all their hostile actions against his Collony."[80]

The boundary between Maryland and Pennsylvania not being clearly defined, and the authorities of both colonies claiming jurisdiction over certain sections, it was but natural that there should be frequent clashes and a generally unsettled condition of affairs.   As both colonies demanded taxes from the settlers in the disputed territory the latter scarcely knew what to do, although some of them

[79] Pennsylvania Archives, First Series, Vol. I., p. 85.
[80] Colonial Records, Vol. I., p. 188.

acknowledged allegiance to that province which seemed most likely to further their own plans.

The lands lying to the west of the Susquehanna river were among the most fertile to be found in either of the two provinces and being, therefore, very desirable, every opportunity was sought to gain access to and settle upon them. When William Penn made his early treaties with the Indians it was agreed that he should have the right to take up lands in that section on either side of the Susquehanna, but it was mutually understood that the lands lying to the west of the Susquehanna should not be settled until they had been formally purchased from the Indians. There was no written agreement to this effect, at least none has ever been found, but frequent references to it indicate that it was in existence, at least verbally. The desirable lands along the west bank of the Susquehanna within the territory in dispute were eagerly desired, and it was in connection with them that the chief trouble arose.

The controversy over the disputed territory became prominent at an early date. At a meeting of the Provincial Council of Pennsylvania, on February 15, 1717,

"the Governr acquainted the Board that the Proprietors Commissioners of Property had lately Represented to him in Writing, that certain persons from Maryland had, Under Colour of Rights from that province, lately Survey'd out Lands not far from Conestogo, & near the thickest of our settlements to the Great Disturbance of the Inhabitants there, and that for preventing the Disorders which might arise from such Incroachments, they Desir'd that magistrates & proper officers should be appointed in those parts in order to Prevent the like for the ffuture. The Governour also imparted to the Board the Copy of a Letter which he had wrote on this Occasion to Collo. Hart, Governour of Maryland, and further added, that this Day the Secretary had shewn him a

Letter from Collo. ffrench, Informing of ffurther Designs of the
same kind, that the same persons from Maryland was Immediately
upon putting in Execucon; That hereupon he thought it necessary fforthwith to Call the Council, as he now did, and Desired
their Advice what methods might be most proper to be taken in
the premises."[81]

The members of the Council recognized the importance
of the matter and ordered that a commission be prepared
appointing Col. French ranger and keeper, with instructions to take such steps as might be agreed upon.   It was
also decided to appoint magistrates for that section.   But
the trouble was not to be so easily allayed.   The settlers
from the south wanted those fertile lands and were determined to have them, if it were possible.

It was not very difficult to prevent the Pennsylvania
settlers from crossing the Susquehanna and occupying
lands to the west of that river, but it was altogether different with those who came up from Maryland.   The
authorities of the latter colony claimed jurisdiction over
the territory in dispute, and if they did not actually issue
warrants for land in that section they at least made no
efforts to prevent the Maryland settlers from taking up
land in the territory which the Pennsylvania authorities
claimed to belong to that province.   Although it had been
agreed between Penn and the Indians that no settlements
should be made to the west of the Susquehanna until the
land was actually purchased, the aggressive actions of the
Marylanders in taking up lands alarmed the Indians, who
complained to Governor Keith, of Pennsylvania, and the
latter, in the hope that further trouble might be avoided
by taking up the land, persuaded the Indians to allow a

[81] Colonial Records of Pennsylvania, Vol. III., p. 37.

large tract of land on the west bank of the Susquehanna to be surveyed into a manor for the use of Springett Penn, and to be known at Springettsbury Manor. Writing to the Pennsylvania Council from Conestoga on June 18, 1722, Governor Keith says:

"Finding the Indians, since I came last here, to be very much alarmed with the noise of an intended survey from Mary Land, upon the Banks of Sasquehannah, I held a Council with them at Conestogoe, upon Tuesday & Saturday last, wherein I proposed to them to Cause a large Tract of Land to be surveyed on the Side of that River for the Proprietor, to begin from the Upper Line of my new settlement six miles back, & extending downwards upon the River as far as over against the mouth of Conestogoe Creek."[82]

He went on to say that the Indians were pleased with the proposition, and that having heard that the Mary-landers proposed setting out for Pennsylvania on that day he intended having the survey made at once. The land was surveyed on June 19 and 20, 1722, but this action did not have the effect intended, in keeping the colonists from Maryland from settling on the land. In the following year a number of people from Maryland took up land in that locality, among them being Edward Parnell, Jeffrey Summerfield, Michael Tanner and Paul Williams, who settled near the Indian town of Conejohela. In 1728 these settlers were driven off by the Pennsylvania authorities, and as no warrants for the land could be issued, the Proprietary land office having been closed from 1718 to 1732, during the minorities of Thomas and Richard Penn, and the land not having been purchased from the Indians, Samuel Blunston, of Wright's Ferry, was authorized to

[82] Ibid., p. 178.

issue licenses to settlers to take up land on the west of the
Susquehanna river.   These licenses were promises to grant
the holders patents for the land they settled, and about
twelve thousand acres were taken up under these licenses,
and after the territory was purchased from the Indians, in
1736, the patents were signed by the Proprietary, Thomas
Penn, at Lancaster.[83]

But even these proceedings could not keep back the
settlers from Maryland.   In March, 1730, Thomas
Cresap received a grant from Maryland for the land from
which the Pennsylvanians had driven Parnell and others a
couple of years before, and settled upon it.   With the
coming of Cresap the trouble among the settlers in the
disputed territory became more acute, and it was not very
long before it culminated in a condition of actual warfare
along the border.   It is difficult at this day to form an
accurate opinion of the character of Cresap.   According
to the Pennsylvanians he was a quarrelsome, lawless individual whose home was a rendezvous for criminals and
fugitives from justice and other disreputable characters,
who were banded together under the leadership of Cresap;
while from the viewpoint of the Marylanders he was a
law-abiding citizen of that province who was continually
being interfered with in his efforts to develop the land
which had been granted to him.   It is a pretty well established fact, however, that either under an agreement with
Governor Ogle, of Maryland, or, at least, with the con-
nivance of the latter, Cresap made his advent and organized a body of followers numbering about fifty for the
express purpose of driving the settlers from the territory
along the west bank of the Susquehanna; those settlers, at
least, who acknowledged the jurisdiction of Pennsylvania,

[83] "History of Waynesboro," by Benjamin M. Nead, p. 29.

and it is evident that whatever the character of Cresap may have been he proposed to accomplish that end, no matter what means might have to be employed. A campaign of bluster was started and many of the settlers were ordered to leave under threats of dire punishment in case they did not heed the notice to leave.

A good idea of the state of affairs may be gathered from a letter written to the Governor of Pennsylvania by John Wright and Samuel Blunston, under date of October 30, 1732, in which they say:

" About two years Since, Thomas Cressop, and some other people of Loose Morals and Turbulent Spirits, Came and disturbed the Indians, our friends and Allies, who were peaceably Settled on those Lands from whence the said Parnel and others had been removed, Burnt their Cabbins, and destroyed their Goods, And with much threatening and Ill-usage, drove them away; and by pretending to be under the Maryland government (as they were got far from their Laws, Sought to Evade ours). Thus they proceeded to play booty, Disturbing the Peace of the Government, Carrying people out of the Province by Violence, Taking away the Guns from our friends, the Indians, Tying and making them Prisoners, without any offence given; And threatening all who should oppose them; And by Underhand and Unfair practices, Endeavoring to Alienate the minds of the Inhabitants of this Province, and Draw them (from Obedience) to their party. Their Insolence Increasing, they Killed the horses of Such of our people whose trade with the Indians made it Necessary to Keep them on that Side of the river, for Carrying their Goods & Skins; Assaulted those who were sent to look after them, and threatened them Highly if they should Come there again."[84]

Among those who sought a refuge in Cresap's house was Samuel Chance, a debtor of Edward Cartlidge, an

[84] Pennsylvania Archives, First Ser., Vol. I., p. 364.

9*

Indian trader. Cartlidge's son arranged to capture
Chance and bring him back. Cresap was operating a
ferry across the Susquehanna river and Chance was helping him in running his boats. On one occasion, on the
last day of October, 1730, when Cresap and Chance were
called to the east side of the river, they found there a
party consisting of Edward Beddock, Rice Morgan, and a
negro belonging to Cartlidge. The party embarked in
the boat and when in mid-stream they attacked Cresap,
threw him overboard and rowed back to land with Chance.
Cresap succeeded in landing on an island in the river,
from which he was later taken by an Indian. He made
a report of this proceeding to the Governor of Maryland,
embodied in a deposition made before Benjamin Tasker,[85]
in which he claimed that Chance was a debtor of his and
was working for him to discharge part of his indebtedness.
In sending this deposition to Governor Gordon, of Pennsylvania, the Governor of Maryland wrote that he had
been told by some Indians "that they were offered a good
reward by one Cartlidge, of Conestogoe, to drive Said
Cresap and his family off his land and burn his home."

Disturbances were continually breaking out, armed
parties coming up from Maryland and threatening the
settlers, and being met by armed posses of Pennsylvanians.
As a rule, these encounters were bloodless battles, although
not always was this the case. In the early part of 1734
John Emerson, a Lancaster lawyer who had been appointed ranger and keeper of Conestoga manor, went to
Cresap's house to arrest him. He took with him his
servant, Knowles Daunt, and five others. Cresap fired on
the party and Daunt received a wound from the effects
of which he died.

[85] Ibid., p. 311.

In July, 1735, Cresap came to the plantation of John Wright with an armed party and announced that they had come to fight, but his blustering attitude had little effect upon Wright and the party retired without opening hostilities. Shortly after this Governor Ogle, of Maryland, ordered the militia of Baltimore and Harford counties, under Colonels Rigsbe and Hall, to muster for the purpose of going up into the disputed territory to distrain for the Maryland levies which had been made among the inhabitants of that region. Information to this effect having reached the Lancaster county magistrates, they induced Benjamin Chambers, of the Conococheague settlement (now Chambersburg), to go to the muster and learn all he could concerning it. Colonel Chambers made the trip and although he was at first regarded as a spy he was finally allowed to depart, and hurrying to Donegal where many of the settlers had gathered for a house-raising, he reported the results of his investigations, and a large party of armed men immediately left for Wright's ferry, where they met the Marylanders, and the latter, considering themselves overmatched, returned to Maryland.[86]

In 1736, in a letter to the President and Council of Pennsylvania, John Wright describes another invasion. Under date of Tuesday, September 7th, he writes:

"After our Sheriff and People had waited some time in expectation of the Marylanders arrival, & were mostly Dispersed, on Saturday night last, the Sheriff of Baltimore and the greater part of their Military officers, with upwards of two Hundred Men, arrived at Cressap's, and about noon on Saturday, came in Arms, on horseback, with Beat of Drum and sound of Trumpet, to Hendricks, their Sheriff, and several other Gentlemen, that afternoon, at different times, came to John Wright, Jun., where about thirty

[86] Pennsylvania Archives, First Ser., Vol. IV., p. 535.

of our People were Lodged, to Demand the Dutch who were some of them in his house. Our sheriff sent them a written message, desireing to know the Reason of their coming in that Hostile manner, to threaten the peace of our Province, They Dated their answer from John Hendricks, in Baltimore County. However, Justice Guest, one of their Company, appointed ten o'clock the next day to speak with some of our People; but about five that evening, they left Hendricks with great Precipitation, and went to Cressap's. Yesterday our Sheriff sent a written message that he had orders to Command them peacably to Depart; But if any of their Company would meet the Magistrates, and some other Persons of our County, who were with him, and endeavour amicably to settle those unhappy Differences at present subsisting in these parts, they sho^d receive no Insults or Ill usage. To which their sheriff return'd a Insolent and threatening answer in writing, & much more by word of mouth. Soon after John Wilkins, one of our Company, unknown to the rest, went down to Cressap's, whom they took prisoner, upon pretence of his having been in a former Riot, & sent under a Guard towards Maryland. Our Magistrates sent them a Letter, to desire Wilkins might be suffered to return home, which they refused to receive. 'Tis said a messenger is sent down to their Governor, who is still waiting in Baltimore County, and is expected up this day wth considerable more force.

" Our Sheriff with about a hundred and fifty people, have been, since Sunday evening, at John Wright's, Jun. No hostilitys have as yet been Committed, except the taking of Wilkins; But they have sent our People word this day to take care of their Buffs. Had we arms & ammunition, of which we are almost Destitute, we Judge, from the Disposition of our People, that we might come of with Honour; But for want of them, they think it not safe to wait upon such a number of armed men to the limits of our promise; But to endeavor to Defend such of his Majesties peaceable subjects, as are fled from their own Houses, and come to them for Refuge. Saml Blunston came home from the other side the River in the night, last night, and Immediately return'd. He desired this account might be sent to you; which for the want of a better Hand to do it, I have very faithfully performed."[87]

The Pennsylvania authorities finally came to the conclusion that matters had been allowed to drift long enough, and decided to have Cresap arrested for the murder of Knowles Daunt. A warrant, dated September 5, 1736, was, therefore, issued by Jeremiah Langhorne and Thomas. Greeme, magistrates of Philadelphia.[88] This was placed in the hands of Samuel Smith, sheriff of Lancaster county, and on the night of November 24, 1736, with a posse of about thirty men, he surrounded Cresap's house. Cresap's party at once opened fire on the posse and in the fight one of the sheriff's party was wounded. Finding that nothing could be accomplished in this way, the sheriff ordered Cresap's house to be set on fire. This was done, and when the fire had gained considerable headway the entire party rushed out, firing as they came. In the confusion of their escape from the burning building, Michael Reisner, one of Cresap's party, accidentally shot and killed Lauchlan Malone, another of the party. As he came from the house Cresap was overpowered, and with several of his party was sent to Philadelphia, where he was confined in jail. It is said that when he was being taken through the streets of Philadelphia he looked around and said: " Why, this is the finest city in the province of Maryland!"[89] He was confined in jail for over a year and when finally released returned to Maryland and settled at Antietam.

[87] Pennsylvania Archives, Second Ser., Vol. VII., p. 213.
[88] Pennsylvania Archives, First Ser., Vol. I., p. 489.
[89] Scharf's " History of Western Maryland," Vol. I., p. 114.

About the same time the following communication was sent to the Governor of Maryland:[90]

LANCASTER COUNTY IN PENSILVANIA

Sir

The Oppression and ill Usage We have met with from the Government of Maryland, or at least from such Persons who have been empowered thereby and their Proceedings connived at, has been a Treatment (as We are well informed) very different from that which the Tenants of your Government have generally met with, which with many other cogent Reasons, give Us good Cause to conclude the Governor and Magistrates of that Province do not themselves believe Us to be settled within the real Bounds of his Lordships Dominions, but we have been seduced & made Use of, first by fair Promises, and afterwards by Threats and Punishments to answer Purposes which are at present unjustifiable, and will if pursued tend to Utter Ruin.

We therefore the Subscribers with many Others Our Neighbours being become at last truly sensible of the Wrong we have done the Proprietors of Pensilvania in settling on their Lands without paying Obedience to their Government do resolve to return to our Duty and live under the Laws and Government of Pensilvania, in which Province We believe Our selves seated.

To this We unanimously resolve to adhere 'till the Contrary shall be determined by a legal Decision of the Disputed Bounds, and Our honest and just Intention we desire may be communicated to the Governor of Maryland or whom else it may concern.

Signed with Our Own hands this Eleventh day of August Anno Dom. 1736:

Michael Tanner Jacob Welshoffer Charles Jones Nicholas Baun
     Henry Lib Hart   Henry Hendrix   Jacob Lawnius
  Martin Schultz Christian Crowler Francis Worley jun[r]
Tobias Fray Balthar Shambargier Jacob Seglaer his X mark
  Martin Fray George Scobell Nicholas Birij Jacob Grable
        Jacob Seglaer Philip Sanglaer Henry Stantz
            Caspar Sanglaer Tobias Bright & al

[90] Archives of Maryland, Vol. XXVIII., p. 100.

Two days later the following communication was sent by the same persons and others to the Governor and Council of Pennsylvania :[91]

The Petition of most of the Inhabitants on the west side of the Sasquehanna River, opposite to Hempfield, in the County of Lancaster, Humbly Sheweth, that your petitioners, two or three years past, (Being many of us newly arrived in America,) and altogether strangers to the Boundaries of the two Provinces of Pennsylvania & Maryland, were, by many plausable pretences and fair promises, persuaded to settle under the Government of the latter, supposing from what we were then told, that these lands were within that Province, And that the River Sasquehanna was the Division. But after we were seated, finding the usage we received was very different from that to the rest of the Government, and what small substance we had, was made a pray to some persons impowered by them. And th° we often made known our cause of complaint, could have no redress, nor the promises, which had been first made us, in the least Regarded. Being also lately told by some in power there that we were worse than Negroes, for that we had no Master, nor were under the protection of any laws, and since informed by them, that the River Sasquehanna, could not be the bounds, as we had been at first told, but that an East and West Line would Divide the Provinces. And also, observing that the People on the East side of said River, Inhabitants of Pennsylvania, who live much more to the Southward than we Do, Enjoyed their possessions peaceably, without any Disturbance or claim from the Province of Maryland. We, from these reasons, Concluded we had been imposed upon and Deluded, to answer some purposes of the Government of Maryland, which are not justifiable, and might, in the end, tend to our Ruin; and that we were not settled within the true and Real bounds of that Province, as we had been made to believe. And from a sense thereof, and of the wrong we were doing to the Proprietors of Pennsylvania, in Living on their

[91] Pennsylvania Archives, Second Ser., Vol. VII., p. 215.

Lands, (as we now conceive we are,) without paying the acknowledgements due to them for the same, and in denying Obedience
to the Laws of your Government, Unanimously Resolved to Return to our Duty.   Your Humble Petitioners, therefore, pray you
would Impute our late Errors to our want of better Information,
And would be pleased to Receive us under the Protection of your
Laws and Government.   To which for the future we promise all
faithful obedience and submission and in Granting this our humble
Petition your petitioners as in Duty bound shall ever pray for
your Health and Prosperity.   Signed with our own hands and
Dated the thirteenth day of August, one thousand seven hundred
and thirty-six.

The receipt of this paper, together with the knowledge
that a similar communication had been sent to the President and Council of Pennsylvania, angered the Maryland
authorities, and at a meeting of the Maryland Council,
held on October 21, 1736, it was put on record that the
Council had good reason to be assured that this action on
the part of the settlers in the disputed territory had been
instigated and countenanced "by some who pretended to
be Magistrates and Residents of Pennsylvania."   The
Council went on to say that such proceedings "may have
the most mischievous Consequences, not only to the Peace
of this Province, but also in the Example which may be
thereby given to any other of his Majestys Subjects daring to refuse Subjection to the Government in which they
live and reside."[92]   They, therefore, adopted a resolution
directing that a proclamation be issued offering a reward
for the arrest of "all who have acted, countenanced or
abetted the Actors in any of the Matters aforesaid."

In accordance with this resolution, on October 21, 1736
Governor Ogle issued a proclamation offering a reward of

[92] Archives of Maryland, Vol. XXVIII., p. 101.

one hundred pounds each for the arrest of Samuel Blunston and John Wright, magistrates, Samuel Smith, sheriff, and Edward Smoute; twenty pounds each for the arrest of Michael Tanner, Christian Crowle, Mark Evans, Charles Jones, the constable, and Joshua Minshall; and ten pounds each for the arrest of the following persons: Jacob Grabill, Jacob Seglaer, Conrad Lowe, Christian Lowe, Jacob Seglaer, Jr., Michael Aringall, Philip Seglaer, Dennis Myer, Hance Stanner, Tobias Spright, Tobias Henricks, Leonard Immel, Balchar Sangar, Michael Wallack, Michael Evat, Michael Miller, Jasper Carvell, George Swope, George Philier, Nicholas Butchiere, Andrew Phlaviere, Henry Stantz, Henry Lephart, Peter Gartner, Jacob Lawnious, Nicholas Conn, Conrad Stricklaer, Henry Bowen, Francis Worley, Junr., Martin Sluys, Jacob Hoopinder, Michael Raishiere, Tobias Fry, Martin Fry, Henry Smith, Jacob Welshoffer, Henry Henricks, Adam Byard, Godfrey Fry, Methusalem Griffith, Bartholomew Shambarriere, Nicholas Hatchey, Yorrick Cobell, Henry Young, Michael Waltz, Kelyon Smith, Caspar Varglass, Martin Wyngall, Nicholas Peery, Bryonex Tandre and Eurick Myer.

Michael Tanner, Joshua Minshall and Charles Jones were arrested and confined in the jail at Annapolis.

In spite of these actions the disorder along the border continued, and finally the matter was brought to the attention of the King, and by an order in council, dated August 18, 1737, the Governors of Maryland and Pennsylvania were commanded to put a stop to the disorders and grant no more warrants for land in the disputed territory until the boundary question was settled. In 1738 an agreement was made for the running of a provisional line between the provinces which was not to interfere with the actual possessions of the settlers, but was merely to suspend all grants in the disputed territory until the final settlement of the boundary question.

This settled the border warfare, but some years later another matter came up which, for a time, threatened to drive a large number of the German settlers from western Maryland. It was but natural that quite frequently some of the settlers were not able to meet the payments of quit-rents as they fell due and at length it became the custom to turn these claims over to the sheriffs for collection, and these officers frequently added such an exorbitant amount as commissions and penalties, that it finally became a question whether many of the Germans would remain in the province. The matter was brought before the Council by Governor Ogle at a meeting held on June 7, 1748. In his statement he says:

"Sometimes Lists (which the People call Black lists) have been Delivered to the Sheriffs of arrears of Rents due and when such lists have been so Delivered, the Sheriffs have not only Charged the People a Commission of Ten p Cent for Receiving the Money but also a fee of 168 pounds of Tobacco, till Lately it has been reduced to 126 or 15 shillings Altho the Money has been Paid them and they never made any Distress; This has been Submitted to by Several because they did not know but that the demand was Iust, and if otherwise they knew not how to obtain any Relief without Puting themselves to a greater expence in seeking Relief than the fees and ten p Cent were worth. But of Late these particulars have been carried to so great a length that it has made a great many People Resolve to Leave their habitations and the Province, rather than to submit to such Impositions (as they have been lately informed they were) and Several are actually gone, and others Intend to follow as soon as they can dispose of what they have, at any rate: The Present Sheriff having one of these

Black Lists on or about the eighth day of March last past, an under sheriff Summoned the Persons to attend the high Sheriff at Frederick Town, which they accordingly did, and Paid down all that was Demanded of them together with Ten p Cent (except Stephen Ranspergen who did not Pay the ten p Cent) and every one of them Paid fifteen shillings to the Sheriff."[93]

The Governor also submitted the names of the following persons who had paid the fifteen shillings penalty: Jacob Foot, Peter Apple, Henry Trout, Melcar Wherfield, Christian Thomas, Peter Hoffman, Christian Getsoner, Stephen Ransbergen, Henry Roads, Conrad Kemp, Francis Wise, Jacob Smith, George Lye, Isaac Miller, Thomas Johnson, Joseph Browner, Henry Browner, Nick Frisk, John Smith, John Browner, Jacob Browner, Ken. Backdolt, Nicholas Reisner, David Delaitre, Martin Wisell, Casper Windred and Peter Shaffer.

In a deposition by Stephen Ransbergen, dated May 6, 1748, he says:

"A Great Number of the Germans and some others were so much alarmed by the Sheriffs Proceedings, that Several of them have already left the Province, and others have declared, that as soon as they could sell what they are Possessed off, they would go away, many of the Germans declaring that they being Oppressed in their Native Country, Induced them to Leave it, and that they were Apprehensive of being Equally oppressed here, and that therefore they would go away to avoid it."[94]

Several other depositions to the same effect were read at this meeting of the Council, and the sheriff of Prince George's county and the farmer of quit-rents being present, Governor Ogle instructed the sheriff that he should be

[93] Archives of Maryland, Vol. XXVIII., p. 420.
[94] Ibid., p. 423.

very careful in exacting no fees from the people and in
doing nothing that was not warranted by law, and to the
farmers he said that "they should use all the lenity possible
in collecting the quit-rents from the people." This disposition of the matter seems to have settled the trouble, as
nothing further is heard of it.

The boundary question was not finally settled, however,
until the two English surveyors, Charles Mason and
Jeremiah Dixon, ran the line which has gone into history
as Mason and Dixon's Line. This survey was started in
December, 1763, and the surveyors were finally discharged
in December, 1767. This line was marked at intervals of
a mile by stone monuments, every fifth monument having
carved on the northern side the arms of Penn and on the
southern side the arms of Lord Baltimore.

CHAPTER XII.

The French and Indian War.

THE amicable relations with the Indians established by the first colonists in Maryland continued for more than a century. There was never any trouble, at least with the southern Indians, and the latter assisted the colonists in defending themselves when the northern Indians became threatening. It was not until the redmen were drawn into the quarrels between England and France that trouble arose for the Marylanders.

The war between England and France was ended by the treaty signed at Aix-la-Chapelle in 1748, but that treaty did not settle the question of the boundaries between the colonies of the two countries in America. At that time the territory under the control of England embraced only a rather narrow strip along the Atlantic coast, and did not extend very far to the westward, although the English

claimed the country westward to the Pacific ocean.   In the
possession of France was Canada, on the north, and the
Louisiana territory, on the south, and the French claims
included all the territory between these two sections.   It
was the design of the French to connect these two colonies
by a line of forts extending from the Bay of Fundy to the
Gulf of Mexico, by way of the St. Lawrence, the lakes,
and the Ohio and Mississippi rivers.   As early as 1745
the Marquis de la Galissonière, the Governor-general of
Canada, had begun putting this scheme into execution.

The British government naturally made its own preparations to check this advance of the French, which would
cut off the English from pushing farther westward, and
in pursuance of its plans in 1749 made a grant of five
hundred thousand acres of land to the Ohio Company, an
association made up of a number of residents of Maryland and Virginia.   The territory covered by this grant
lay on the south side of the Ohio river, between the
Kanawha and Monongahela rivers.   According to the
terms of this grant a large part of the land was to be
settled immediately, one hundred families were to settle
upon it within seven years and a fort was to be erected and
maintained as a defense against the Indians.

When the Marquis Du Quesne de Menneville succeeded
the Marquis Galissonière as Governor-general, in 1752,
he continued the policy of his predecessor and rapidly extended the fortifications along the lakes, and in 1753
erected a fort at Presque Isle, now Erie, Pennsylvania, and
one on the Rivière aux Bœufs, now French Creek.   In
working out their plan the French endeavored as far as
possible to make friends with the Indians and turn the
latter against the English.   In this design they were
largely successful, being aided by the fears of the Indians

on account of the encroachment of the English settlers on the redmen's domain. Through the intrigues of the French, on the one hand, and the spreading out of the English settlements, on the other, it required but a small spark to fire the train already laid and cause it to break out into a fierce conflagration.

The Ohio Company proceeded to carry out the terms of its grant and at the beginning of 1754 a small company of militia furnished by Governor Dinwiddie, of Virginia, started to build a fort at the Forks of the Ohio. The officers of this company were William Trent, captain; John Frazer, Lieutenant, and Edward Ward, Ensign. On April 17, 1754, during the absence of both the captain and lieutenant, Contrecœur, the French commander at Rivière aux Bœufs, made his appearance with a force of several hundred men and compelled Ensign Ward to surrender. The Frenchman at once went ahead with the erection of the fort, enlarging it and making it more formidable, and named it Fort Du Quesne. At the time of the surrender a body of three hundred militia, sent by Governor Dinwiddie to garrison the fort, were on their way to the Forks of the Ohio. These troops were under the command of Colonel Joshua Fry and Lieutenant-colonel George Washington. News of the surrender of the fort by Ensign Ward reached these officers while at Will's Creek, and they advanced very cautiously. Hearing that a French force under Coulson de Jumonville was not far away, Washington went out to meet them, and in the fight that ensued de Jumonville and a number of his men were killed and the rest of them taken prisoners. Not long after this Colonel Fry being killed by a fall from his horse, Washington became the commander of the expedition. When Contrecœur, the commander at Fort Du

Quesne, heard of this fight, he sent a party of six hundred men against Washington's force The latter hastily constructed a fortification at Great Meadows, which he called Fort Necessity. Here he was attacked on July 3, 1754, and not being able to hold the place against a superior force, he was compelled to surrender. He retreated to Will's Creek, now Cumberland, where his force went into camp, and he returned to Virginia to acquaint Governor Dinwiddie with the result of the expedition.

This was the beginning of the struggle that was to last for years and to almost depopulate some sections of the country. The German settlers of western Maryland were nearest to the scene of hostilities and they were, for a time at least, to endure all the horrors of a bloody warfare with a savage foe. They did their part, too, in defending the country against the invaders, in spite of the fact that Governor Sharpe did not have much faith in their willingness to do so. On November 3, 1754 he wrote:

" It is expected I apprehend from your letter that the Germans who have imported themselves into these Provinces will be found as ready as they are capable of bearing Arms on the Occasion, but I can assure you that whatever Character they may deserve for Courage or military skill I despair of seeing any of them so forward as to offer themselves Voluntiers under my Command unless the Enemy was to approach so far as actually to deprive them of their Habitations & Possessions of which alone they are found tenacious."[95]

The provinces of Pennsylvania and Virginia were the ones which were chiefly interested in holding back the French, for the reason that French occupation of the territory along the Ohio would prevent their expansion to the

[95] Archives of Maryland, Vol. VI, p. 110.

westward; and for this reason, because the territory belonging to Maryland was not involved in the contest, the Maryland assembly was lukewarm in making preparations for taking part in the war. The perennial controversy between the upper and lower houses also had a great deal to do with the negligence of the authorities in this respect. On the part of all the colonies there was a feeling that this was a war between England and France, although the scene of it was on the western continent, and this being the case, it was thought that the mother country should provide for the expenses of carrying it on. The Maryland assembly put itself on record as being opposed to helping in a war of conquest but was ready to do its part in defending the province against invasion. The German settlers on the frontier, however, knew only too well what to expect, and at once made what preparations they could to protect themselves, no matter what the attitude of the authorities might be. Companies of riflemen and rangers were organized and scouts were sent out to give warning of approaching danger. Many of the settlers of the more outlying sections abandoned their homes and with their families went to the more thickly-settled regions

As soon as the news of the defeat of the provincials at Fort Necessity reached the east Governor Sharpe called the Maryland assembly into session on July 17th, and asked for an appropriation for raising troops. The legislature passed an act appropriating six thousand pounds to be used by Governor Sharpe "for his majesty's use, towards the defence of the colony of Virginia, attacked by the French and Indians, and for the relief and support of the wives and children of the Indian allies that put themselves under the protection of this government." Three companies were raised to be sent to Will's Creek,

10*

where Colonel Innes, who commanded the North Carolina troops, had erected a fort which was named Fort Cumberland Besides the men from North Carolina the troops under Colonel Innes' command consisted of three companies from New York, one company from South Carolina and a company of one hundred Marylanders, altogether a little more than one thousand men.[96]

In the autumn of 1754 Governor Sharpe was appointed commander-in-chief of all the forces engaged against the French on the Ohio, and he at once set out for Fort Cumberland, where he arrived in November He proceeded to prepare for active operations in the spring and gathered large quantities of military stores and provisions, although he was greatly handicapped by the refusal of the assembly to appropriate money to carry on the war, except under such conditions as the Governor could not approve.   In December the assembly passed a law for levying troops and provided that if in the service any citizen should be so maimed as to be incapable of maintaining himself he should be supported at the public expense There was no difficulty in obtaining volunteers.   The settlers in the western part of the province promptly enrolled themselves, and even in the eastern section calls for volunteers were promptly met.

In February, 1755, Major General Edward Braddock arrived from England to take command of the forces engaged against the French.   Braddock's plan of campaign was laid out for him before he left England,[97] and on his arrival he called a council of the colonial governors, which was held at Alexandria, before which the plans were dis-

[96] Archives of Maryland, Vol. XXVIII., p. 77.
[97] See secret instructions to Gen. Braddock from George III., Pennsylvania Archives, Second Ser., Vol. VI., p. 223.

cussed and three expeditions were arranged for: the one against Fort Duquesne, to be commanded by Gen. Braddock, with the regulars, reinforced by troops from Maryland and Virginia; one against Niagara and Fort Frontenac, to be led by Governor Shirley, of Massachusetts, and one against Crown Point, under Sir William Johnson. In preparing for his campaign Braddock made his headquarters at Frederick. The expedition started for the Ohio on May 30, and after it had left large numbers of Maryland troops marched to the frontiers to garrison the posts and protect the settlers As the assembly failed to appropriate money for maintaining these troops the expense was met by private subscription.

The details of the disastrous Braddock campaign are outside the scope of this work and cannot be given here. The effects of it were prompt and overwhelming. The extreme western settlements of Maryland were abandoned, the settlers flying for protection to more eastern points, some of them, however, stopping at Fort Cumberland and others at the block-house of Col. Thomas Cresap. Terror and desolation reigned everywhere. Hostile bands of Indians made raids on unprotected outposts, massacreing the garrisons and such settlers as they were able to capture. Even before the defeat of Braddock the Indian raids had begun. On June 28 Governor Sharpe sent the following message to the lower house:

I have just received letters from Col. Innes at Fort Cumberland, and from the back inhabitants of Frederick County, advising me that a party of French Indians last Monday morning (June 23) fell on the inhabitants of this province, and killed two men and one woman (who have been since found dead), eight other persons they have taken prisoners and carried off. The names of the persons who were murdered and left are John Williams, his wife, and grandson, and with their bodies also was found that of a French Indian. The persons carried off are Richard Williams (a son of John who was murdered), with two children, one Dawson's wife and four children. Richard William's wife and two brothers of the young man that is killed have made their escape. This accident, I find, has so terrified the distant inhabitants that many of them are retiring and forsaking their plantations. Another letter from Winchester, in Virginia, informs me that a party of Indians have also attacked the back inhabitants of that province, of whom they have killed eleven and carried away many captives. Apprehending the French would proceed in this manner as soon as Gen. Braddock and the troops under his control should have passed the mountains, and being confirmed in my opinion by an intimation in the general's letter, I issued a proclamation near a month since, cautioning the distant and other inhabitants of this province to be on their guard, and unite for their common defence and safety. At the same time I sent peremptory orders and instructions to the officers of the militia of Frederick County frequently to muster and discipline their several troops and companies, once a fortnight at least, and in case of alarm that the enemy was approaching or had fallen on the inhabitants, to march out and act either offensively or defensively, and use all means to protect and defend the inhabitants from the devastations of the French or Indians. However, I find neither the proclamation nor instructions will be effective unless the militia can be assured that they shall receive satisfaction, and be paid for the time they are out on duty. I should consider it highly proper for us to have about one hundred, or at least a company of men, posted or constantly ranging for some time on the frontiers for our protection. In this I desire your advice, and that you will enable me to support such a number.

Shortly after this a party of settlers on their way to Fort Cumberland was attacked and fifteen of them killed, three escaping. The following account from the *Maryland Gazette* of October 9, 1755, gives some idea of the state of affairs that followed Braddock's defeat:

By a person who arrived in town last Monday from Col Cresap's, we are told that last Wednesday morning the Indians had taken a man prisoner who was going from Frazier's to Fort Cumberland, and had also carried off a woman from Frazier's plantation, which is four miles on this side Fort Cumberland. The same morning they fell in with a man and his wife who had left their plantations, and were retiring into the more populous part of the country; they shot the horse on which the man was riding, but as it did not fall immediately he made his escape. The woman, it is supposed, fell into their hands, as neither she or the horse on which she was riding have been seen since or heard of. The same party of Indians also have carried off or killed Benjamin Rogers, his wife, and seven children, and Edmund Marle, one family of twelve persons, besides fifteen others, all in Frederick County. On Patterson's Creek many families have within this month been murdered, carried away, or burnt in their houses by a party of these barbarians, who have entirely broke up ' that settlement.

Another person, who left Stoddert's fort last Sunday, acquaints us that the inhabitants in that part of the country were in the greatest consternation. That near eight persons were fled to the said fort for protection, and many more gone off in the greatest confusion to Pennsylvania. This, it seems, had been occasioned by a dispatch sent to Lieut. Stoddert and the neighborhood by Col. Cresap, advising them that a party of seventeen Indians had passed by his house and had cut off some people who dwelt on the Town Creek, which is a few miles on this side of Cresap's. One Daniel Ashloff, who lived near that creek, is come down towards Conococheague, and gives the same account. He also says that as himself and father, with several others, were retiring from their plantations last Saturday they were attacked by the same Indians, as he supposes, and all but himself were killed or taken prisoners. It is said that Mr. Stoddert, who has command of fifteen men, invited a few of the neighbors to join him and to go in quest of the enemy, but they would not be persuaded, whereupon he applied himself to Maj. Prather for a detachment of the militia, either to go with a party of his men in pursuit of the savages, or garrison his fort while he made an excursion. We hope there will be no backwardness in the militia to comply with such a reasonable request, especially as any party or person that shall take an enemy prisoner will be rewarded with six pounds currency, and the person who will kill an enemy, with four pounds, provided he can produce witnesses, or the enemy's scalp, in testimony of such action.

The whole country to the west was in a condition of terror. Indian raids were constantly occurring, small parties attacking the settlers whenever their unprotected condition made it possible. Even the severity of winter did not serve to lessen the danger. In a resumé of the operations of the French Governor-General Vaudreuil writes:

"A detachment commanded by M. de Niverville came, after a campaign of thirty-three days, within reach of Fort Cumberland, and though it was impossible for him to approach it, in consequence of the dread our Indians had of being surrounded, there being considerable snow on the ground, he nevertheless, took four prisoners in the settlements bordering on the river called Potŏmak, in Virginia, about fifteen leagues from Fort Cumberland; burned ten houses and the like number of barns full of wheat; killed twenty horses or cows. This trifling success ought to show the enemy that the severest season of the year does not protect them against our incursions."[98]

With the opening of the year 1756 the attacks became more frequent. Captain Dagworthy still occupied Fort Cumberland, but the territory around it was almost deserted. In March, the commander at Fort Duquesne sent a small force of Indians under Ensign Douville with orders to "make it his business to harass their convoys and

[98] Pennsylvania Archives, Second Ser., Vol. VI., p. 422.

endeavor to burn their magazines at Canagiechuie [Cono-
cocheague] if possible."[99]   Commenting on this order,
Washington wrote to Governor Dinwiddie, on April 7,
" I have ordered the party there to be made as strong as
time and our present circumstances will afford, for fear
they should attempt to execute the orders of Dumas."[100]
On the 16th Washington wrote:

All my ideal hopes of raising a number of men to scour the
adjacent mountains have vanished into nothing. Yesterday was
the appointed time for a general rendezvous of all, who were
willing to accompany me for that desirable end, and only fifteen
appeared. . . . I have done everything in my power to quiet the
minds of the inhabitants by detaching all the men I have any command over to the places more exposed. There also have been
large detachments from Fort Cumberland in pursuit of the enemy
these ten days past, yet nothing, I fear will prevent the people from
abandoning their dwellings and flying with the utmost precipitation.[101]

Again, on the 22d, he says:

The supplicating tears of the women and moving petitions of
the men melt me into such deadly sorrow, that I solemnly declare,
if I know my own mind, I could offer myself a willing sacrifice
to the butchering enemy, provided that would contribute to the
people's ease.[102]

The *Maryland Gazette* of March 11 contains the following letter from Isaac Baker, dated at Conococheague:

My last was of the 26th instant. On our march to Toonaloways, about five miles this side Stoddert's Fort, we found John
Meyers' house in flames, and nine or ten head of large cattle

[99] Ibid., p. 361.
[100] Ford, " The Writings of George Washington," Vol. I., p. 238.
[101] Sparks's Washington, Vol. II., p. 138.
[102] Ford's Washington, Vol. I., p. 250.

killed. About three miles and a half farther up the road we found a man (one Hynes) killed and scalped, with one arm cut off and several arrows sticking in him; we could not bury him, having no tools with us for that purpose. Half a mile farther (within a mile of Stoddert's Fort) we found Ralph Watson's house burnt down, and several hogs and sheep killed. When we came to Stoddert's Fort we found them all under arms, expecting every minute to be attacked. From thence we went to Combe's Fort, where we found a young man about twenty-two years of age killed and scalped; there were only four men in this fort, two of which were unable to bear arms, but upwards of forty women and children, who were in a very poor situation, being afraid to go out of the fort, even for a drink of water. The house caught fire during the time the Indians were surrounding the fort, and would have been burnt down, but luckily there was some soapsuds in the house, by which they were extinguished. The young man mentioned above was one Lynn's son, and was sitting on the fence of the stockyard with Combe's son, when they discovered the Indians, upon which they ran to get into the fort, and before they reached it Lynn's son was shot down, and an Indian pursued the other man with a tomahawk within thirty yards of the fort, but he luckily got into the fort and shot the Indian. We searched the woods to see if we could see where the Indian was buried (as they supposed him to be mortally wounded). We found in two places great quantity of blood, but could not find the body. We saw several creatures shot, some dead, and others going around with arrows sticking in them. About half a mile on this side Mr. Kenney's (in Little Toonaloways) we found a load of oats and a load of turnips in the road, which two boys were bringing to Combe's, and it is imagined the boys are carried off by the Indians. When we came to Mr. Kenney's we saw several sheep and cattle killed. From thence we went to one Lowther's, about two miles farther, where we found his grain and two calves burnt, two cows and nine or ten hogs killed, and about fifty yards from the house found Lowther dead and scalped, and otherwise terribly

THE PENNSYLVANIA-GERMAN SOCIETY.

FORT FREDERICK AS IT IS TO-DAY.

mangled; his brains were beat out, as it is supposed, with his own gun barrel, which we found sticking in his skull, and his gun broken; there was an axe, two scythes, and several arrows sticking in him. From here we returned to Combe's and buried the young man, and left ten of our men here to assist them to secure their grain, which soon as they have done they purpose to leave that fort and go to Stoddert's, from hence we went to Stoddert's Fort, where we laid on Friday night and yesterday. On our way down here we buried the man we left on the road.

The two houses of the legislature continued their wrangling over appropriating money to carry on the war, the lower house insisting that the estates of the Proprietor should bear their share of the taxes, while the upper house and the governor refused to consent to this, and the result was that nothing was done. The settlers became exasperated at this do-nothing policy, and finally a body of armed men assembled at Frederick, under the leadership of Col. Thomas Cresap, and threatened that unless the legislature ceased wrangling and made some effort to provide for the defense of the province, they would march to Annapolis and compel action A bill was then passed appropriating forty thousand pounds. Of this amount eleven thousand pounds were to be used in building a fort and several block-houses on the western frontier, and for levying, arming, paying and maintaining a body of troops, not exceeding two hundred men, to garrison these posts. As Fort Cumberland was too far to the westward to afford much protection to the settlers Governor Sharpe determined to build another fort nearer the frontier, and in 1756 Fort Frederick was erected, concerning which more will be said later.

All through the summer of 1756 the Indians raids continued, many of the settlers being killed and others carried

off prisoners.   On August 29, Washington wrote to Lord
Fairfax:

"It is with infinite concern, that I see the distresses of the
people, and hear their complaints, without being able to afford
them relief.   I have so often troubled your Honor for aid from the
militia, that I am almost ashamed to repeat my demands; nor
should mention them again, did I not think it absolutely necessary at this time to save the most valuable and flourishing part of
this county from immediate desertion.   And how soon the remainder part, as well as the adjacent counties, may share the same
fate, is but too obvious to reason, and to your Lordship's good
sense, for me to demonstrate.   The whole settlement of Conococheague in Maryland is fled, and there now remain only two
families from thence to Fredericktown which is several miles below
the Blue Ridge.   By which means we are quite exposed and have
no better security on that side, than the Potomac River, for many
miles below the Shenandoah; and how great a security that is to
us, may easily be discerned, when we consider, with what facility
the enemy have passed and repassed it already.   That the Maryland settlements are all abandoned is certainly a fact, as I have had
the accounts transmitted to me by several hands, and confirmed
yesterday by Henry Brinker, who left Monocacy the day before,
and also affirms, that three hundred and fifty wagons had passed
that place to avoid the enemy, within the space of three days."[103]

Ten days later he wrote to Gov. Dinwiddie that the
frontiers of Maryland were abandoned for many miles
below the Blue Ridge, as far as Frederick.

Wherever it was possible the settlers raised companies
of rangers for their protection.   At Conococheague a subscription was raised and a company of twenty men, under
Lieutenant Teagard, was equipped.   "Their services
were soon required," says Scharf,[104] "for on August 18th

[103] Ford's Washington, Vol. I., p. 329.
[104] History of Western Maryland, Vol. I., p. 97.

the enemy plundered the settlers near Baker's Ridge, and on the 20th attacked a funeral train, killing two persons, George Hicks and Lodovick Claymour. They were followed by a party of thirteen of Teagard's men, under Luke Thompson, until they came within two miles of the mouth of the Conococheague, on the Pennsylvania road, when five shots were heard about three hundred yards in advance, which threw the pursuing party into some confusion; but Matthias Nicholls, a young man of eighteen, insisted that they should run up and come upon the enemy while their pieces were unloaded, and set off immediately. The others, however, ran off, but he continued the pursuit, and rescued William Postlewaite, who had been seriously wounded by the Indians."

That the French looked with equanimity on the outrages committed by the Indians is shown by a letter written to his brother by the Rev. Claude Godfroy Cocquard, in which he says:

"You will learn, first, that our Indians have waged the most cruel war against the English; that they continued it throughout the spring and are still so exasperated as to be beyond control; Georgia, Carolina, Marrelande, Pensilvania, are wholly laid waste. The farmers have been forced to quit their abodes and to retire into the town. They have neither ploughed nor planted, and on their complaining of the circumstance to the Governor of Boston, he answered them that people were ploughing and planting for them in Canada. The Indians do not make any prisoners; they kill all they meet, men, women and children. Every day they have some in the kettle, and after having abused the women and maidens, they slaughter or burn them."[105]

Up to this time the war had been allowed to drag along in a desultory sort of way, no really active operations being

[105] Pennsylvania Archives, Second Series, Vol. VI., p. 409.

undertaken, but in 1758 William Pitt became prime minister and he determined that a very different sort of campaign should be started.   There had been great diffi-culty in securing enough troops to carry on the war, and in 1756 the British government decided to enlist a regi-ment made up of the foreign settlers in the British posses-sions in America, principally Germans.   In order that those who enlisted in this regiment might have over them officers who were able to speak their own language, an act of parliament was passed authorizing the king to grant commissions to a certain number of German, Swiss and Dutch officers   This regiment, when formed, was known as the Sixty-second, or Royal American Regiment of Foot, and was made up almost entirely of Germans from Mary-land and Pennsylvania.   Later it was changed to be the Sixtieth Regiment, and is in existence today.   The first battalion of the regiment was placed under the command of Colonel Henry Bouquet,[106] a native of Switzerland who had settled in Pennsylvania.   This battalion was made up of Germans from Pennsylvania and Maryland.

At the beginning of the year 1758 plans were made for an expedition against Fort Duquesne, under the command of General John Forbes.   The troops under his command numbered between six and seven thousand and consisted of provincials from Pennsylvania, Maryland, Virginia and North Carolina, some Highlanders and the Royal Ameri-cans.   The expedition started from Philadelphia the latter part of June, the Maryland troops, with those from Vir-ginia and North Carolina, assembling at Winchester, Va., under Colonel George Washington.   Colonel Bouquet reached Raystown, now Bedford, Pa., early in July but

---

[106] H. A. Rattermann in "Deutscher Pionier," Vol. X., p. 217, says that Bouquet's real name was Strauss.

the main body of troops did not arrive until September. The details of this expedition cannot be entered into here, but there was one engagement in which the Maryland troops played a conspicuous part At the earnest solicitation of Major James Grant, of the Highlanders, Colonel Bouquet allowed the former to make a reconnoissance in order, if possible, to discover the position of the enemy at Fort Duquesne This expedition started on September 9, and consisted of thirty-seven officers and 805 privates, among whom were eighty-one Marylanders. With the usual disregard shown by the British officers of the Indian methods of warfare, Major Grant allowed his force to be led into an ambuscade, and on the 14th he was attacked by the French and Indians with disastrous results, 270 of his men being killed and 42 wounded. As usual under such circumstances, the British troops became demoralized under the Indian method of attack, but the Marylanders conducted themselves gallantly. As one account of the affair gives it, "the Carolinians, Marylanders, and Lower Countrymen, concealing themselves behind trees and the bushes, made a good defence; but were overpowered by numbers, and not being supported, were obliged to follow the rest."[107] Of the Maryland force of eighty-one men, twenty-seven privates and one officer, Lieutenant Duncan McRae, were killed.

The French, knowing that Colonel Bouquet's troops were only the advance guard, determined to attack them before the arrival of the main body, and on October 12 a force of 1,200 French and 200 Indians attacked Bouquet's camp at Loyalhanna. After several hours of hard fighting the enemy was repulsed. In this attack the Marylanders had three men killed, Lieutenant Prather and two

[107] Penna. Archives, Second Series, Vol. VI., p. 455.

privates, six privates were wounded and eleven were miss-
ing.   General Forbes did not reach Loyalhanna until November.   Numerous skirmishes followed, but the French
realizing that they could not hold Fort Duquesne, set fire
to it and abandoned it   The English pushed forward, and
on November 25, 1758, took possession of the ruins of
Fort Duquesne, which was rebuilt and named Fort Pitt.

With the abandonment of Fort Duquesne by the French
the troubles of the settlers of western Maryland were
greatly modified, although there were occasional raids by
bands of hostile Indians until the end of the war, in 1763.
With the end of the war the settlers began to return to
their deserted homes and advance further toward the west.
Seeing this, Pontiac, an Ottawa chief, determined to prevent it and drive the English from the western frontier.
With this end in view he secretly traveled from tribe to
tribe and formed an alliance, and without any warning the
blow fell upon the unsuspecting settlers.   The savages
planned to attack the settlers during harvest and destroy
their crops and cattle and kill the men   This plan was put
into execution in June, 1763.   Bands of raiding Indians
spread over western Maryland, killing the settlers and destroying their property.   Describing the condition of
affairs at this time, in a letter to Robert Stewart, dated
August 13, 1763, Washington wrote:

" Another tempest has arisen upon our frontiers, and the alarm
spread wider than ever.   In short, the inhabitants are so apprehensive of danger, that no families remain above the Conococheague road, and many are gone from below it.   The harvests
are, in a manner lost, and the distresses of the settlements are
evident and manifold."[108]

[108] Sparks' Washington, Vol. II., p. 339.

The condition of the settlers at this time is well shown in a letter in the *Maryland Gazette,* written at Frederick, under date of July 19, 1763, which says:

Every day, for some time past, has offered the melancholy scene of poor distressed families driving downwards through this town with their effects, who have deserted their plantations for fear of falling into the cruel hands of our savage enemies, now daily seen in the woods. And never was panic more general or forcible than that of the back inhabitants, whose terrors at this time exceed what followed on the defeat of Gen. Braddock, when the frontiers lay open to the incursions of both French and Indians. While Conococheague settlement stands firm we shall think ourselves in some sort of security from their insults here. But should the inhabitants there give way, you would soon see your city and the lower counties crowded with objects of compassion, as the flight would in that case become general. Numbers of those who have betaken themselves to the fort, as well as those who have actually fled, have entirely lost their crops, or turned in their own cattle and hogs to devour the produce, in hopes of finding them again in better condition should it hereafter appear safe for them to return. The season has been remarkably fine, and the harvest in general afforded the most promising appearance of plenty and goodness that has been known for many years. But alas! how dismal an alteration of the prospect! Many who expected to have sold and supplied the necessities of others now want for themselves, and see their warmest hopes defeated, the fruits of their honest industry snatched from them by the merciless attack of these blood-thirsty barbarians, whose treatment of such unhappy wretches as fall into their hands is accompanied with circumstances of infernal fury, too horrid and shocking for human nature to dwell upon even in imagination. We were so sensible of the importance of Conococheague settlement, both as a bulwark and supply to this neighborhood, that on repeated notice of their growing distress Capt. Butler, on Wednesday last, called the town company together, who appeared under arms on the court-house green with great unanimity. Just as the drum beat to arms we had the agreeable satisfaction of seeing a wagon sent up by his excellency (whose tender care for the security of the province raised sentiments of the highest gratitude in the breast of every one present) loaded with powder and lead,—articles of the greatest importance at this critical juncture, when the whole country had been drained of those necessary articles by the diligence of our Indian traders, who had bought up the whole for the supply of our enemies, to be returned, as we have dearly experienced, in death and desolation among us. A subscription was then set on foot and cheerfully entered into, in consequence of which twenty stout young men immediately enlisted under Mr. Peter Grosh to march immediately to the assistance of the back inhabitants, and with other volunteers already there raised, to cover the reapers, in hopes of securing the crops. Had not the Governor's supply arrived so reasonably it was doubted whether the whole town could have furnished ammunition sufficient for that small party, half of which marched backwards in high spirits on Thursday, and the remainder on Friday morning. And on Sunday subscriptions were taken in the several congregations in town for sending up further assistance. On Sunday afternoon we had the pleasure of seeing Mr. Michael Cresap arrive in town with mokosins on his legs, taken from an Indian whom he had killed and scalped, being one of those who had shot down Mr. Wilder, the circumstances of whose much-lamented murder and the success of Col. Cresap's family you no doubt have received from other hands. Money has been cheerfully contributed in our town towards the support of the men to be added to Col. Cresap's present force, as we look upon the preservation of the Old Town to be of great importance to us, and a proper check to the progress of the savages; but notwithstanding our present efforts to keep the enemy at a distance, and thereby shelter the whole province, our inhabitants are poor, our men dispersed, and without a detachment from below it is to be feared we must give way, and the inundation break upon the lower counties.

The Indian depredations continuing, early in 1764 two expeditions were planned, one under Colonel Bradstreet, against the Wyandots, Ottawas, Chippewas and other nations near the great lakes; the other, under Colonel Bouquet, against the Delawares, Shawnese, Mingoes, Mohickans, and other nations between the Ohio and the lakes. Colonel Bouquet's force was made up of part of the Forty-second and Sixtieth Regiments, some troops from Pennsylvania, and two companies of volunteers from Maryland, riflemen from Frederick county,. one commanded by Captain William McClellan, the other by Captain John Wolgamott These two companies were made up as follows:

Captain.
William McClellan.

Lieutenants.

John Earl,   James Dougherty.

Ensigns.

David Blair,   John Mcran,
Edmund Moran.

Sergeants.

Joseph Hopewell,   Henry Graybill.

Privates.

David Shelby,   James Ross,
George Rout,   Isaac Flora,
William Beadles,   Richard Coomore,
John Dean,   William Sparks,
Richard Arsheraft,   Thomas Clemens,
Nicholas Carpenter,   John Sealon,
Thomas Vaughan,   John Doughland,

11*

Patrick O'Gullen,
Robert Ford,
Joseph Clemens,
James Small,
Joshua Young,
George Mathison,
Isaac Wilcocks,
William Hanniel,
John Dougherty,
William Colvin,
William Flora,

Thomas Edington,
James Bradmore,
William Lockhead,
James Ware,
Thomas Williams,
John Masters,
John Murray,
Felix Leer,
Bartholomew Pack,
Charles Hays,
William Polk.

Captain.
John Wolgamott.
Lieutenant.
Matthew Nicholas.
Ensign.
John Blair.
Privates.

James Booth,
James Dulany,
William Fife,
William Dunwidie,
Peter Ford,
Thomas Davis,
David Johnson,

Samuel McCord,
Robert Blackburn,
Abraham Enocks,
James Myers,
William Marshal,
James Fox.

The Indians did not make any resistance, but sued for peace, and thus ended, for the time being, the Indian troubles which for years had made the western frontiers of Maryland the scene of terror and bloodshed.

CHAPTER XIII.

FORT FREDERICK.

WHEN the first settlement was made by the Ohio Company, about the middle of the eighteenth century, upon the land they had obtained under their grant, in accordance with the terms of that grant a minor fortification was built at the junction of Will's Creek with the Potomac river, for the purpose of affording protection to the settlers. At this time that section of territory was supposed to be in the colony of Virginia. After the defeat at Great Meadows, Washington retreated to Will's Creek, and while he went back to Virginia to report to Governor Dinwiddie, he left his force in charge of Colonel Innes, who commanded several companies of North Carolina troops. Acting under instructions from the Virginia government, during the autumn of 1754 Colonel Innes constructed a fort at this point, which he called Fort Mount Pleasant. This fort was little more than a blockhouse, and a series of stockades. About the close of the year Governor Dinwiddie received instructions from England to build a fort at Will's Creek of such dimensions and character of construction as the importance of the position seemed to require. These instructions were transmitted to Colonel Innes, who proceeded to build the fort. The men engaged in its construction were three companies from North Carolina, under Colonel Innes, two companies from New York, one from South Carolina and one from Maryland. When it was completed it was named, at the request of General Braddock, Fort Cumberland, in honor of the commander-in-chief of the British army. This fort was under the jurisdiction of the Virginia government. For some time it was the sole protection for the western frontier of Maryland against the hostile Indians. The Maryland settlement did not extend beyond the mouth of the Conococheague creek, in what is now Washington county, and this left a wide extent of territory, about sixty miles, which was without protection.

After the defeat of Braddock the Indian raids became more frequent and a number of blockhouses were built between Fort Cumberland and the western frontier to which the settlers could flee upon the raising of an alarm. These, however, had but little effect in preventing the raids or in affording protection to the settlers. As Judge Stockbridge says, " a period of terror and desolation ensued. The borders of Maryland, Pennsylvania and Virginia became one extended field of petty battles, murder und devastation. The outposts were driven in, and some of the smaller posts captured and their garrisons massacred; and Frederick, Winchester and Carlisle became the frontiers of the colonies. Fort Cumberland was still held by the troops under Captain Dagworthy, but this isolated fortress could afford no protection against roving bands of savages who passed around it to seek their prey in the settlements beyond. The panic spread by the flying British troops spread even to the bay shore. Many of the inhabitants of the interior fled to Baltimore, and there preparations were made by the citizens to embark their women and children on board the vessels in the harbor preparatory to a flight to Virginia, while some of the Virginians even believed that there was no safety short of England itself."[109]

The need of further defenses was evident and Governor Sharpe did all in his power to procure the means of securing them, but the assembly was slow in meeting the need of the hour. Finally, in response to the appeals of the Governor and the urgent demands of the people, on March 22, 1756, a bill was passed appropriating forty thousand pounds for the defense of the colony, of which eleven thousand pounds were to be used for the erection of a fort and several blockhouses on the western frontier, and for the levying, arming, paying and maintaining a body of troops to garrison these posts. Governor Sharpe at once proceeded to put into execution the plans he had formulated. He purchased from Peter and Jacob Cloine a tract of land consisting of about one hundred and forty acres, in Frederick county, near where Hancock, Washington county, now stands. The deed for the land is dated August 19, 1756, but Sharpe was so anxious to provide defenses that he secured possession of the land and began the erection of the fort before the deed was executed. On August 21, 1756, he wrote to Lord Baltimore:

As I apprehended that the French would e'er long teach their Indian Allies to approach & set fire to our Stoccado or Wooden

[109] "American Historical Register," Vol. II., p. 748.

Forts I thought proper to build Fort Frederick of Stone, which steps I believe even our Assembly now approve of tho I hear some of them sometime since intimated to their Constituents that a Stoccado would have been sufficient & that to build a Fort with Stone would put the Country to a great & unnecessary Expence, but whatever their Sentiments may be with respect to that matter I am convinced that I have done for the best & that my Conduct therein will be approved by any Soldier & every impartial person. The Fort is not finished but the Garrison are well covered & will with a little Assistance compleat it at their leisure. Our Barracks are made for the Reception & Accommodation of 200 Men but on Occasion there will be room for twice that number. It is situated on North Mountain near Potowmack River, about 14 miles beyond Conegocheigh and four on this Side of Licking creek. I have made a purchase in the Governor's Name for the use of the Country of 150 Acres of Land that is contiguous to it, which will be of great Service to the Garrison & as well as the Fort be found of great use in case of future Expeditions to the Westward for it is so situated that Potowmack will be always navigable thence almost to Fort Cumberland, and the Flatts or Shallows of that River lying between Fort Frederick and Conegocheigh. It is probable this Fortification will cost the Province £2000, but I am told that one is raising at Winchester in Virg^a that will not be built for less than four times that Sum, and when finished will not be half so good.[110]

This structure was named Fort Frederick in honor of the proprietor, Frederick, sixth Lord Baltimore. Some confusion has arisen from the fact that there were two structures known as Fort Frederick. During the Revolution the general assembly of Maryland, in 1777, passed an act providing that there should be erected "in or near Fredericktown in Frederick County, a number of fit, convenient and proper barracks of plain brick or stone work,

[110] Archives of Maryland, Vol. VI., p. 466.

with a block house at each corner and ditched and palisaded in, sufficient for the reception of two battalions, with officers." Schultz says: "There is ground for the belief, however, that there was a stockade fort, or something of that character, ôn or near their site at the time of the French and Indian Wars, similar to those erected by the early settlers near the present Clearspring and Williamsport, to which the women and children retreated when the Indians became troublesome."[111]

Fort Frederick was built on a hill about one hundred feet above the level of the Potomac and about one-third of a mile from the river. From its position it commanded the surrounding country. Describing its construction, Scharf says:

"The old fort occupied an acre and a half of ground, and its massive walls of hard magnesian limestone are four feet thick at the bottom, and two feet at the top. The stone, which is mostly in large, irregular blocks, was brought from the mountain three miles distant, and is laid in such excellent mortar that nothing but an earthquake or the hand of man will ever shatter the walls. These are seventeen and a half feet in height at the highest point, and are very fairly preserved. The greatest damage that has been done was the cutting of a wagon-gate through the west curtain sixty years ago, and now Nathan Williams, its present owner, has pulled down the west bastion to make room for his barn. The fort is square, with a bastion at each angle. The south bastion is the best preserved, but the whole structure is very far from being a ruin. The portal was twelve feet wide, and the immensity of the gates may be judged by the fact that one of the iron hinges, which Williams kept until a few years ago,. weighed forty-two pounds. There is not a piece of the old wood-work left, some curiosity-seekers having carried off the last bit in 1858. Gen. Kenly's First Maryland Regiment occupied the fort in 1861, and

[111] "First Settlements of Germans in Maryland," p. 56.

knocked a hole in the wall through which to point a gun for taking pot shots at the Confederates across the Potomac. The original armament of the fort was a gun in each bastion, worked *en barbette,* and within the enclosure were the barracks."[112]

But Governor Sharpe's troubles over the building of Fort Frederick were far from being ended. His original estimate of the cost of building the structure fell far short of the actual cost, and he was compelled to ask the assembly for more money with which to complete it. Then, too, the cost of maintaining the garrison and paying the troops was no small item. The residents of the eastern section of the colony, at a distance from the scene of the Indian raids, did not realize just what they meant, and could not see why so much money was required for the protection of the western settlers. Their idea was to keep down the expenditures as much as possible, so that there were constant disputes between the executive and the assembly on the question of providing means to carry on the war. On December 15, 1757, the House of Delegates made the following address on the subject of Fort Frederick:

"Near the sum of £6000 has been expended in purchasing the ground belonging to and constructing Fort Frederick, and though we have not any exact information what sum may still be wanting to complete it (if ever it should be thought proper to be done), yet we are afraid the sum requisite for that purpose must be considerable, and we are apprehensive that the fort is so large that, in case of attack, it cannot be defended without a number of men larger than the province can support, purely to maintain a fortification."

On June 9, 1758, Governor Sharpe wrote to General Forbes,[113] giving a detailed account of the trouble over

---

[112] History of Western Maryland, Vol. II., p. 1298.
[113] Archives of Maryland, Vol. IX., p. 198.

the payment of the troops. Lord Loudoun had proposed that Maryland should raise and support five hundred men to garrison Fort Cumberland and Fort Frederick, but instead of agreeing to this proposal the assembly included in the bill which they passed a provision which prohibited the Maryland troops from garrisoning Fort Cumberland, or at all events, giving fair warning that if these troops did go to Fort Cumberland they would not be paid by the province of Maryland. Fuel was added to the flames of the dispute by Virginia turning over Fort Cumberland to Maryland. When the Virginia troops retired from the fort it was necessary for their place to be taken by Marylanders, but the Maryland assembly absolutely refused to agree to this. However, Governor Sharpe took the matter into his own hands and sent Captain Dagworthy with one hundred and fifty of his men from Fort Frederick, to garrison Fort Cumberland. As the assembly would not authorize the enlistment of more troops, Governor Sharpe called for volunteers and his call was promptly answered by the settlers of Frederick county, so that Fort Frederick was soon garrisoned by a force of two hundred and fifty hardy pioneers, under Captain Alexander Beall. As the assembly refused to appropriate money to pay and maintain the garrison, the cost had to be met by private subscriptions. Writing to Sir John St. Clair, on March 27, 1758, Governor Sharpe says:

I am obliged to you for encouraging General Forbes to entertain a favourable opinion of me & of my Desires to forward the Service, but I am much afraid that it will not be in my power to confirm it. In short, I cannot promise him any men from this Province unless He or General Abercromby will engage to pay them & I have taken the Liberty to tell him as much in the Letter I have now sent. It is well Capt Dagworthy & the Rest of our

Officers taught their men to live without Victuals last Summer; otherwise they may not have found it so easy a matter to keep them together 6 months without pay in the Winter. How much longer they will be contented to serve on this Footing I cannot tell, but lest Accidents should happen I hope some other Troops will be ordered to Fort Cumberland as soon as possible.[114]

The difficulty about the payment of the troops was partially overcome by taking some of them into the king's service, and on one occasion General Forbes advanced sufficient money to pay them something, although he said that he could not undertake to take care of the arrearage.

The road between Fort Frederick and Fort Cumberland was a rough and circuitous one, and several attempts to remedy this were made. Writing to Governor Sharpe from " Conigogegh," on June 13, 1758, Colonel Bouquet says:

As it will be of the greatest benefit to His Majesty's Service, to have a road of communication open from Each of the Provinces to Fort Cumberland I am under the necessity of requesting you to have the straightest Road reconnoitred, leading from Fort Frederick to Fort Cumberland: Recommanding to those you appoint to mark it out to report the time that 500 men will take to cut it: any Expence you may be at shall be paid by Sir John St Clair; as he will be the nearest to you. Please to send him the Report of it, that if found practicable he may send Troops to work at it.[115]

Two days later Sharpe directed Captain Evan Shelby to survey a route for a road and make a report as to the cost and the time required to make it, and on the 25th of the same month Captain Shelby reported that " Upon

114 Archives of Maryland, Vol. IX., p. 164.
115 Archives of Maryland, Vol. IX., p. 205.

the whole, it is my opinion that a Road might be made between the two Forts which will not be 60 miles in Length & there will be no bad Pinches for Waggons to ascend nor any bad Fords." The road was evidently not constructed at that time, for in the following December the assembly appointed a commission to determine whether a better road could not be built. This commission consisted of Colonel Thomas Cresap, Joseph Chapline, E. Dorsey, Josias Beall, Francis King and Captain Crabb. After investigating the subject the commission reported as follows:

Your committee have made an inquiry into the situation of the present wagon-road from Fort Frederick to Fort Cumberland, and are of the opinion that the distance by that road from one fort to the other is at least eighty miles, and find that the wagons which go from one fort to the other are obliged to pass the river Potowmack twice, and that for one-third of the year they can't pass without boats to set them over the river.

Your committee have also made an inquiry into the condition of the ground where a road may be made most conveniently to go altogether on the north side of the Potowmack, which will not exceed the distance of sixty-two miles, at the expense of £250 current money.

Your committee are of the opinion that a road through Maryland will contribute much to lessen the expense of carrying provisions and warlike stores from Fort Frederick to Fort Cumberland, and will induce many people to travel and carry on a trade in and through the province, to and from the back country.[116]

This report was accompanied by an itemized account of the distances and the probable cost of building each stretch of the road. This road was eventually built, and, as the commission's report had indicated, did prove of great advantage to the province.

[116] Scharf's "History of Western Maryland," Vol. II., p. 1328.

The erection and occupation of Fort Frederick gave the settlers in that section the protection they needed. The Indians soon learned to avoid the locality of the fort. Writing to Lord Loudoun, on October 12, 1756, Governor Sharpe says: "No Indians have been down among the Inhabitants for a considerable time, nor appeared on this side of Fort Frederick." After the fall of Fort Duquesne and the withdrawal of the French from the Ohio river, the necessity for the continued maintenance of Fort Frederick ceased. Governor Sharpe accordingly leased the property on which it was built to Henry Heinzman, for a rental of thirty pounds yearly. The lease was dated December 25, 1762, and provided that "whereas there is not any garrison or soldiers at the said Fort Frederick, and several persons who live at or near the said fort do, and if not prevented, will continue to make great waste and destruction of the said fort and improvements by burning the plank and other materials,"[117] possession of it was to be given, the Governor reserving the right to enter upon the property and annul the lease at any time when he might need the same for military purposes.

Scarcely had Fort Frederick been turned over to the uses of peace when another war-cloud began to gather on the horizon. The tension between the colonies and the mother-country grew greater and greater, and finally the cords which bound them together were broken and the struggle was on; but still the tide of warfare did not surge near the old fort. Its walls looked down upon peace and quiet, for the German settlers in western Maryland were not slow in going to the defense of the liberties of their adopted country, and many of the fields and plantations in the neighborhood were almost deserted.

[117] Stockbridge in "American Historical Register," Vol. II., p. 754.

During the earlier years of the Revolutionary War the British and Hessian prisoners were confined at various points in Pennsylvania: Reading, Lancaster, York, Bethlehem and Lebanon, but after the occupation of Philadelphia by the British, particularly as there were rumors of an uprising among the prisoners, the War Office decided to transfer some of the prisoners to some point further inland, and Fort Frederick was investigated to determine whether it would be a suitable place for the purpose. On December 16, 1777, the following letter was written to Colonel Moses Rawlins:

As you are about returning home by way of Fort Frederick in Maryland, the Board of War request you will take a view of the situation of that place and represent the state you find it in immediately. As it is proposed to send a number of prisoners of war thither, you will examine it with a view to this design. You will see how many men it is capable of holding, what repairs are wanting, how soon those repairs can be made, whether workmen can be procured in this vicinity to do the work, and whether materials are within reasonable distance. You will also report how many men you think it will be necessary to employ as guards for the number of prisoners the place is capable of receiving, and every other matter which shall occur to you as necessary for the information of the Board.

Colonel Rawlins reported that the fort could easily be put in condition for the confinement of the prisoners, and the Maryland assembly directed that the necessary repairs be made. The assembly also provided for a guard for the prisoners. During part of the time this guard consisted of Captain John Kershner's company. On July 27, 1778, this company was made up as follows:

Captain.

John Kershner.

Lieutenants.

Jno. McLaughlin,   Peter Backer.

Ensign.

Wm. Conrod.

Sergeants.

Luke Sholly,   David Wolgamot,
Martain Phipher,   George Fanglar.

Corporals.

Jacob Craver,   Peter Conn,
Jacob Barnt,   John Conn.

Drum and Fife.

John Oster,   Peter Lighter.

Privates.

Michael Hartly,   Christiain Kirgery,
George Stuart,   James Flack,
George Hudson,   George May,
Jno. Shriber,   Chris. Shock,
Elias Reeter,   Jno. Robinson,
George Carter,   Jacob Geerhert,
Abraham Bower,   David Fosney,
Martain Harry (or Narry), Richd. Menson,
Andrew Miller,   Peter Oster,
Peter Haflegh (Hoeflich), Thos. McCullim,
Fredk. Craft,   Casper Snider,
Henry Tyce,   Peter Rough,
Goodhert Tressel,   Adam Sydey,

Jacob Binkler,
Abraham Troxal, Jr.,
Jacob Ridenour,
Peter Adams,
Abraham Leedy,
Jno. Gable,
Michael Kernam,
Danl. Kemmer,
Adam Coon,
Jacob Adams,
Jno. Fiche,
Mathw. Williams,
Wm. Allin,

Abraham Feeter,
John Augusteen,
Jacob Rorer,
Peter Sybert,
Michl. Spesser,
Fredk. Deefhem (or Deef-
herr),
Fredk. Shackler,
Phillip Criegh,
David Wirley,
Christiain Nockey
(or Hockey),
Jacob Tysher.

A number of prisoners from various points in Pennsylvania were transferred to Fort Frederick. At first some of the prisoners were allowed to work for the neighboring farmers, but it was found that this plan had disadvantages and in the autumn of 1778 the Board of War directed Colonel Rawlins to " call in all the prisoners in the neighborhood of your post or its dependencies and, as the practice of letting them out to farmers and suffering them to go at large is attended with great mischiefs, you will in future keep them in close confinement."

After the surrender of Cornwallis a large number of the prisoners taken at that time were sent to Fort Frederick.

In September, 1791, by direction of the Legislature of Maryland, Fort Frederick was sold to Robert Johnson, of Frederick county, for three hundred and seventy-five pounds, ten shillings, since which time it has belonged to a number of different people. For a short time during the Civil War the fort was occupied by some of General Kenly's command.

CHAPTER XIV.

THE PRE-REVOLUTIONARY PERIOD.

WITH the end of Pontiac's war and the signing of the treaty between England and France peace and quiet returned to the western part of Maryland, and the settlers returned to their deserted homes. Many of them, however, were in almost a destitute condition. Not only had their crops been destroyed and their domestic animals driven off or killed, but, in many cases, all their buildings with their contents had been burned. Then, too, many of them had fallen in arrears in the payment of their rents, so that their situation was deplorable. Their poverty was emphasized by the fact that there were constant demands upon them for fees and taxes. The British government, at the close of the French and Indian

War, found itself staggering under an immense debt, and as it had been incurred in a war in America, although the underlying principles which led to it had their foundations at home, it was speciously assumed that the colonies should defray the expenses of the war, and steps were taken to bring this about.

In March, 1765, the Stamp Act was passed. This provided that all bills, bonds, leases, notes, ships' papers, insurance policies, and legal documents, to be valid in the courts, must be written on stamped paper. The passage of this act was instantly resented by the colonists, and nowhere were the indignation and determination to resist the enforcement of the law more pronounced than among the German settlers in western Maryland. Indeed, the first open stand against the use of the stamped paper and the determination to transact business without the use of stamps was made in Frederick county, which at that time included the whole of western Maryland.

Zachariah Hood, a native of Maryland, and a merchant of Annapolis, who was in England at the time, was appointed stamp distributor for the province of Maryland. So intense was the feeling of the inhabitants of Maryland that when Hood returned with the stamps and a cargo of goods he was not allowed to land. Knowing that the open threats of the people to burn the stamps if they were brought on shore would be carried out, the authorities deemed it advisable that no opportunity should be given for such proceedings, and the stamps were kept on board ship and finally taken to Virginia, where they could be held under the protection of a British ship of war. In the meantime business of all kinds was held up. There were many legal papers which could not be issued except on stamped paper, and there were no stamps in the colony.

12*

Indignation meetings were held everywhere and resolutions were passed condemning the passage of the Stamp Act and refusing to use the stamps, and in many places Zachariah Hood, the stamp distributor, was burned in effigy. The matter was brought to a head in Frederick county. At a meeting of the Frederick county court, on November 18, 1765, Judges Joseph Smith, David Lynn, Charles Jones, Samuel Beall, Joseph Beall, Peter Bainbridge, Thomas Price, Andrew Hugh, William Blair, William Luckett, James Dickson and Thomas Beatty being present, the following order was made:

Upon application of Michael Ashford Dowden, bail of James Veach, at the suit of a certain Stephen West to surrender said James Veach in discharge of himself, which the court ordered to be done, and an entry of the surrender to be made accordingly, which John Darnall, Clerk of the Court, refused to make, and having also refused to issue any process out of his office, or to make the necessary entries of the Court proceedings, alleging that he conceives there is an Act of Parliament imposing stamp duties on all legal proceedings, and therefore that he cannot safely proceed in exercising his office without proper stamps,

It is the unanimous resolution and opinion of this Court that all the business thereof shall and ought to be transacted in the usual and accustomed manner, without any inconvenience or delay to be occasioned from the want of Stamped Paper, Parchment, or Vellum, and that all proceedings shall be valid and effectual without the use of Stamps, and they enjoin and order all Sheriffs, Clerks, Counsellors, Attorneys, and all officers of the Court to proceed in their several avocations as usual, which Resolution and Opinion are grounded on the following and other reasons:

1st. It is conceived that there has not been a legal publication yet made of any Act of Parliament whatever imposing a Stamp Duty on the Colonies. Therefore this Court are of opinion that until the existence of such an Act is properly notified, it would be culpable in them to permit or suffer a total stagnation of business, which must inevitably be productive of innumerable injuries to individuals, and have a tendency to subvert all principles of civil government,

2d. As no Stamps are yet arrived in this Province, and the inhabitants have no means of procuring any, this Court are of opinion that it would be an injustice of the most wanton oppression to deprive any person of a legal remedy for the recovery of his property for omitting that which it is impossible to perform.[118]

The clerk of the court, to protect himself, refused to comply with this order, whereupon the Court ordered

That John Darnall, clerk of this Court, be committed to the custody of the sheriff of this county for a contempt of the authority of this court, he having refused to comply with the foregoing order of this Court relative to the execution of his office in issuing processes and making the necessary entries of the Court's proceedings; and that he stands committed for the above offense until he comply with the above mentioned order.[119]

On the issuance of this order the clerk submitted to the order of the court, paid the costs and was discharged. This was the beginning of the overthrow of the Stamp Act, and on November 30 a celebration in honor of the decision of the court was held at Frederick. The *Maryland Gazette* of December 16, 1765, gives an extended account of this celebration, which is quoted by Scharf.[120] The action taken in Frederick county was followed in other parts of the province, so that so far as Maryland was concerned the Stamp Act was absolutely disregarded. The law was repealed on March 18, 1766.

The next year, however, a law was passed imposing

[118] Scharf's "History of Western Maryland," Vol. I., p. 122.
[119] Ibid.
[120] History of Western Maryland, Vol. I., p. 122.

duties on glass, paper, pasteboard, white and red lead, painters' colors, and tea imported into the colonies. The passage of this act quickly revived the opposition of the colonists, and associations were formed to oppose the collection of the taxes, the members pledging themselves to non-importation. These pledges were generally strictly adhered to, although occasionally some merchant, seeing a chance to make a good profit, violated the conditions of the agreement. But the punishment for such actions was swift and sure, and the instances of it were rare. "In October, 1769, a number of wagons of contraband goods, valued at three hundred pounds, were shipped from Pennsylvania to Frederick, and not being accompanied with the proper certificates, they were stored at the risk and cost of the owners."[121]

Meetings to protest against the imposition of these taxes were held in all the counties. The *Maryland Gazette* gives an account of a meeting held in Frederick county on August 28, 1770. The place of meeting was a school house, near Troxell's mill, on Tom's creek. Among those present were William Blair, James Shields, Sr., William Shields, Charles Robinson, Patrick Haney, Robert Brown, Henry Hockersmith, William Elder, son of Guy, Samuel Westfall, Moses Kennedy, Alexander Stewart, William Curran, Jr., Charles Carroll, William Koontz, Christian Hoover, John Smith, Daniel McLean, John Faires, John Long, Arthur Row, John Crabs, Moses Ambrose, George Kelly, Walter Dulany, Thomas J. Bowie, James Park, Robert Agnew, John Corrick, Frederick Troxell, Rudolf Nead, Octavius S. Taney, George Ovelman, Dominick Bradley, Thomas Hughes, Philip Weller, Jacob Valentine, William Brawner, Thomas Martin, Daniel Morrison, William Munroe, and

[121] Scharf's "History of Western Maryland," Vol. I., p. 124.

Henry Brook. At this meeting the following resolution was adopted:

Resolved, by the inhabitants of Tom's Creek, Frederick County, in the province of Maryland, loyal to their king and country that we reaffirm the great Magna Charta of our Civil and Religious Rights, as granted by Charles of England to Lord Baltimore and the inhabitants of this colony, as reaffirmed on the first landing of the Pilgrim Fathers of Maryland, that there shall be a perfect freedom of conscience, and every person be allowed to enjoy his religious and political privileges and immunities unmolested.

The opposition of the colonists to the imposition of these taxes and the adoption of a policy of non-importation were so general that the British government found it impossible to enforce the law, and with the exception of the tax on tea it was allowed to fall into abeyance. With the destruction of the cargo of tea in Boston harbor and the subsequent passage of the Boston Port Bill, in 1774, the indignation of the colonists and their determination to oppose the oppressive measures of the British government became so intense that the majority of the people were ready to follow any one who would take a determined stand against the unpopular measures. At that period the majority of the population of Maryland lived in the western part of the province, within the limits of what was then Frederick county, and of these by far the greater number were the Germans who had come down from Pennsylvania, and their descendants. These people had abondoned their homes across the ocean and had come to America to escape from just such oppression, and it was but natural, therefore, that they should quickly resent any attempts of the British government to enforce what appeared to be unjust laws, particularly in the matter of taxation. The inhabitants of Frederick county, therefore, generally took the lead in proposing measures for the relief of the people. Their action following the passage of the Boston Port Bill was prompt. On June 11, 1774, the inhabitants of the lower part of Frederick county held a largely attended meeting at the tavern of Charles Hungerford. They elected Henry Griffith moderator and adopted the following resolutions:

Resolved unanimously, That it is the opinion of this meeting that the town of Boston is now suffering in the common cause of America.

Resolved, unanimously, That every legal and constitutional measure ought to be used by all America for procuring a repeal of the act of Parliament for blocking up the harbor of Boston.

Resolved, unanimously, That it is the opinion of this meeting that the most effectual means for the securing American freedom will be to break off all commerce with Great Britain and the West Indies until the said act be repealed, and the right of taxation given up on permanent principles.

Resolved, unanimously, That Mr. Henry Griffith, Dr. Thomas Sprigg Wootton, Nathan Magruder, Evan Thomas, Richard Brooke, Richard Thomas, Zadok Magruder, Dr. William Baker, Thomas Cramphin, Jr., and Allen Bowie be a committee to attend the general committee at Annapolis, and of correspondence for the lower part of Frederick county, and that any six of them shall have power to receive and communicate intelligence to and from their neighboring committees.

Resolved, unanimously, That a copy of these our sentiments be immediately transmitted to Annapolis, and inserted in the *Maryland Gazette.*   Signed per order,

ARCHIBALD ORME, *Clerk.*[122]

Nine days later, on June 20, a meeting was held in the court house at Frederick, at which John Hanson presided, and the following resolutions were adopted:

[122] Force's "American Archives," Series IV., Vol. I., p. 403.

I. *Resolved,* That it is the opinion of this meeting that the town of Boston is now suffering in the common cause of America, and that it is the duty of every colony in America to unite in the most effectual means to obtain a repeal of the late act of Parliament for blocking up the harbor of Boston.

II. That it is the opinion of a great majority of this meeting that if the colonies come into a joint resolution to stop all imports from, and exports to, Great Britain and the West Indies till the act of Parliament for blocking up the harbor of Boston, as well as every other act oppressive to American liberty, be repealed, the same may be the means of preserving to America her rights, liberties and privileges.

III. That, therefore, this meeting will join in an association with the several counties in this province and the principal colonies in America to put a stop to all exports to, and imports from, Great Britain and the West Indies, shipped after the 25th day of July next, or such other day as may be agreed on, until the said acts shall be repealed, and that such association shall be upon oath.

IV. That we, the inhabitants of Frederick county, will not deal or have any connections with that colony, province, or town which shall decline or refuse to come into similar resolutions with a majority of the colonies.

V. That no suit shall be commenced after the stop shall be put to imports and exports for the recovery of any debt due to any person whatsoever, unless the debtor be about to abscond, or being appealed to shall refuse to give bond and security.

VI. That Messrs. John Hanson, Thomas Price, George Scott, Benjamin Dulany, George Murdock, Philip Thomas, Alexander C. Hanson, Baker Johnson, and Andrew Scott be a committee to attend the general congress at Annapolis, and that those gentlemen, together with Messrs. John Cary, Christopher Edelen, Conrad Groth, Thomas Schley, Peter Hoffman, and Archibald Boyd, be a committee of correspondence to receive and answer letters, and in any emergency to call a general meeting, and that any six shall have power to act.

Ordered, that these resolves be immediately sent to Annapolis, that they may be printed in the *Maryland Gazette.*

Signed per order,

ARCHIBALD BOYD, *Cl. Com.*[122]

The inhabitants of the upper part of Frederick county met at Elizabeth-Town, now Hagerstown, on July 2. The *Maryland Gazette* gives the following account of this meeting:

On Saturday, the 2d of July, 1774, about eight hundred of the principal inhabitants of the upper part of Frederick County, Md., assembled at Elizabeth Town, and being deeply impressed with a sense of the danger to which their natural and constitutional rights and privileges were exposed by the arbitrary measures of the British Parliament, do think it their duty to declare publicly their sentiments on so interesting a subject, and to enter into such Resolutions as may be the means of preferring their freedom. After choosing John Stull, Esq., their Moderator, the following resolves were unanimously entered into:

I. That the Act of Parliament for blocking up the harbor of the Town of Boston is a dangerous invasion of American liberty, and that the town of Boston is now suffering in the common cause, and ought to be assisted by the other Colonies.

II. That the stopping all commercial intercourse with Great Britain will be the most effectual means for fixing our Liberties on the footing we desire.

III. That a general congress of Delegates from the several colonies to effect a uniform plan of conduct for all America is highly necessary, and that we will strictly adhere to any measure that may be adopted by them for the preservation of our Liberties.

IV. That the surest means for continuing a people free and happy is the disusing all luxuries, and depending only on their own fields and flocks for the comfortable necessaries of Life.

[122] Force's "American Archives," Series IV., Vol. I., p. 433.

V. That they will not, after this day, drink any Tea, nor suffer the same to be used in their Families, until the Act for laying duty thereon be repealed.

VI. That they will not, after this day, kill any sheep under three years old.

VII. That they will immediately prepare for manufacturing their own clothing.

VIII. That they will immediately open a subscription for the relief of their suffering Brethren in Boston.

After choosing John Stull, Samuel Hughes, Jonathan Hager, Conrad Hogmire, Henry Snebley, Richard Davis, John Swan, Charles Swearingen, Thomas Brooke, William McGlury, and Elie Williams as a committee, they proceeded to show their disapprobation of Lord North's Conduct with regard to America by Hanging and burning his Effigy, after which a subscription was opened for the relief of the Poor of Boston. In consequence of the Fifth Resolve, a number of mercantile Gentlemen solemnly declared that they would send off all the Tea they had on hand and that they would not purchase any more until the Act laying a duty thereon be repealed, among which number was a certain John Parks.

A great deal has been written concerning the "Boston Tea-party," but there were tea-parties in other parts of the colonies which, while they may not have been so spectacular as the one at Boston, were just as effective in the results obtained. As McSherry says "Long before the destruction of tea in Boston harbor by disguised men the patriots of Maryland calmly, openly, and in the presence of the governor and the provincial officers discussed and set at defiance this obnoxious act and prevented its execution."[124] The most spectacular occurrence of this kind in Maryland was the destruction of the brig *Peggy Stewart*. In October, 1774, that vessel arrived at Annapolis having among its

[124] "History of Maryland," revised ed., p. 136.

cargo several packages of tea consigned to Thomas Williams & Co. The vessel was owned by Anthony Stewart, who paid the duty on the tea. As soon as this became known a public meeting was called at which the greatest indignation was expressed. The merchants who received the tea were present at the meeting and publicly apologized for having done so and agreed to burn the tea. But this did not entirely satisfy the people, who openly made threats against the vessel and its owner. Mr. Stewart, in order to quiet the people, offered to destroy the vessel himself. This proposition was accepted and Mr. Stewart, accompanied by the merchants to whom the tea was consigned, went aboard the *Peggy Stewart*, ran her aground at Windmill Point, and set fire to her in the presence of a great crowd of people.

In the account given above of the meeting at Elizabeth-Town "a certain John Parks" is mentioned. It seems that Parks did not abide by the agreement not to buy any more tea, and when it was discovered that he had a chest of tea in his possession he was summoned before the Committee. He admitted the fact and agreed to deliver the tea to the Committee. The *Maryland Gazette* of December 22, 1774, gives the following account of the subsequent proceedings in this case:

The committee for the upper part of Frederick county, Maryland, having met at Elizabeth Town, on the 26th of November, which was the day appointed for the delivery of John Park's chest of tea, in consequence of his agreement published in the Maryland Journal of the 16th ult. After a demand was made of the same, Mr. Parks offered a chest of tea, found on a certain Andrew Gibson's plantation, Cumberland County, Pennsylvania, by the committee for that place, which tea he declared was the same he promised to deliver.

The committee are sorry to say that they have great reason to believe, and indeed with almost a certainty, that the said chest of tea was in Cumberland county at the time Parks said upon oath it was at Christen Bridge.

After mature deliberation, the Committee were of opinion, that Parks should go with his hat off, and lighted torches in his hands, and set fire to the tea, which he accordingly did, and the same was consumed to ashes, amongst the acclamations of a numerous body of people. The Committee were also of opinion that no further intercourse should be had with the said Parks. Every friend to liberty is requested to pay due attention to the same.

Voted, the thanks of this committee to that of Cumberland county, for their prudent and spirited behaviour upon this occasion.

Signed by order of the committee,

JOHN STULL, President.

N. B. The populace thought the measures adopted by the committee were inadequate to the transgression, and satisfied themselves by breaking his door and windows.[125]

On November 18, 1774, a meeting of the qualified voters of Frederick county was held at the court house in Frederick and the following gentlemen were named to represent the county, and to carry into execution the association agreed upon by the Continental Congress: Charles Beatty, Henry Griffith, Thomas Sprigg Wooton, Jacob Hunk, Nath. Magruder, Richard Thomas, Evan Thomas, Richard Brooke, Zadock Magruder, William Baker, Thomas Cramphin, Jr., John Murdock, Thomas Jones, Allen Bowie, Jr., William Deakins, Jr., Bernard O'Neal, Brook Beall, Edward Burgess, Charles G. Griffith, Henry Griffith, Jr., Wm. Bayley, Jr., Samuel W. Magruder, Nath. Offutt, Archibald Orm, Joseph Threlkeld, Walter Smith, Thos. Beall of George, Richard Crab, William

---

[125] Force's "American Archives," Fourth Series, Vol. I., p. 1009; Ridgely's "Annals of Annapolis," p. 164.

Luckett, William Luckett, Jr., Greenbury Griffith, Samuel Griffith, John Hanson, Thomas Price, Thomas Bowles, Conrad Grosh, Thomas Schley, Jonathan Wilson, Francis Deakins, Casper Schaaf, Peter Hoffman, George Scott, Baker Johnson, Philip Thomas, Alexander C. Hanson, Archibald Boyd, Arthur Nelson, Andrew Scott, George Stricker, Adam Fisher, Wm. Ludwick, Weltner Van Swearengen, William J. Beall, Jacob Young, Peter Grosh, Æneas Campbell, Elias Bruner, Frederick Kemp, John Haas, John Romsburg, Thomas Hawkins, Upton Sheredine, John Lawrence, Basil Dorsey, Charles Warfield, Ephraim Howard, Joseph Wells, David Moore, Joseph Wood, Norman Bruce, William Blair, David Schriver, Roger Johnson, Henry Cock, Robert Wood, William Albaugh, Jacob Mathias, Henry Crawle, Jacob Ambrose, David Richards, William Winchester, Philip Fishburn, William Hobbs, Thomas Cresap, Thomas Warren, Thos. Humphreys, Richard Davis, Jr., Charles Clinton, James Prather, George Brent, James Johnson, James Smith, Joseph Chapline, John Stull, Samuel Beall, Jr., William Baird, Joseph Sprigg, Christian Orendorf, Jonathan Hager, Conrad Hogmire, Charles Swearengen, Henry Snavely, Richard Davis, Samuel Hughes, Joseph Perry, John Jugerhorn, Joseph Smith, Thomas Hog, Thomas Prather, William McClary, John Swan, Eli Williams, Stophall Burkett, and Thomas Brooke.[126] Any five of them had power to act.

At the same time the following were named as a Committee of Correspondence: Charles Beatty, Thos. Sprigg Wooton, John Hanson, Thomas Bowles, Casper Shaaf, Thomas Price, Baker Johnson, Philip Thomas, George Murdock, Alexander C. Hanson, Thomas Cramphin, Jr., William Bayley, Jr., Evan Thomas, Richard Brooke,

---

[126] Force's "American Archives," Fouth Series, Vol. I., p. 986.

Thomas Johns, Walter Smith, William Deakins, John Murdock, Bernard O'Neal, John Stull, Samuel Beall, Jr., James Smith, Joseph Chapline, Joseph Sprigg, Charles Swearengen, Rich. Davis, Jonathan Hager, and Joseph Perry.

The following were also elected to attend the Provincial Convention: Charles Beatty, Henry Griffith, Thos. Sprigg Wooton, Jacob Funk, Evan Thomas, Richard Brooke, Upton Sheredine, Baker Johnson, Thomas Price, Joseph Chapline, and James Smith.

The Provincial Convention, which met on December 8, adopted resolutions recommending that the inhabitants of the province, from sixteen to fifty years of age, form themselves into companies of sixty-eight men, and elect a captain, two lieutenants, an ensign, four sergeants, four corporals, and a drummer for each company, and to use their utmost endeavors to make themselves masters of military exercise. It was also recommended that each man be provided with a good firelock and bayonet fixed thereon, half a pound of powder, two pounds of lead, and a cartouch-box or powder-horn, and a bag for ball, and be in readiness to act in any emergency.

When they had made up their minds to act, the citizens of Frederick county were fired with enthusiasm, and in order that all the necessary precautions might be taken another meeting of the citizens of the county was called to be held at the court house on Tuesday, January 24, 1775. At this meeting John Hanson was made chairman, and Archibald Boyd, secretary. The association and resolves of the American Congress and the proceedings of the last Provincial Convention were read and unanimously approved, and the following resolutions adopted:[127]

---

[127] Force's "American Archives," Fourth Series, Vol. I., p. 1173.

I. *Resolved,* That Messrs. Charles Beatty, Henry Griffith, Thomas Sprigg Wooton, Jacob Funk, and Nathan Magruder, Richard Brooke, Zadock Magruder, William Baker, Thomas Cramphin, Jr., Alexander Bowie, Jr., William Deakins, Jr., John Murdock, Thomas Johns, Bernard O'Neal, Brooke Beall, Edward Burgess, Charles G. Griffith, Henry Griffith, Jr., William Bayley, Jr., Samuel Magruder, Nathaniel Offutt, Archibald Orme, Joseph Threlkeld, Walter Smith, Thomas Beall of George, Richard Crabb, William Luckett, William Luckett, Jr., Greenbury Griffith, Samuel Griffith, John Hanson, Thomas Price, Thomas Bowles, Conrad Grosh, Thomas Archley, Jonathan Wilson, Francis Deakins, Casper Schaaff, Peter Hoffman, George Scott, Baker Johnson, Philip Thomas, Alexander C. Hanson, Archibald Boyd, Arthur Nelson, Andrew Scott, George Stricker, Adam Fisher, Wm. Ludwick, Weltner Van Swearengen, Wm. M. Beall, Jacob Young, Peter Grosh, Æneas Campbell, Elias Brunner, Frederick Kemp, John Haas, John Remsburg, Thomas Hawkins, Upton Sheredine, Basil Dorsey, John Lawrence, Charles Warfield, Ephraim Howard, Joseph Wells, David Moore, Joseph Wood, Norman Bruce, William Blair, David Schriver, Roger Johnson, Henry Cock, Robert Wood, William Albaugh, Jacob Mathias, Henry Crawle, Jacob Ambrose, David Richards, William Winchester, Philip Fishburn, William Hobbs, Thomas Cresap, Thomas Warren, Thomas Humphreys, Richard Davis, Jr., Charles Clinton, James Prather, George Bent, James Johnson, James Smith, Joseph Chapline, John Stull, Samuel Beall, Jr., William Baird, Joseph Sprigg, Christian Orendorff, Jonathan Hager, Conrad Hogmire, Charles Swearingen, Henry Snavely, Richard Davis, Samuel Hughes, Joseph Perry, Joseph Smith, Thomas Hog, Thomas Prather, William McClary, John Swan, Eli Williams, Christopher Burkett, Thomas Brooke, Michael Raymer, Nicholas Tice, John Adlum, Samuel Norwood, Bartholomew Booth, Jacob Boyer, Michael Jacob Miller, Andrew Bruce, John Darnall, John Remsburg, William Dorran, John Key, John Beall, John McCallister, Charles Beall, Lewis Kemp, John Stoner, Thomas Beatty, Thomas

Gilbert, Abraham Hoff, P. Henry Thomas, Jacob Good, Westel Ridgely, Samuel Carrick, Abraham Hosteter, Baltzer Kelcholumer, Samuel Emmet, John Cary, Christopher Edelin, Amos Riggs, John Grimber, Leonard Smith, Nicholas Hower, Richard Northcraft, John Herriot, Richard Smith, Zacharias Ellis, Azel Waters, Martin Cassil, James Johnson, George Bare, Benjamin Johnson, and Abraham Paw be a committee of observation, with full powers to prevent any infraction of the said institution, and to carry the resolves of the American Congress and of the Provincial Convention into execution; that any seventy-five of those gentlemen have power to act for the county, and any five in each of the larger districts be authorized to act in any manner that concerns such Division only.

II. *Resolved,* That the gentlemen appointed at the last meeting of this County a committee of Correspondence be hereby continued, and that the duration of their authority be limited to the second Tuesday in October next.

III. *Resolved,* As the most convenient and effectual method of raising the sum of $1,333, being this County's proportion of the $10,000 which the provincial convention has appointed to be raised for the purchase of arms and ammunition, that a subscription be immediately opened in every part of the County, and the following gentlemen be appointed to promote such subscriptions in their several Hundreds:

For Salisbury Hundred, Jonathan Hager, Henry Snavely and Jacob Sellers.

For Upper Catoclin, Peter Bainbridge, Benjamin Eastburn, Caspar Smith, and Thomas Johnson.

For the Lower part of New Foundland, Edward Burgess, Walter Beall, Joseph Perry.

For Skipton, Thomas Cresap, Moses Rawlings, and Richard Davis, Jr.

For Georgetown, William Deakins, Thomas Johns, Walter Smith.

For Sharpsburg, Joseph Chapline and Christian Orendorf.

For Lower part of Potomack Hundred, William Bayley, Samuel Wade Magruder, Andrew Hugh, and Charles Jones.

For Tom's Creek Hundred, William Blair, William Sheales, and Benjamin Ogle.

For Catoclin Hundred, George Stricker, William Luckett, Jr., and Westel Ridgely.

For Upper Antietam Hundred, Jacob Funk, Conrad Hogmire, Joseph Perry, John Ingram.

For Linton Hundred, Martin Johnson, and Joseph Flint.

For Cumberland Hundred, Charles Clinton.

For Middle Monocacy, Thomas Beatty, Mathias Ringer, Christopher Stull, and T. Flemming.

For Rock Creek Hundred, Thomas Cramphin, Zadock Magruder, W. Baker, and Allen Bowie.

For Sugar Loaf Hundred, Francis Deakins, R. Smith, L. Plummer, Z. Waters, and Z. Linthicum.

For Burnt Woods Hundred, Ephraim Howard, Charles Warfield, David Moore, John Lawrence, Henry Crowle, and William Hobbs.

For Lower Antietam Hundred, Thomas Hog, Henry Butler, and Thomas Cramphin.

For Linganore Hundred, John Beall, Charles G. Griffith, Nicholas Hobbs, Basil Dorsey, and William Duvall.

For Conococheague, David Jones Isaac Baker, and Jacob Friend.

For Piney Creek Hundred, Jacob Good, John McCallister, Samuel McFarren, Abraham Hiter, and John Key.

For Lower Monocacy Hundred, Lewis Kemp, John Darnall, Thomas Nowland, and Leonard Smith.

For Northwest Hundred, Samuel Harwood, Peter Becraft, and Richard Beall, of Samuel.

For Marsh Hundred, Charles Swearingen, Eli Williams, James Smith, Richard Davis, and George Swimley.

For Upper Part of Potomac Hundred, Brooke Beall, Samuel West, Nathaniel Offutt, and Alexander Clagett.

For Seneca, Charles Perry, Richard Crabb, Gerard Briscoe.

For Pipe Creek Hundred, Andrew Bruce, William Winchester, David Schriver, and Nathaniel Norris.

For Manor Hundred, William Beatty, Joseph Wood, Jr., Azel Waters, John Remsburg, Abraham Hoff, and Valentine Creager.

For Upper Part of Monocacy Hundred, Henry Cox, Roger Johnson, Richard Butler.

For Upper Part of New Foundland Hundred, Henry Griffith, Richard Brooke, and Henry Gaither, Sr.

For Elizabeth Hundred, John Stull, Otho Holland Williams, John Swan, and John Rench.

For Fredericktown Hundred, Phil. Thomas, Thomas Price, Baker Johnson, Peter Hoffman, and Ludwick Weltner.

For Fort Frederick Hundred, Ezekiah Cox.

For Sugar Land Hundred, Æneas Campbell, John Fletcher, John Luckett, Alexander Whitaker, and Solomon Simpson.

The said gentlemen are instructed to apply personally, or by Deupty, to every freeman in their respective Districts, and to solicit a generous contribution.

They are ordered to state accounts of money received, and pay it to the Committee of Correspondence, which is hereby appointed to meet at Fredericktown, the 23d day of March next: and they are further ordered to report to the said Committee the names of persons (if any) who shall refuse to subscribe.

IV. That Messrs. Thomas Johnson, William Deakins, Charles Beatty, George Murdock, John Stull, and John Swan, or any one of them, be empowered to contract, in behalf of the Committee of Correspondence, for any quantity of powder and Lead, to be paid for on the said 23d day of March.

V. In order that a committee of observation may be more conveniently chosen, and a more proper representation of the people may be had, the several collectors in each Hundred are desired to give notice to those qualified by their estates to vote for Representatives of some time and place of meeting in the Hundred, to elect members for a Committee, agreeably to the following regulation.

13*

When the number of taxables exceed two hundred, and amounts to not more than four hundred, the District shall elect three members. The Collectors are ordered to return such Representatives to the Committee of Correspondence on the 23d day of March; the Committee so chosen shall then meet, and the authority of the present Committee of Observation shall be dissolved.

VI. *Resolved,* That Messrs. John Hanson, Charles Beatty, Upton Sheredine, Baker Johnson, Philip Thomas, Jacob Funk, Samuell Beall, Joseph Chapline, John Stull, James Smith, Henry Griffith, Thomas Sprigg Wootton, Richard Brooke, William Deakins, and Thomas Cramphine, or any five of them, shall represent this County to any Provincial convention to be held at the city of Annapolis before the second Tuesday of October next. A petition from the People called Dunkers and Mennonists was read. They express a willingness freely to contribute their money in support of the common cause of America, but pray an exemption from the Military Exercise on the score of their Religious Principles.

Resolved, That this petition be referred to the Committee to be chosen agreeably to the fifth Resolve. In the mean time it is strictly enjoined that no violence be offered to the person or property of any one, but that all grounds of complaint be referred to said Committee.

ARCH. BOYD, *Clerk.*

Although making preparations to be ready for any contingency, the German citizens of Maryland were not, as a rule, prepared to go to the length of severing their connection with Great Britain. They considered that their rights had been invaded, but they also thought that this matter could be adjusted by the British government without going to the length of a separation of the colonies from the mother country. In the latter part of 1774 the magistrates of Frederick county adopted the folowing address to their representatives in the Provincial Convention:

Address of the Magistrates of Frederick County, Maryland, to the Honourable Matthew Tilghman, Thomas Johnson, Robert Goldsborough, William Paca and Samuel Chase, Esquires.

We the Subscribers, Magistrates of Frederick County, sensible of the disinterested services you have rendered your county on many occasions, but particularly as Deputies from this Province to the Continental Congress, beg leave to return you our sincere acknowledgements. The whole of the proceedings of that important Assembly are so replete with loyalty to the King; with tenderness to the interest of our fellow-subjects in Great Britain; and above all, reverential regard to the rights and liberties of America, that they cannot fail to endear you to every American, and your memory to their latest posterity.[128]

The magistrates who signed this address were chiefly of English extraction, but at the same time the Grand Jury, made up partly of German citizens, also forwarded an address to the same representatives. In this address, after endorsing the action of the Continental Congress, the Grand Jury goes on to say: "Permit us, gentlemen, to observe, that Councils tampered with such filial loyalty to the Sovereign, such fraternal delicacy for the sufferings of our friends in Great Britain, and at the same, with such unshaken zeal for the preservation of the inestimable privileges derived from our admirable Constitution, cannot fail to give weight and influence to the cause, and must moderate and relax the minds of our most poignant enemies."[129]

But, as Dr. Steiner says, "The 'most poignant enemy' was King George, and when the men of Frederick discovered that fact, all 'filial loyalty' was lost and they girded themselves for the fray."

[128] Force's "American Archives," Series IV., Vol. I., p. 992.
[129] Ibid., p. 993.

CHAPTER XV.

LEXINGTON and Bunker Hill will always be brilliantly illuminted pages in the history of America, and the Minute Men who had the temerity to contest the advance of Major Pitcairn and his regulars, and the farmer boys behind the fence on Breed's Hill who twice drove back the crack Welsh Fusileers, will always be entitled to their due meed of praise. They were the advance guard in the struggle with the mother country, and were steadfast in the hour of need, and are justly honored for the part they played. But after they had begun the contest and others were needed to reinforce them and continue the work, it was the sturdy Germans from the south: from Pennsylvania and Maryland, who hurried to their aid. The first troops from the other provinces to reach Cambridge after the battle of Bunker Hill were the two companies from Frederick county, Maryland, made up largely of Germans. This was but the beginning, and although many of these Germans were opposed to war and had come to this country to escape from the burdens imposed upon them by it, they left their homes and their untilled fields and joined the bands of patriots, prepared to back their desire for the freedom they had been promised with the rifle and bayonet. It is impossible to estimate the full value of their services, but considering the numbers of them who served in the patriot army throughout the war, it can be stated as an incontrovertible fact that without the aid of the Germans from Pennsylvania and Maryland the issue of the Revolutionary War would have been more than doubtful.

The news of the fight at Lexington reached Annapolis on the morning of April 26th, and couriers rapidly carried it to all parts of the colony. The excitement produced by the information that the war had been begun had scarcely begun to subside when news was received of the battle of Bunker Hill, which was fought on June 17, 1775. Three days before the Continental Congress had adopted a resolution providing for a battalion of riflemen, two companies of which were to be raised in Maryland, two in Virginia, and six in Pennsylvania. The two Maryland companies were assigned to Frederick county, and it was ordered that as soon as they were enlisted they were to be marched to Boston. A meeting of the Committee of Observation for Frederick county was held in the court-house at Frederick on June 21, and at this meeting John Hanson, chairman of the Maryland delegation to the Continental Congress, read the resolution adopted by that body just a week before. The committee at once adopted a resolution direct-ing that the two companies of expert riflemen be forthwith raised and named the following officers for the companies:

First Company.—Michael Cresap, captain; Thomas Warren, Joseph Cresap, Jr., and Richard Davis, Jr., lieutenants.

Second Company.—Thomas Price, captain; Otho Holland Williams and John Ross Key, lieutenants.

These companies were promptly recruited from among the expert riflemen of Frederick county, a large proportion of whom were Germans. Unfortunately the muster rolls of these companies have not been preserved, or at least cannot be found, so that the names of these patriots cannot be given. So prompt was the organization of these companies that by the middle of July they were ready to start on their march to Boston. The appearance of these riflemen and their skill as marksmen attracted attention everywhere. Writing to a friend in Philadelphia, under date of August 1, 1775, a gentleman in Frederick says:[130]

Notwithstanding the urgency of my business, I have been detained three days in this place by an occurrence truly agreeable. I have had the happiness of seeing Captain Michael Cresap marching at the head of a formidable company of upwards of one hundred and thirty men, from the mountains and backwoods, painted like Indians, armed with tomahawks and rifles, dressed in hunting-shirts and moccasins, and though some of them had travelled near eight hundred miles from the banks of the Ohio, they seemed to walk light and easy, and not with less spirit than at the first hour of their march. Health and vigour, after what they had undergone, declared them to be intimate with hardship and familiar with danger. Joy and satisfaction were visible in the crowd that met them. Had Lord North been present, and been assured that the brave leader could raise thousands of such like to defend his Coun-

130 Force's "American Archives," Fourth Series, Vol. III., p. 2.

try, what think you, would not the hatchet and block have intruded upon his mind? I had an opportunity of attending the Captain during his stay in Town, and watched the behaviour of his men, and the manner in which he treated them; for it seems that all who go out to war under him do not only pay the most willing obedience to him as their commander, but in every instance of distress look up to him as their friend or father. A great part of his time was spent in listening to and relieving their wants, without any apparent sense of fatigue and trouble. When complaints were before him he determined with kindness and spirit, and on every occasion condescended to please without losing his dignity.

Yesterday the company were supplied with a small quantity of powder from the magazine, which wanted airing, and was not in good order for rifles; in the evening, however, they were drawn out to show the gentlemen of the Town their dexterity at shooting. A clapboard, with a mark the size of a dollar, was put up; they began to fire offhand, and the bystanders were surprised, few shots being made that were not close to or in the paper. When they had shot for a time in this way, some lay on their backs, some on their breasts or side, others ran twenty or thirty steps, firing, appeared to equally certain of the mark. With this performance the company were more than satisfied, when a young man took up the board in his hand, not by the end, but by the side, and holding it up, his brother walked to the distance, and very coolly shot into the white; laying down his rifle, he took the board, and holding it as it was held before, the second brother shot as the former had done. By this exercise I was more astonished than pleased. But will you believe me, when I tell you, that one of the men took the board, and placing it between his legs, stood with his back to the tree while another drove the centre. What would a regular army of considerable strength in the forests of America do with one thousand of these men, who want nothing to preserve their health and courage but water from the spring, with a little parched corn, with what they can easily procure in hunting: and who wrapped in their blankets, in the damp of night, would choose the shade of a tree for their covering, and the earth for their bed.

These two companies of riflemen marched from Frederick on July 18, 1775, and although their journey of 550 miles was over rough and difficult roads, they reached Boston on August 9, without the loss of one man. These troops were the first from the south to reach Cambridge, and they naturally attracted considerable attention. Thatcher says:[131] " Several companies of riflemen, amounting, it is said, to more than fourteen hundred men, have arrived here from Pennsylvania and Maryland; a distance of from five hundred to seven hundred miles. They are remarkably stout and hardy men; many of them exceeding six feet in height. They are dressed in white frocks, or rifle shirts, and round hats. These men are remarkable for the accuracy of their aim; striking a mark with great certainty at two hundred yards' distance. At a review, a company of them, while on a quick advance, fired their balls into objects of seven inches diameter at a distance of two hundred and fifty yards. They are now stationed on our lines, and their shot have frequently proved fatal to British officers and soldiers, who expose themselves to view, even at more than double the distance of common musketshot."

The next year these companies were incorporated in a regiment of riflemen commanded by Colonel Stephenson, of Virginia. Upon his death Moses Rawlings became colonel of the regiment, and Otho Holland Williams, major. Both of these officers were from that part of Frederick county which is now Washington county, Maryland.

Although, as has been said, a large number of the citizens of Maryland were not in favor of a separation from Great Britain, events were moving so rapidly as to compel them to abandon this position. On July 26, 1775, the

131 " A Military Journal during the American Revolutionary War," p. 37.

Provincial Convention determined to take the government of the Province into its hands, and adopted the following declaration:

The long premeditated, and now avowed, design of the British government, to raise a revenue from the property of the colonists without their consent, on the gift, grant, and disposition of the Commons of Great Britain; and the arbitrary and vindictive statutes passed under color of subduing a riot, to subdue by military force and by famine the Massachusetts Bay; the unlimited power assumed by Parliament to alter the charter of that Province and the constitutions of all the colonies, thereby destroying the essential securities of the lives, liberties, and properties of the colonists; the commencement of hostilities by the ministerial forces, and the cruel prosecution of the war against the people of Massachusetts Bay, followed by General Gage's proclamation, declaring almost the whole of the inhabitants of the united colonies, by name or description, rebels and traitors; are sufficient causes to arm a free people in defence of their liberty, and justify resistance, no longer dictated by prudence merely, but by necessity; and leave no other alternative but base submission or manly opposition to uncontrollable tyranny. The Congress chose the latter; and for the express purpose of securing and defending the united colonies, and preserving them in safety against all attempts to carry the above mentioned acts into execution by force of arms, resolved that the said colonies be immediately put into a state of defence, and now supports, at the joint expense, an army to restrain the further violence, and repel the future attacks of a disappointed and exasperated enemy.

We therefore inhabitants of the Province of Maryland, firmly persuaded that it is necessary and justifiable to repel force by force, do approve of the opposition by arms to the British troops employed to enforce obedience to the late acts and statutes of the British Parliament for raising a revenue in America, and altering and changing the charter and constitution of the Massachusetts Bay, and for destroying the essential securities for the lives, liberties, and properties of the subjects in the united colonies. And we do unite and associate as one band, and firmly and solemnly engage and pledge ourselves to each other, and to America, that we will, to the utmost of our power, promote and support the present opposition, carrying on as well by arms as by the continental association restraining our commerce.

And as in these times of public danger, and until a reconciliation with Great Britain on constitutional principles is effected, (an event we ardently wish may soon take place) the energy of government may be greatly impaired, so that even zeal unrestrained may be productive of anarchy and confusion, we do in like manner unite, associate, and solemnly engage, in maintenance of good order and the public peace, to support the civil power in the due execution of the laws, so far as may be consistent with the present plan of opposition; and to defend with our utmost power all persons from every species of outrage to themselves or their property, and to prevent any punishment from being inflicted on any offenders other than such as shall be adjudged by the civil magistrate, the Continental Congress, our Convention, Council of Safety, or Committees of Observation.

The Maryland delegates to the Continental Congress had been forbidden, except under certain circumstances, to agree to any declaration of independence, but it soon became evident that the sentiment of that body was in favor of such a declaration. Consequently, when a resolution to that effect was introduced the Maryland delegates were recalled and the question was referred to the people so that delegates to the Provincial Convention could be elected and given instructions upon the matter. The people of the various counties held their meetings and elected delegates to the convention and instructed these delegates to repeal the restrictions imposed upon the delegates to Congress and to allow them to unite with those of the other colonies in declaring their independence and the formation of a confederacy. Less than a week before the adoption of the

Declaration of Independence the Maryland Convention rescinded the restrictions placed upon their delegates, so that the latter were able to join in voting for its passage. The Maryland Convention, however, determined to put itself on record, and on July 3, 1776, adopted the following:

A Declaration of the Delegates of Maryland.

To be exempted from Parliamentary taxation, and to regulate their internal government and polity, the people of this colony have ever considered as their inherent and unalienable right; without the former, they can have no property; without the latter, no security for their lives or liberties.

The Parliament of Great Britain has of late claimed an uncontrollable right of binding these colonies in all cases whatsoever; to enforce an unconditional submission to this claim the legislative and executive powers of that State have invariably pursued for these ten years past a steadier system of oppression, by passing many impolitic, severe, and cruel acts for raising a revenue from the colonists; by depriving them in many cases of the trial by jury; by altering the chartered constitution of our colony, and the entire stoppage of the trade of its capital; by cutting off all intercourse between the colonies; by restraining them from fishing on their own coasts; by extending the limits of, and erecting an arbitrary government in the Province of Quebec; by confiscating the property of the colonists taken on the seas, and compelling the crews of their vessels, under the pain of death, to act against their native country and dearest friends; by declaring all seizures, detention, or destruction of the persons or property of the colonists, to be legal and just.

A war unjustly commenced hath been prosecuted against the united colonies with cruelty, outrageous violence, and perfidy; slaves, savages, and foreign mercenaries have been meanly hired to rob a people of their property, liberties and lives; a people guilty of no other crime than deeming the last of no estimation without the secure enjoyment of the former; their humble and dutiful petitions for peace, liberty, and safety have been rejected with scorn; secure of, and relying on foreign aid, not on his national forces, the unrelenting monarch of Britain hath at length avowed, by his answer to the city of London, his determined and inexorable resolution of reducing these colonies to abject slavery.

Compelled by dire necessity, either to surrender our properties, liberties, and lives into the hands of a British King and Parliament, or to use such means as will most probably secure to us and our posterity those invaluable blessings,—

WE, THE DELEGATES OF MARYLAND, in Convention assembled, do declare that the King of Great Britain has violated his compact with this people, and they owe no allegiance to him. We have therefore thought it just and necessary to empower our deputies in congress to join with a majority of the united colonies in declaring them free and independent States, in framing such further confederation between them, in making foreign alliances, and in adopting such other measures as shall be judged necessary for the preservation of their liberties; provided the sole and exclusive rights of regulating the internal polity and government of this colony be reserved for the people thereof. We have also thought proper to call a new Convention, for the purpose of establishing a government in this colony. No ambitious views, no desire of independence, induced the people of Maryland to form an union with the other colonies. To procure an exemption from parliamentary taxation, and to continue to the legislatures of these colonies the sole and exclusive right of regulating their internal policy, was our original and only motive. To maintain inviolate our liberties and to transmit them unimpaired to posterity, was our duty and first wish; our next, to continue connected with and dependent on, Great Britain. For the truth of these assertions, we appeal to that Almighty Being who is emphatically styled the Searcher of hearts, and from whose omniscience nothing is concealed. Relying on His divine protection and affiance, and trusting to the justice of our cause, we exhort and conjure every virtuous citizen to join cordially in the defence of our common rights, and in maintenance of the freedom of this and her sister colonies.

CHAPTER XVI.

THE FLYING CAMP.

THROUGHOUT the summer of 1775 the citizens of western Maryland, comprising chiefly the German element of the population of the Province, were actively engaged in preparing for the war which they now knew was inevitable. Men enrolled themselves into companies and perfected themselves in military tactics under officers of their own choosing. Four of these companies were officered as follows:

Captain, William Blair.
1st Lieutenant, George Hockersmith.
2d Lieutenant, Henry Williams.
Ensign, Jacob Hockersmith.

Sergeants.

William Curran, Jr.   John Smith,
George Kelly,   Christian Crabbs.

Corporals.

John Crabbs,   Arthur Row,
George Matthews,   James Park.

Drummer, Daniel McLean.

Captain, William Shields.
1st Lieutenant, John Faires. *2d Lieutenant,* Michael Hockersmith.
Ensign, John Shields.

Sergeants.

Charles Robinson,   Patrick Haney,
James Shields, Sr.,   Robert Brown.

Corporals.

Moses Kennedy,   John Long,
John Hawk,   Thomas Baird.

Captain, Jacob Ambrose.
1st Lieutenant, Peter Shover. *2d Lieutenant,* Henry Bitzell.
Ensign, John Weller.

Sergeants.

Martin Bartz,   John Gump,
Frederick Schultz,   Casper Young.

Corporals.

John Protzman,   George Kuhn,
Dominick Bradley,   Laurence Creager.
Drummer, John Shaw.   *Fifer,* Philip Weller.

Captain, Benjamin Ogle.
1st Lieutenant, Henry Matthews. *2d Lieutenant,* George Nead.
Ensign, James Ogle.

Sergeants.

John Syphers,	Peter Leonard,
Lawrence Protzman,	Conrad Matthew.

Corporals.

Jacob Valentine,	Adam Knauff,
Daniel Protzman,	William Elder.

Drummer, John Roche.   *Fifer,* Daniel Linebaugh.

These companies, numbering over 250 men, were attached to one of the battalions raised in Frederick county and performed active service throughout the war.

On the first day of January, 1776, the Convention resolved to immediately put the Province in the best state of defence and to raise an armed force sufficient for this purpose. It was decided that this force should consist of 1,444 men, with the proper officers, and that it should be divided into a battalion of eight companies of sixty-eight men each, with officers, and the remainder of the troops formed into companies of one hundred men each. On January 14 this was changed so that there was to be a battalion of nine companies, seven independent companies, two companies of artillery and one company of marines. The Council of Safety was empowered to order these troops into Virginia, Delaware and Pennsylvania. Officers for the battalion were elected as follows: Colonel, William Smallwood; major, Thomas Price; paymaster, Charles Wallace; clerk to colonel, Christr. Richmond; 1st Surgeon's mate, Dr. Michael Wallace; quarter master, Joseph Marbury; acting adjutant, Jacob Brice. These companies were enlisted chiefly in the eastern section of the Province, and while there were many Germans among the officers and privates there was no grouping of that nationality.

On June 3, 1776, the Continental Congress resolved

"That a flying camp be immediately established in the middle colonies; and that it consist of 10,000 men; to complete which number . . . the colony of Pennsylvania be requested to furnish of their militia 6,000, Maryland of their militia 3,400, Delaware government, of their militia, 600."

On the 21st the Maryland Convention resolved "that this province will furnish 3,405 of its militia, to form a flying camp, and to act with the militia of Pennsylvania and the Delaware government in the middle department." These troops were to serve until the first of the following December.

The organization of the companies for the Flying Camp was promptly undertaken, and no class of citizens was more prompt in enlisting than the German residents of Frederick county. Some of the companies were made up almost entirely of Germans, while in all of them there was a fair proportion of that nationality. Following are the muster rolls of the companies enlisted in Frederick county for the Flying Camp:

LOWER DISTRICT, NOW MONTGOMERY COUNTY.
Captain Edward Burgess' Company in the Flying Camp.
Captain, Edward Burgess.
1st Lieutenant, Thomas Edmonston.
2d Lieutenant, Alexander Estep.
Ensign, Zephaniah Beall.
Privates.

Nathan Orme,	Miles Mitchell,
Richard Weaver Barnes,	Thomas Wood,
Charles Gartrell,	Charles Maccubin Reynolds,
Alexander Lazenby,	Joseph Estep,
Edward Harden,	John Tuckker,

Zachariah Aldridge,
Samuel Beall White,
Nathan Waters,
Benjamin Fitzjarrald,
Gilbert Bryan,
Nathan Musgrove,
James Burgess,
Benjamin Burgess,
Arthur Legg,
Thomas Freeman,
John Sheekels, or Shukels,
John Ray,
Shadrach Penn, or Peen,
Zephaniah Browning,
George Fryback,
John Hanson Wheeler,
Samuel Wheeler,
Thomas Culver,
Henry Lazenby,
Jeremiah Beall,
John Harding,
Samuel Taylor Orme,
Thomas Wallis,
John Lashyear (Layzare),
Reson Hollon,
Alexcious Simms,
Thomas Nichols,
Laurance Hurdle,
William Crow,
Lenard Wood,
Saml. Carter,
Thomas Beall,
Kinsey Hanee,
Joseph Gartrell,
John Geehan, or Guhan,

14*

Jeremiah Ferrell,
Samuel Purnal,
Thomas Sheekels, or Shukels,
Thomas Gittings,
Archibald Hoskinson,
Alexander Barratt,
Owen Haymon,
Alexander Edmonston Beall,
John Beaden,
Alexander Tucker,
John Wilcoxen,
Richard Burgess,
John Fryback,
Daniel Lewis,
John Ryan,
Benj. Tucker,
Wevour Waters,
Morris Brashears,
Obed Willson,
Stephen Gatrell,
James Beall (of Roger),
John Elwood,
James Carter,
Josiah Harding (Harden),
Henry Clark,
John Nichols,
Alexander Robert Beall,
William Garten,
Solomon Dickerson,
William Young Conn,
Marthew Lodgeade,
Leaven, (Leven) Beall,
John Ferrell,
William Hicke,
Dennis Marhay,

James Hurvey,
Edward Trout,
Samuel Solamon,
William Hopkins,

John Crook,
Samuel Taylor,
William Blackburn,
Richard Nicholsson.

Captain Leonard Deakins' Company in the Flying Camp.
Captain, Leonard Deakins.
1st Lieutenant, Thomas Nowland.　*2d Lieutenant,* Elisha Williams.
Ensign, John Griffith, resigned, Dennis Griffith.
Privates.

Lloyd Beall,
Zachariah Askey,
William Lanham,
Richard O'Daniel,
David Green,
John Taylor,
Thomas Lightfoot,
James McDeed,
Samuel Spycer,
Bartholomew Edelin,
William Draper,
Henry Allison,
Leonard Hagon,
Charles Mahoney,
John Baptis Gauff,

James Gauff,
John Yates,
Jacob Veatch,
William Longley,
Dennis Griffith,
Thomas Stewart,
John Stewart,
William Walker,
James McCulloch,
William Lovet,
Jessee Woodward,
Nathan Wilson,
Robert Wilson,
Edward Jinkings,
William Hays.

Captain Benjamin Spyker's Company in the Flying Camp.
Captain, Benjamin Spyker.
1st Lieutenant, Greenbury Gaither.
2d Lieutenant, Richard Anderson.
Ensign, Nicholas Scybert.
Privates.

Zachariah Rily,
John Gorman,
John McDavid,

Thomas Wise,
William House,
Geor. Sybert (Scybert),

Edward Northcrafft,
Neil Dogherty,
Michael Stanly,
William Carlin,
Peter Hoey (Hoy),
Strutton Hazel,
Henry Burton,
John Smith,
Archibald Trail,
Nathan Green,
John Currington,
William Murphy,
Joseph Crawly,
Edward Goodwin,
Timothy Maclamary,
John Turner,
William Glory,
John Reynolds,
William Hollands,
Allan Mackabee (Mockbee),
Francis Downing,
James Wilson,
Nathan Traill,
James Artis,
Aaron Wood,
John Keemer,
William Leitch,
William Baitson,
Charles Saffle,
Nicholas Gaither,
Lodowick Davis (Davies),
Bennett Herd,
Henry Mackee (Mackey),
Michael Rily (Riley),
Walter Nichols (Nicholl),

Nathan Roberts,
Stephen Harper,
John Cook,
Joseph Ross,
Patrick Murphy,
George Heater,
Dennis Clary,
Thomas Love,
Thomas Knowlar,
Abraham Booker,
Joseph Penny,
John Wilson,
Richard Short,
Thomas Chattell, (Chattle),
John Haymond Nicholls,
Richard Cooke,
Lewis Mullican,
James Pelly,
Eli Smith,
John Collins,
William Lowry,
Osborn West,
Leven Kersey,
William Jerbo,
John Lowry,
John Langton,
John Evans,
Henry Atchison (Hutchingson),
John Madding,
Robert Rickets,
Zachariah Evans,
Benjamin Holland,
Richard Kisby,
Michael Carter,
Thomas Sheppart,

Edward Waker,
Thomas Malloon,
John Gaskin,
Robert Drake,
Patrick Carroll,

William Pack,
John Cavenor (Cavernor),
Philip Hindon,
Stephen Warman,
George Heathman.

Captain Richard Smith's Company in the Flying Camp.
Captain, Richard Smith.
1st Lieutenant, Walter White.   *2d Lieutenant,* Thomas Hayes.
Ensign, Thomas Sprigg.
Privates.

Levi Hayes,
Henry Clagett,
John Patrick,
Matthias Henistone,
Andrew Hughes,
Jesse Harris,
William Summers,
Joseph Lewis,
John Davies,
John Smith,
Alexander Read,
Matthew Read,
William Norris, son of Benjn,
William Wallace,
Levin Hayes,
John Raynolds,
George Windom,
Peter Night,
William Madden,
Henry Atcheson,
Andrew Keath,
Samuel Queen Windsor,
John Bennett,
John Hinton,

Thomas Fanning,
Ezekiel Harris,
Herbert Alex^r Wallace,
Robert Moore,
Henry Kuhnes,
Anthony Murphy,
Jacob Irissler,
William Veal Steuart,
Michael Clancy,
James Long,
Charles Steuart,
James Nolland,
John Gibson,
William Sutton,
John Harriss,
John Fitzgerrald,
John Carroll,
John Burgess,
Jeremiah Leitch,
Denmas Mannan,
Nicholas Rodes,
Zepheniah Wallace,
Nicholas Rodes, Jr.,
William Pruett,

William Johnston,
John Bowen,
Robert Muckleroy,
William Pollard,
Jacob Hesse,
William Preston,

Alexander Mason,
James Jordan,
John Hennes,
Robert Robinson,
Thos. Hays.

MIDDLE DISTRICT, NOW FREDERICK COUNTY.
Captain Philip Maroney's Company in the Flying Camp.
Captain, Philip Maroney.
1st Lieutenant, Elisha Beall.   *2d Lieutenant,* John Hellen.
Ensign, William Beatty, Jr.
Privates.

Garah Harding,
William Jacobs,
John McCrery,
Daniel Shehan,
John Churchwell,
George Holliday,
George Hill,
William Gilmour (Gilmore),
Patrick Murphy,
Francis Quynn,
Samuel Wheeler,
John Shank,
James McKinzie,
Thomas Gill,
William Calvert,
John McClary,
William Skaggs,
John Marshall,
Bennett Neall,
John Test,
Thomas Kirk, Jr.,
Ninion Nichols (Nickols),

George McDonald,
James Hutchcraft,
Jacob Holtz,
Henry Smith,
Richard Wells,
Elisha Rhodes,
Paul Boyer,
Samuel Busey,
John Kenneday,
William Chandler,
William Hilton,
Warran Philpot,
Christopher Wheelen,
James Buller,
John Jones,
James Carty,
John Hutchinson,
Luke Barnet,
William Barnitt,
Samuel Silvor,
Edward Salmon,
James McCoy,

William Cash,
James Burton,
Thomas Bayman,
Thomas Hillery,
James Beall (Ball),
John Brease (Breeze),
Patrick Scott,
William McKay (McKoy),
Zadock Griffith,
Henry Meroney,
Henry Clements,
Thomas Fenly (Finley),
James McCormack Beall,
Patrick Connan,
Chas. Philpott Taylor,
James Lowther,
Henry Barkshire,
John Maynard,
James Beckett,
James Tannehill,
John Miller,
James Bryant,
Michael Arran,
Jacob Barrack,
John Donack,
James Kelam,

John Sehom,
Robert McDonald,
Richard Tongue,
Herbert Shoemaker,
John Myer,
Richard Fletcher,
Joseph McAllen,
Thomas Harrison,
John Alsop,
Charles Dullis,
Joshua Pearce,
Jacob Rhodes,
George Kelly,
William Louden,
Christian Smith,
Frederick Beard,
Henry Fisher,
James Hudson,
Michael Hale,
John Rite,
William Byer,
Francis Freeman,
John Cash,
William Hollings,
Jacob Burton.

Captain Jacob Good's Company in the Flying Camp.

Captain, Jacob Good.
1st Lieutenant, John Baptist Thompson.
2d Lieutenant, John Ghiselin.
Ensign, John Smith.
Privates.

Christeen Clisce,
George Obalam,

Henry Brawner,
Patrick Money,

Tobias Hammer,
George Rice,
Philip Fletcher,
Martin Fletcher,
Christeen Gobble,
Adam Keller,
John Dwyre,
John Billow,
John Chamberlin,
William Trace,
Jacob Freeman,
James Collins,
Thomas White,
Charles Freind,
James Estup,
John O'Bryan,
John Wimer,
George Gobble,
Henry Miller,
Ludwick Mober,
Peter Giddy,
Jacob Horine,
Philip Pepple,
Daniel Means,
George Free,
Daniel McTier,
Patric McIntire,
Danl. McIntire,
Danl. Merfey,
Thomas Adams,
John Sill,
Anthony Thomas,
Matthew King,
Joseph McClaine,
David Jones,
John Harrison,
John Money,
Peter Penroad,
James Campbell,
Leonard Macatee,
Thomas Anderson,
Jacob Bearae,
Philip Jacob,
William McClane (McClame),
Peter Havclay,
Philip Cenedy,
Patrick Deneley,
Joseph McCracken,
William Linch,
John Toughman,
Edward Pegman,
John Wart,
Michael Dodson,
Benj. Norris,
George Bonagal,
George Ettleman,
James Vaughan,
Wm. Brown,
Geo. Spunogle,
Peter Weaver,
Saml. Hamilton,
William Price,
Henry Fanslar,
William Boe,
Jacob Martin,
Jonathan McDonall,
Zachariah Ward,
John Slagel,
Danl. Benning,
John Robertson,
George Carroll,
John Henderson,

Fettea Stuffle,
Jacob Ridingour,
George Benter,
Joseph Ray,
John Duncan,

Patrick White,
John Test,
Robert McLeod,
Wm. Drome,
Wm. Brinsford.

Captain Peter Mantz' Company in the Flying Camp.

Captain, Peter Mantz.

1st Lieutenant, Adam Grosh.   *2d Lieutenant,* Peter Adams.

Ensign, John Richardson.

Privates.

William Richardson,
John Shelman,
Andrew Loe,
Henry Bear,
Andrew Wolf,
John Kellar,
John Martin,
Andrew Speak,
Charles Smith,
John Newsanger (Neswangher),
John Gombare, Jr.,
Jacob Bayer,
George Siegfried,
Jacob Stevens,
William Mills,
Mathias Overfelt,
David Eley,
Henry Smith,
Peter Bell,
John Twiner,
John Netsley,
Geo. Mich. Hawk,
John Conrad,
Joseph Pinnall (Pannell),
Frederick Kallenberger,

John Snider,
John Lock,
Saml. Yaulet,
James Adams,
Peter Walts,
Henry Huffman,
Jacob Crapell (Creppell),
Mathew Rudrieck,
Christ. Stanley,
Thomas Stanley,
Chr. Kallenberger,
Jacob Kern,
George Hower,
David Nail,
George Tennaly,
Jonathan Jones,
Frederick Heeter,
Rudolph Morolf,
John Mouer (Mourrer),
John Dutterer,
Martin Heckentom,
Abraham Boucher (Bucher).
Philip Bowman,
George Stoner,
Henry Hulsman,

Valentine Brunner,
John Foster,
Mich. Cramer,
Laurence Myers,
John Bennett,
John Gisinger,
Henry Teener,
John Striser,
Henry Myer,
John Shenk,
John Smith, dyer,
Jos. Williams,
Philip Flack,
John Hendrickson,
Dennis Realley,
Thomas Smith,
Jacob Carnant,

Henry Grose,
George Plummer,
Peter Wagoner,
Thomas Tobiry,
Philip Aulpaugh,
Jacob Shade,
Peter Snowdenge (Snowdeigel),
Henry Berreck,
John Baker,
Daniel Hinds,
George Boyer,
Joseph Shame,
Michael Baugh,
Nicholas Becketh (Beckwith),
Jacob Bowman,
Andrew Ringer.

Captain Vallentine Creager's Company in the Flying Camp.

Captain, Vallentine Creager.
1st Lieutenant, Phillip Smith, Jr.
2d Lieutenant, George Need (Neet).
Ensign, John Parkinson (Pirkinson).

Sergeants.

Solomon Bentley,
Aquilla Carmack,

Josiah Hedges,
Christian Cumber.

Corporals.

John Brattle,
Solomon Rowlins,
Drummer, Joseph Allsop.

Charles Menix,
John Link.
Fifer, Peter Trux (Trucks).

Privates.

Thomas Edison,
Christian Smith,
George Dotts,
Jacob Bostion,

Edward Hossilton,
John Smith,
Laurence Stull,
Samuel Hulse,

Matthias Andess,
John Springer,
Oliver Linsey,
Ludwick Moser (Mouser),
James Silver,
Michael Fox,
George Burrawl (Burrol),
Jacob Barrick (Barrack),
Jonothan Beard,
Christopher Cooper,
Patrick Daugherty (Daugerty),
Jacob Holtzman,
Peter Lickliter,
John Mortt,
William Slick,
Thomas Tumbleson (Tombleson),
Adam Russ,
Jacob Weyant (Wicant),
John Ciferd,
James Cammell (Campbell),
Henry Decamp,
James Buckhannon (Buchanan),
Peter Heveron,
Jacob Rignall (Rignell),
Peter Dick,
Cornelius Downey,
William From,
George Younger,
Lodwick Woller (Wooler),
Daniel Moore,
William Weier,
James Smith,
Joseph Smith,
Thomas Parkinson (**Pirkinson**),
Henry Fogle,
Henry Fox,
Frederick Hardman,
John Waggoner,
Adam Waggoner,
Adam Simmon (Simon),
George McDonald,
Henry Clice (Clise),
Thomas Nailor (Nalor),
George David,
Henry Reich,
Patrick Dayley,
James Branwood,
Thomas Cook,
Philip Greenwood,
Robert Sellers (Sellors),
John White,
David Barringer,
Patrick Rowin,
George Serjeant,
Evan Morris,
William Preston,
Robert Parson,
John Langley,
Daniel Bryan,
Jacob Ringer.

UPPER DISTRICT, NOW WASHINGTON COUNTY.

Captain Æneas Campbell's Company in the Flying Camp.

Captain, Æneas Campbell.

1st Lieutenant, Clement Hollyday.

2d Lieutenant, John Courts Jones.

Ensign, David Lynn.
Privates.

John Moxley,
Levi Walters,
George Hoskins,
William Frankline,
William Davis,
John Gillam (Gillum),
Henry Beeding (Beading),
Michael Hagan,
Daniel Moxley,
George Gentile (Gentle),
William Dixon,
Mark Chillon,
Martin Kiezer,
Shedereck Locker,
John Steel,
James Williams,
Samuel Lintridge (Lentarage),
Benjamin Osburn (Ozenburn),
William Veatch,
William Lucas (Luckas),
Charles Byrn (Burn),
William Housley (Owsley),
Notley Talbot (Talbort),
John Martin (Martain),
Charles Hoskins,
Barton Lovelass
        (Charles Loveless),
Grove Tomlin (Tamlane),
William Stallings (Stalion),
Thomas Gillam (Gillum),
John Henry,
Richard Lewis,
Aneas Campbell, Jr., cadet,
James Raidy,

Ignatius Maddox,
William Carroll,
John Snowden Hooke,
Richard Sarjeant, Jr.,
James Weakley,
George Kingston,
John Simpson Aldridge,
Charles Thomas Philpot,
Jeremiah Fulsome,
John Heart,
Edward Cane,
Robert Beall Crafford,
Philip Tracy,
Henry Jones,
Thomas Chappell,
Jacob Mills,
Hezekiah Speake,
Walter Raley (Raleigh),
Zephaniah Mockbee,
John Higdon, Jr.,
William Lewis,
Henry Allison,
Nathan Thompson,
James Glaze,
Archibald Chappell,
Hugh Elder,
Arthur Carns,
William Windham,
Samuel Busey,
Alexander Adams,
Lewis Peak (Speake),
Stephen West,
Thomas Owen,
John Jeans,

John Williams,
John Compton,
Peter Boardy,
William Poland,
Cornelius Harling,
Josh. Harbin,
Charles Lucas (Luckas),
John Ellis,
Stephen Gentile,
Joseph Beeding,
Philip Sulivane,
John Ferrell,
Patrick Rine,
Benjamin Ellit,

William Lamar,
William Thompson,
Stephen West,
William Briggs,
Francis Kitely,
Nathaniel Glaze,
Peter Hardesty,
Thomas Barrett,
Daniel Ferguson,
John Self,
William Oliver,
John White,
Abraham Chapman.

Captain John Reynolds' Company in the Flying Camp.

Captain, John Reynolds.

1st Lieutenant, Moses Chapline. *2d Lieutenant,* Christian Orndorff.

Ensign, Nathan Williams.

Privates.

William Walker,
Moses Hobbins,
John Ferguson,
Wm. Bradford, volunteer,
Jacob Hosler,
Thomas Fowler,
John Been,
David Grove,
Thos. Bissett,
Wm. Messersmith,
Wm. Patrick,
Archibald Mullihan,
Edward Pain,
Wm. Coffeeroth,
John Wade,
Thomas Stogdon,

Philip Wyonge,
Allexander Sparrow,
Christian Weirich,
Nicholas Weirich,
Peter Loar,
Jacob Long,
Nicholas Pinkely,
Mathias Wolf,
John Randle,
Michael Edelman,
Joseph Emrich,
Jacob Brunner,
Edward Kerny,
Nathaniel Linder,
Hermon Consella,
Nicholas Hasselback,

Silus Tomkins,
John Class,
John Hurley,
Thomas Pitcher,
Edward Brown,
Henry Coonse,
George Deale,
Benedict Eiginor,
Edward Dumatt,
Daniel Murphey,
Ludowick Kiding,
Christopher Curts (Cortz),
Henry Knave,
Thomas McKoy, D. S. T.
Henry Saftly,
John Berry,
Rinear Bennett,
Francis Thornbourgh,
Peter Seaburn,
Thomas Sands,
James Cunningham,
James Nowles, D. S. T.
Edward Nowles,
Thomas Barrett, D. S. T.
Christian France,
Jacob Weisong,
Joseph Finch,
John Hood,
William Baumgartner,
George Baumgartner,
Teeter Waltenback,
James Thompson,
George Reynolds,

Philip Loar,
Nicholas France,
Thomas Wilkins,
George Flick,
George Bowersmith,
Robert Wells,
John Walker,
Garrett Closson,
Basill Williams,
Simon McClane,
Joseph Carrick,
John Peirce Welsh,
John McKenny,
Benjamin Dye,
Jacob Forsythe,
Edward Gardner, D. S. T.
Joseph Moor,
Laurance Williams,
Bennett Madcalf,
Ephraim Skiles,
John Powell,
Michael Cortz,
Clement Howard,
John Teeter,
Jacob Teeter,
William Fanner,
John Iden,
William Kerney,
John Eove (Cove?)
Jacob Linder,
Rodger Dean,
James Stewart.

Captain Henry Hardman's Company in the Flying Camp.

Captain, Henry Hardman.

1st Lieutenant, Daniel Stull.   *2d Lieutenant,* Peter Contee Hanson,
Jona. Morris.

Ensign, John Rench.

Privates.

Chs. White,	Paul Schley,
Francis Frumantle,	Wm. Crale,
Daniel Matthews,	James Martin,
James Jordon,	Danl. Fisher,
George How,	Phil. Flack,
Thomas West,	James Green,
Jno. Kirk,	Isaac Hardey,
Maurice Baker,	Wm. Casey,
Daniel Cline,	Saml. Smith,
Jno. Newman,	Wm. Wallis,
Jno. Brown,	Thos. Jones,
Livie Jones,	Danl. Henderson,
Thomas Fish,	John Ward,
John Lindsey,	George Morrison,
Jno. Troxel,	Chr. Hart,
Jno. Collins,	Jno. Welsh,
Thos. Smith,	Jno. Moor,
Chas. Feely,	Jno. Aim,
Abm. Miller,	Jno. Barry,
George Colley,	Stephen Preston,
Jno. Mowen,	Rhd. Noise,
Martin Rickenbaugh,	Mathias Houks,
Pat. Ryley,	Stephen Rutlidge,
Robert English,	William Davis,
James Crale,	Thomas Collins,
Jno. Stoner,	William Divers,
Jacob Hirsh,	Chr. Metts,
Jno. Bemhart,	Danl. Wicks,
Jno. Grant,	Jno. Dicks,

Thos. Robison,
James Duncan,
Peter Haines,
Phil. Brugh,
Peter Fiegley,
Chr. Neal,
George Fiegley,
Phil. Berener,
Abm. Troxel,
Samuel Sprigg,
Barny Riely,
John Closs,
Peter Digman,
Chn. Berringer,
Thomas McGuyer,

Jacob Storam,
Saml. Richardson,
Conomus Acre,
Daniel Carty,
Rhd. Morgon,
Wm. Campian,
Isaac Barnet,
Chr. Fogely,
Michael Pote,
George Rismel,
Chr. Alinger,
Peter Splise,
Chr. Walker,
John Hager,
Jas Munn.

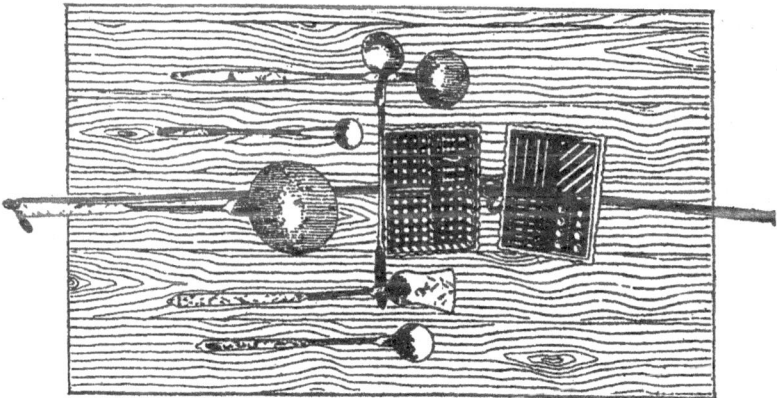

CHAPTER XVII.

The German Regiment.

THE Continental Congress having considered the question of raising a regiment to be composed entirely of Germans, on June 27, 1776, adopted the following resolution:

That four companies of Germans be raised in Pennsylvania and four companies in Maryland, to compose the said regiment: That it be recommended to the convention, or in their recess, to the council of safety of Maryland, immediately to appoint proper officers for, and direct the inlistment of, the four companies to be raised in that colony.

The Convention of Maryland promptly ratified this action by directing that two companies of Germans be raised in Baltimore county and two in Frederick county. The officers for the German regiment named by Congress were as follows: Nicholas Haussegger, colonel; George Stricker, lieutenant-colonel; Ludwick Weltner, major. The proceedings of Congress state that "the committee appointed to settle the rank of the captains and subalterns in the German battalion, reported the same as follows, which was agreed to:

"Captains, Daniel Burkhart, Philip Graybill, George Hubley, Henry Fister, Jacob Bonner, George Keeports, Benjamin Weiser, William Heyser, and David Woelpper.

"First-lieutenants, Frederick Rolwagen, John Lora, Peter Boyer, Charles Bulsel, William Rice, Jacob Kotz, Jacob Bower, Samuel Gerock, and Bernard Hubley.

"Second-lieutenants, George Hawbacker, Christian Meyers, John Landenberger, Michael Bayer, George Schaeffer, Adam Smith, Frederick Yeiser, William Ritter, and Philip Schrawder.

"Ensigns, John Weidman, Martin Shugart, Christian Helm, Jacob Crummet, Jacob Cramer, Paul Christman, Christopher Godfrey Swartz, and John Landenberger."

Of the officers of the regiment, Lieutenant-colonel George Stricker and Major Ludwick Weltner were from Frederick county. The Maryland captains were William Heyser, Philip Graybill, Henry Fister and George Keeports. The *Pennsylvania Archives*[132] state that Colonel Haussegger deserted to the British after the battle of Monmouth, but Dr. H. M. M. Richards has shown this to be a mistake. "This is evidently false," says Dr. Richards, "as he returned to his home at Lebanon, where he died in July, 1786. His heirs participated in the donation land-grants, awarded by the State of Pennsylvania to its meritorious and brave officers and soldiers of the Revolution, which would not have been the case were he a

[132] Second Series, Vol. XI., p. 73.

15*

traitor. It is more probable that, on account of his age, he became sick and incapacitated from active duty, and was given a lengthy furlough, which he spent at his Lebanon home."[133]

The *Maryland Archives*[134] give the following as a portion of the roster of the German regiment:

Sergeants.

Jacob Alexander,
John Cole,
Richard Gaul,
Jacob Hose,
John Heron,
Charles Jones,
William Johnson,
Daniel Jacquett,
Jacob Keyser,

Jacob Lowe,
John Ladder,
William Lewis,
Wm. Rummelson,
George Stauffer,
Christr. Stanty,
Frederick Sollers,
John Truck.

Corporals.

Philip Beam,
John Brieger,
John (or Jas.) Burk,
William Croft (Kraft),
Jacob Etter,
Bernard Frey,
Joseph Hook,

John Hochshield,
Patrick Kelly,
John Michael,
Thomas Polhouse,
James Smith,
S. Fredk Shoemaker.

Drummer.

Thomas Hutchcraft,
John Roach (or Rock),
Michael Smith.

Fifer.

John Brown,
Henry Ferrins.

Privates.

Levy Arrings,
James W. L. Ashly,

Daniel Kettle,
Francis Kerns,

---

133 "The Pennsylvania-German in the Revolutionary War," p. 399.
134 Archives of Maryland, Vol. XVIII., p. 184 et seq.

John Armstrong,
John Abel,
George Arnold,
Leonard Aberly,
George Bough (or Buck),
Saml. Bauswell,
Peter Backer,
Michael Benner,
Henry Bender (or Painter),
Jacob Bishop,
Jacob Beltzhover,
Danl. Baylor,
John Bower,
Michael Brodbech,
George Bantz,
Conrad Beam,
John Bennett,
Philip Bates,
Michael Bowerd,
Timothy Cahill,
Jacob Caufman,
Benjamin Cole,
George Crothorn,
Owen Curley,
Henry Cronise,
John Croft,
Thomas Clifton,
Michael Cambler (or Gambler),
Christopher Casner,
Rudolph Crower,
Michael Cowley,
Chas. Champness,
Jacob Cromer (or Cramer),
Michael Crush,
John Cline,
James Dyer,

Peter Koons,
Geo. Keephart,
Michael Kershner,
Jacob Kline,
Jacob Kentz,
Jacob Kaufman,
John Lecrose,
Thomas Larmore,
Charles Lago,
George Leithusier,
Fredk. Larantz,
Vendel Lorantz,
Fredk. Locker,
Martin Lantz,
Leonard Ludwick,
Galfried Lawrey,
Henry Michael,
Fredk. Mongaul,
John Miller,
Jacob Miely,
Jacob Miller, Jr.,
Lewis McColough,
William Mummart,
Jacob Miller, Sr.,
Henry Martin,
Wm. Maunsel,
William Nerving,
John Nevitt,
Richd. O'Quin,
Thomas Proctor,
William Pointer,
Robert Porter,
Henry Painter,
William Rider,
Chas. Ronenberger,
Michael Ritmire,

John Dalton,
James Dunkin,
John Dretch,
Godlb. Danruth,
Benja. Elliott,
John Eissell,
Wolfgn. Ellsperger,
Paul Elsing,
John Etnier,
Jas. Ensey,
Peter Engelle (or Angel),
Bartel Engle,
John Fennell,
John Folliott,
Henry Fisher,
Charles Fulham,
Patrick Fleming,
John Franklin,
Jacob Frymiller,
Abram Frantz,
John Fleck,
Philip Fisher,
Fredk. Filler,
David Finch,
James Forney,
Philip Fisher,
Philip Fitzpatrick,
Michael Grosh,
John Grupp,
George Getig,
Francis Gavan,
Edward Gould,
Adam Gantner,
Corns. Grunlin (or Quinlin),
Peter Grice,
Michael Gambler,

Conrad Riely,
Edward Robinson,
Andrew Robinson,
Chs. or Chrisr. Raybert,
Jacob Ruppert,
George Rittlemeyer,
Henry Rumfell,
George Regalman,
Jacob Ricknagle,
John Richards,
Christr. Raver,
Bernard Riely,
John Smitherd,
John Shively,
George Silver,
Christian Smith,
Mathias Smith,
James Slite (or Fite),
John Stanton,
Robert Smith,
Chr. Settlemeyer,
John Smith,
Alexander Sealors,
John Shrayock,
Joseph Slreiter,
John Slife,
John Shotts,
Michael Shoemaker,
Philip Studer,
Philip Smith (or Smithly),
John Smith,
Henry Strome,
John Shark,
Jacob Shutz,
Mathias Shrayer,
Henry Smith,

Richd. Hazelip,
Thos. Halfpenny,
Michael Hartman,
Jno. W. Hammersly
(or Amersly),
F. William Haller,
John Harley,
Joseph Hook,
Henry Herring,
Casimer Hull,
Jacob Haseligh,
Thos. Hazlewood,
Jacob Heffner,
Jonathan Hockett,
Peter Hewer (or Hoover),
Peter Hemerick (or Emerick),
John Hatfield,
Conrad Hile,
Jacob Hoover,
James Hughes,
Conrad Hausman,
Dedrick Haninghouse,
James Johnston,
Peter Kruise,
Philip Kuntz,
John Kibber,
Mathias Keyer (Keiser),
John Kendrick,
John Kline (Cline),
Chresn. Keplinger,
Abram Kettle,

John Shaffer,
John Snider,
Adam Stonebraker,
Adam Shaffer,
Fredk. Switzer,
John Smithly (or Smith),
Henry Statler,
Michael Stoner,
Conrad Stoyle,
William Selwood,
Andrew Selas,
John Timblin,
Fredk. Tawney,
William Taylor,
James Tite,
Henry Wilstock,
John Wade,
Danl. Williams,
John Welty,
Saml. Wright,
John Walker,
Thomas Woolford,
Joseph Williams,
Michael Weaver,
Chrisr. Waggoner,
Ludk. Witsinger,
Jacob Wink,
George Wilhelme,
Jacob Wagoner,
Michael Yakely,
John Zimmerman.

Captain Henry Fister's Company in the German Battalion, Commanded by Colonel Nicholas Haussegger, 1776.

Captain, Henry Fister.

Lieutenants.

Charles Balzel,   Michael Bayer.

Ensign, Jacob Grommet.

Sergeants.

John Balzel,   Philip Shopper,
Philip Shroop,   George Wintz.

Corporals.

George Hoover,   Jacob Tudderow,
Fredk. Wilhite,   Jacob Low.

Drummer, John Heffner.

Privates.

Henry Delawter,   Adam Charles,
Henry Hawk,   Abraham Fettie,
Fredk. Mittag,   John Imfeld,
Jacob Fantz,   George Shrantz,
Peter Copple,   Adam Smeltzer,
Jacob Kuntz,   John Bird,
John Ridenhour,   Gottlieb Klein,
Willm. Snider,   Peter Graff,
Adam Froshour,   John Ringer,
Christn. Sheafer,   Jacob Croumer,
Leonard Everly,   Philip Stouder,
John Wachtel,   Peter Hoover,
George Studdlemeier,   Peter Americk,
Philip Colour,   Conrad Houseman,
Valentine Shotter,   John Klein,
Henry Ziegler,   Henry Hain,
Jacob Tabler,   Jacob Kurtz,
Mathias King,   John Zimmerman,
Jacob Miller,   Henry Smith,
Philip Isingminger,   Adam Gentner,

John Leather,
Henry Hilderbrand,
Anthony Miller,
Jacob Farber,
Michael Moser,
Ludwick Visinger,
Jacob Hammer,
Martin Watkins,
Nicholas Frye,
Jacob Weaver,
Jacob Eggman,
John Beckerson,
George Clinton,
Christopher Slender,
Michael Beiker,
Anthony Hamilton,
Jacob Sheafer,

Henry Cronies,
Leonard Ludwick,
John Snider,
Henry Herring,
Peter Kuntz,
Justinius Hogshield,
Edward Robertson,
John Shatz,
Michael Stiener,
John Able,
Michael Shoemaker,
Frederick Henninghouse,
Thomas Polehouse,
Bartle Engle,
John Klein,
John Miller.

PAY ROLL OF CAPT. MICHAEL BAYER'S COMPANY IN THE GERMAN REGIMENT, CONTINENTAL TROOPS IN THE UNITED STATES.

Commanded by Lt. Col. Ludwick Weltner.

For the months of July, August, September and October, 1779.

Capt. Michael Bayer (Boyer),
Corp. ———— Polehouse,
Corp. ——k Shoemaker,
Corp. —rew Robinson,
Corp. John Hoshied,
Corp. John Shotz,
Drum. Thomas Hatchcraft,
Drum. Henry Ferrins.
Privates.
Thomas Mahony,
George Kepphard,
Peter Kuntz,
Abraham Kettle,

John Abel,
Adam Gantner,
Jacob Miller, Sr.,
Jacob Cramer,
Leonard Ludwick,
Michael Shoemaker,
Peter Emerick,
Henry Herring,
Michael Moser,
Henry Cronise,
Phillip Fisher,
John Snider,
John Wachtel,

Henry Fisher,
John Foliott,
Owen Curley,
Charles Fullim,
James Johnson,
——— Wade,
——— Mallady,
Edward Robinson,
Ludwick Wesinger,
Rudolph Marolf,
Jacob Miller, Jr.,

Phillip Strider,
Jacob Riggnagle,
Casemar Hill,
Conrad Houseman,
Michael Stoner,
William Taylor,
John Zimmerman,
John Cline,
Peter Hewer,
Bartle Engle.

MUSTER ROLL OF CAPT. GEO. P. KEEPORT'S COMPY. OF THE
FIRST GERMAN BATTALION CONTINENTAL TROOPS.

Commanded by Colonel Nicholas Haussegger.

Philadelphia, Sept. 19, 1776.

George P. Keeports, Capt.,
Saml. Gerock, 1 Lt.,
Willm Ritter, 2 Lt.,
John Lindenberger, Ensign,
Jacob Smith, 1st Serjt.,
Henry Speck, 2nd Serjt.,
John Keener, 3rd Serjt.,
Christn. Kearns, 4th Serjt.,
George Cole, 1st Corpl.,
Fredk. Moppes, 2nd Corpl.,
Ulrich Linkenfetter, 3rd Corpl.,
Philip Bitting, 4th Corpl.,
Benja. England, Drummer.

Privates.

Michael Brubacher,
Michael Grosh,
Michael Dochterman,
Christn. Settlemires,
Peter Kries,
Peter Koefflich (Hoefflich),

John Weller,
Gotfried Loure,
Jacob Wagner,
Peter Bast,
Jacob Stein,
John Schorcht,
George Schesler,
Danl. Fuhrman,
Henry Traut,
Jacob Schütz,
Peter Hahn,
George Miller,
Peter Anckle,
Jacob Wink,
Danl. Boehler,
John Harring,
John Franken,
John Cole,
Adam Schaeffer,
Mathias Schreier,

Adam Markel,
David Streib,
Joseph Carrol,
David Levy,
Willm. Trux,
Jacob Bigler,
Jacob Burk,

Conrad Reitz,
John Brown,
Fredk. Mongoal,
John Bauer,
Conrad Boehm,
John Miller,
John Smith.

Roll of Capt. William Heyser's Company.
Dated October 23, 1776.

William Heyser, Captain,
Jacob Kortz, 1st Lieut.,

Adam Smith, 2nd Lieut.,
Paul Christman, Ensign.

Sergeants.

David McCorgan (Morgan),
Jacob Hose,
Daniel Jaquet (or Jaques),
Jacob Miller,
George Gittin, Drum,

Corporals.

Andrew Filler,
Philip Reevenach,
Barnard Frey,
William Lewis,
Jacob Gittin, Fife.

Privates.

Peter Sheese,
Henry Stroam,
Adam Stonebreaker,
John Fogle,
Jacob Klien,
George Miller,
Phillip Fisher,
Jonathan Hecket,
Henry Tomm,
Jacob Hoover,
Michael Cambler,
George Harmony,
Thomas Clifton,
Michael Boward,
Henry Wagner,

George Buch,
Stuffle Reever,
George Wise,
John Michael,
John Robertson,
Adam Lieser,
Robt. Hartness,
Henry Benter,
John Armstrong,
Simon Fogler,
Jacob Grass,
Phillip Smithly,
George Wilhelm,
James Duncan,
John Breecher,

John Crafft,
John Shoemaker,
Mathias Gieser,
Mathias Dunkle,
Frederick Filler,
John Kibler,
Stuffle Wagner,
Jacob Heefner,
Conrad Hoyle,
Balsor Fisher,
John Smith,
Michael Weaver,
Jacob Belsoover,
John Rothe,
Wentle Strayly,
John Flick,
John Mettz,
Henry Michael,
George Riggleman,
Nicholas Baird,
John Hottfield,
Jacob Greathouse,

Fredk. Switzer,
Jacob Fowee,
Thomas Burney,
John Itnier,
Phillip Greechbaum,
Jacob Bishop,
Alex. Sailor,
Martin Pifer,
Peter Gittin,
Frances Myers,
Melcher Benter,
Tobias Friend,
Jacob Heefner,
John Smithly,
Everheart Smith,
Godfrey Young,
Frederick Locher,
Michael Yeakly,
James Furnier,
Henry Queer,
Henry Statler,
John Cropp.

Captain Heyser's company, which was enlisted in Washington county, was arranged as follows on May 22, 1777:[135]

William Heyser, Captain,
Jacob Kortz, First Lieut.,

Adam Smith, Second Lieut.,

Sergeants.

David Morgan,
Jacob Hose,
John Jaquet,
Jacob Miller.

Corporals.

Andrew Tiller, discharged by
    the Surgeon,
Philip Reevenacht,
Bernard Frey,

[135] Richards' "The Pennsylvania-German in the Revolutionary War," p. 225.

William Lewis,
John Breecher.

Privates.

Henry Stroam,
Adam Stonebreaker,
John Flick,
Henry Michael,
Philip Fisher,
Jonathan Hacket,
Henry Tomm,
Jacob Hoover,
Michael Camler,
Henry Wagner,
Melchior Benner,
John Fogle,
Francis Myers,
Jacob Kliene,
John Michael,
Simon Fogler,
John Robinson,
Jacob Beltzhoover,
Peter Sheese,
George Harmony,
Michael Bawart,
John Croft,
Frederick Filler,
John Kibler,
John Smith,
Math's Keyser,
Michael Weaver,
Nicholas Beard,
John Hatfield,
Conrad Hoyle,
Christian Reaver,
Adam Lower,
Ph. Greechbaum,

Frederick Locher,
Michael Yockley,
James Fournier,
Henry Quir,
John Cropp,
H'y Statler,
George Gitting,
Thomas Clifton,
George Riggleman,
Thomas Burney,
John Metz,
John Shoemaker,
Tobias Friend,
Adam Leiser,
Jacob Greathouse,
Robert Hartness,
Martin Piffer,
George Miller,
Christopher Wagner,
Mathias Dunkle,
John Roth,
Jacob Piffer,
George Bouch,
Henry Panthar,
Jacob Grass,
George Wilhelm,
George Wise,
Jacob Heffner,
Everhard Smith,
John Armstrong,
Godfried Young,
Peter Gitting, died March 18,
1777,

James Duncan,
John Etnier,
Philip Smithly,
Christian Sides,
Jacob Bishop,
Alexander Saylor,
John Smithley,

Archibald Fleegert,
Wentle Strayley, died January
    15, 1777,
Balzer Fisher, died March 15,
    1777,
Frederick Switzer.

Scharf[136] gives another arrangement of this company from a roll in the possession of Captain Heyser's descendants.

PAY ROLL OF LT. COL. WELTNER'S COMPANY IN THE GERMAN REGT. OF THE CONTINENTAL FORCES OF THE UNITED STATES. *Commanded by Lt. Col. Ludwick Weltner.*

July, August, September and October, 1779.

Capt. Philip Shrawder,
Serjt. William Lewis,
Serjt. Jno. Danl. Jacquet,
Serjt. Jacob Hose,
Corpl. James Smith,
Corpl. John Michael,

Corpl. John Brucher,
Corpl. Adam Stonebraker,
Corpl. Bernard Fry,
Drum. Moses McKinsey,
Drum. Joshua McKinsey.

Privates.

Michael Gambler,
James Ashley,
William Pointer,
Jacob Mosen,
Jonathan Hackett,
Henry Straam,
James Duncan,
George Wilhelm,
Melcher Benner,
Fredrik Schwidzer,
Michael Yockley,

Francis Gavin,
Jacob Kline,
John Kebler,
Mathias Keiser,
John Armstrong,
John Etnier,
Jacob Bishop,
Chris. Raver,
Philip Fisher,
Fredk. Locker,
Alex. Taylor,

136 "History of Western Maryland," Vol. II., p. 1190.

Conrod Hoyle,
John Fliet,
Fredrik. Filter,
Michl. Weaver,
James Forney,
Jacob Beltzhoover,
John Groop,
George Getting,
John Hatfield,
Henry Michael,
Thomas Clifton,
John Craft,

Patrick Fliming,
George Regliman,
Henry Stalter,
Christopr. Waggoner,
John Smith,
Henry Benter,
Philip Smithly,
Jacob Heefner,
John Smithly,
Jacob Haver,
Henry Quier.

A ROLL OF CAPT. PHILIP GRAYBELL'S COMPANY. 1776.

Philip Graybell, Captain,
John Lohra (Lorah), 1st Lieut.,
Christian Myers, 2d Lieut.,
Martin Shugart, Ensign.
Privates.
Ferdinand Lorentz,
Philip Miller,
Henry Millberger (Millburger),
John Freymiller (Frymiller),
James Cappelle (Caple),
John Rick,
Lorentz Kneary,
Jacob Etter,
Peter Baker,
Rudolph Crower,
Adam Rohrbach (Rohhbaugh),
Rowland Smith,
John Shriock (Shryock),
William Rommelsem, Serjt.,
Jacob Striter,
Martin Lantz,
John Hearly (Harley),

Jacob Hoffman,
Charles Zarrell,
Charles Charles,
Joseph Procter,
Joseph Braeter,
Christian Apple,
George Myers (Myer),
Henry Willsdaugh,
George Lighthauser, (Leithauser),
Joseph Smith,
Henry Wilstock,
Henry Rumfield,
George Hyatt, Fifer,
Thomas Kimmel (Kemmell),
Anthony Miller,
Joseph Hook,
Jacob Miley,
Jacob Miller,
Frederick Heller, Serjt.,
Andrew Gorr (Gore),
William Speck, Corpl.,
Henry Hargeroder (Hergeroder),

Wolfgang Ettsperger,
Christopher Regele (Regle),
Frederick Wm. Haller,
John Moore,
Wendell Andrews (Andreas),
Michael Kearshner,
Wolfgang Ettzinger,
John Shaffer,
David Mumma (Muma),
Abraham Frantz,
Frederick Weger,
Henry Hartman,
Wendel Lorentz,
John Hartenstein (Hardenstein),
William Altimus,
Jacob Burke,
Jacob Kintz (Keintz),
George Rittlemyer,
Philip Kautz,
Jacob Myer (Myers),
John Shlife,
John Machenheimer, Sjt.,
George Stauffer, Corpl.,
Gottlieb Danroth,
Lorentz Danroth,
Henry Decker,

Michael Growley,
Frederick Sollers, Corpl.,
Nicholas Frey,
Jacob Kerns (Kearns),
Simon Rinehart (Reinhart),
Mathias Boyer (Byer), Corpl.,
Jacob Ruppert,
Nicholas Keyser,
John Welty,
John Summers,
Michael Huling,
John Eyssell,
William Litzinger, Serjt.,
Fredk. Downey (Tawney),
William Cunius (Cunnius),
James Smith,
Peter Finley, Drummer,
John Smith,
John Bartholomew Deitch (Dych),
William Kraft,
Joseph Williams,
Henry Sprengle,
Henry Smith,
John Stricker, Cadet,
Peter Segman.

A LIST OF RECRUITS BELONGING TO THE GERMAN REGIMENT.

Commanded by Lieut. Colonel Weltner.

White Plains, September 5, 1778.

Names	Time of Service.	Names.	Time of Service.
John Kendrick	3 yrs.	William Johnston	do.
James Champness	War.	John Richards	do.
George Buch	3 yrs.	Albert Hendricks	9 mos.
Adam Mussler	do.	Philip Bates	do.
William Vincent	do.	George Arnold	do.

Names.	Time of Service.	Names.	Time of Service.
Stephen McGrouch	do.	Adam Mattrit, fifer	War.
William Neving	War.	Michael Smith, drummer	War.
James Woolford	3 yrs.	John Malady	do.
James Stiles	War.	Thomas Mackall	do.
Peter Batolomey	do.	Charles Fulham	do.
Richard Hazlip	3 yrs.	John Hughmore	do.
Robert Porter	do.	Thomas Hutchcrofft	do.
William Mummard	War.	John Wade	do.
Hugh McKoy	do.	Alexander Smith	do.
John Ammersly	do.	Frederick Shoemaker	do.
John Stanton	do.	James Johnston	do.
John Bennet	do.	Casimir Hill	3 yrs.
John Roach	do.	Thomas Mahony	do.
Benj. Elliott	do.	John Smadern	do.
Cornelius Quinlin	3 yrs.	Jacob Dolton	do.
Philip Fitzpatrick	9 mos.	John Timhen	do.
Francis Carns	3 yrs.	Michael Hardman	do.
Charles Jones	War.	Henry Ferrins	do.
Samuel Barts	War.	James Dyer	3 yrs,
Mathias Smith	do.	Henry Fisher	do.
William Rider	do.	Jacob Alexander	do.
William Malinia	do.	Christian Kepplinger	9 mos.
Benj. Cole	do.	Philip Hinkel	do.
Timothy Cahill	do.	Thomas Polehouse	do.
Robert Smith	do.	Abraham Miller	do.
Cornelius Vaughan	do.	Bernhard Ridenhour	do.
James Murphy	do.	Levy Aaron	3 yrs.
Christian Castner	do.	Moses McKinsey	do.
William Pope	do.	Joshua McKinsey	do.
John Fennell	do.	Jacob Moser	do.
Jacob Kauffman	3 yrs.	Richard O'Quin	War.
Thomas Proctor	do.	James Ashley	do.
Richard Gaul	do.	James Smith	do.
John Shively	do.	Thomas Rowlands	9 mos.
Thomas Halfpenny	do.	George Bantz	do.
Thomas Hazelwood	War.	On furlough.	

Remarks.

Names	Time of Service	Remarks
Richard Hopkins	9 mos.	Died 7 July.
Christn. Mumma	do.	Died July 27, '78.
William White	War.	Was a Deserter from Carolina.
James Connoway	3 yrs.	Ditto of Col. Chambers.

Name.	Time of Service.	Remarks.
Thomas Holdup	War.	Ditto of Carolina.
Mathias Custgrove	3 yrs.	Deserted.
John Waldon	do.	ditto.
Andrew Shuler	War.	ditto.
John Stout	do.	ditto.
Robert Barnet	do.	Sick, absent.
George Kephard	3 yrs.	Deserted.
Edward Connoly	do.	Taken by the Virginia Artillery.
Frederick Stone	do.	Given up to the Laboratory.
John Weeguel	do.	Left at Frederick Town.

These rolls do not contain the names of all the Germans from Maryland who served in the Revolutionary War. Many of them were to be found in the different regiments of the Maryland Line, some of the companies being made up almost entirely of Germans. But they are so scattered and their names are so changed in the spelling that it is impossible to pick them out.

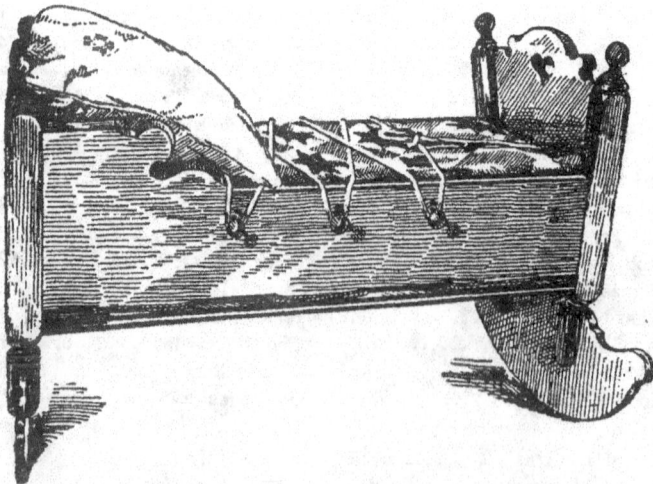

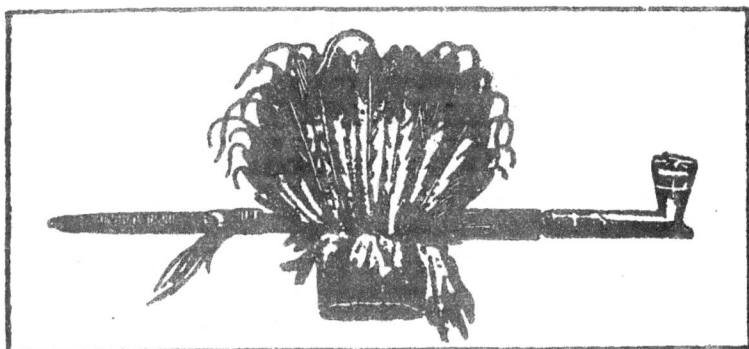

CHAPTER XVIII.

SERVICE OF THE MARYLAND TROOPS.

TO every call for troops made by the Continental Congress the response from Maryland was prompt and enthusiastic, and, as a rule, that province furnished more men than were called for; indeed, in comparison with the other colonies, Maryland contributed more than her share. But there was very little call for the services of her sons at home, as the fighting was all done in other sections of the country, and the Maryland companies, as soon as they were enrolled, were hurried to the point where they were most needed.

After the evacuation of Boston General Howe conceived the idea of dividing the country into two sections, the northern part from the southern, and with that end in view quickly landed a large force on Long Island for the purpose of capturing New York. The exact number of men making up the British commander's army is not known, but it was between 20,000 and 27,000. General Washington's force consisted nominally of about 24,000 men, but of these about one-third were invalids and another third were not properly furnished with arms and ammunition. Then, too, this force was scattered over a large section of country, for while Washington knew something of the intention of the British commander, it was not known just where he would strike his blow.

The Maryland battalion had been placed under the command of Colonel William Smallwood and sent to join Washington's army in the vicinity of New York. As other companies were raised they were hurried forward under orders to join Smallwood's command, so that by August 20, 1776, the whole Maryland force was under the command of that officer. They were attached to the brigade commanded by Lord Stirling. The British troops landed on Long Island between the 21st and 27th of August. On the 20th the Maryland troops, with those from Delaware, were ordered to advance. Colonel Smallwood and Lieutenant-Colonel Ware were in New York as members of a court-martial, and although they asked Washington to be allowed to join their command they were not permitted to do so, and the troops went forward under the command of Major Mordecai Gist.

The American army under Putnam was drawn out to occupy the passes and defend the heights between Flatbush and Brooklyn. During the night of the 26th General Clinton, with the van of the British army, silently seized one of the passes and made his way, about daybreak, into the open country in the rear of the Americans. He was immediately followed by another column under Lord Percy. To divert the Americans from their left another division

THE PENNSYLVANIA-GERMAN SOCIETY.

BATTLE OF LONG ISLAND.

under Grant marched slowly along the coast, skirmishing with the light parties on the road. Putnam being surrounded Stirling was ordered with two regiments, one of which was the Maryland regiment, to meet the army on the route to the narrows. About break of day he took his position advantageously upon the summit of the hills and was joined by the troops driven in by the advancing columns of the enemy. For several hours a severe cannonade was kept up on both sides and Stirling was repeatedly attacked by the brigades under Cornwallis and Grant, who were as often gallantly repulsed. At length the left wing of the American force having been completely turned by Clinton, and the center under Sullivan broken at the first attack of General De Heister, the position of Stirling's brigade on the right became perilous in the extreme. The passes to the American lines at Brooklyn were in the possession of an overpowering British force; two strong brigades were assailing him in front, and in his rear lay an extensive marsh traversed by a deep and dangerous creek, eighty yards in width at its mouth. Nearer its head, at the Yellow Mills, the only bridge which might have afforded the brigade a safe retreat had been burned by a New England regiment under Colonel Ward in its very hasty retreat, although it was covered by the American batteries. The only hope of safety, therefore, for the gallant troops who still maintained the battle and held the enemy at bay was to surrender, or else to cross the dangerous marsh and creek at its mouth, where no one had ever been known to cross before. Colonel Smallwood, having arrived from New York and learning of the perilous situation of his battalion, applied to General Washington for some regiments to cover their retreat. After a moment's hesitation as to the prudence of risking more troops on a lost battle, unwilling to abandon these brave men to their fate, he detached him with Captain Thomas' independent company from New England which had just arrived from New York, and two field pieces, to take a position on the banks of the stream and protect the remnant of the brigade in the attempt to cross it.

The scene of the conflict was within a mile of the American lines, and while Smallwood was hastening to their aid Stirling prepared to make a last effort to check the advance of the enemy and give time to a portion of his command to make good its retreat. For this purpose he selected four hundred men from the Maryland battalion, under Major Gist, placed himself at their head, and having ordered all the other troops to make the best of their way through the creek, advanced against Cornwallis' brigade. As they drew out between the two bodies of the enemy it was thought by those looking on from the camp that they were about to surrender, but as with fixed bayonets they rushed to the charge upon the overwhelming force opposed to them fear and sorrow filled every heart, and Washington is said to have wrung his hands and examined: "Good God! What brave fellows I must this day lose."[137]

The following account of the battle of Long Island was sent to the Maryland convention by Colonel Smallwood:

CAMP OF THE MARYLAND REGULARS,
HEAD QUARTERS, October 12th, 1776.

Sir:—Through your hands I must beg leave to address the Hon'ble Convention of Maryland, and must confess not without an apprehension that I have incurred their displeasure, for having omitted writing when on our march from Maryland to New York, and since our arrival here; nor shall I in a pointed manner urge anything in my defence, but leave them at large to condemn

[137] McSherry's "History of Maryland," p. 165.

or excuse me, upon a presumption that should they condemn, they will at least pardon, and judge me perhaps less culpable, when they reflect in the first instance on the exertions necessary to procure baggage wagons, provisions and house-room for 750 men, marched the whole distance in a body, generally from 15 to 20 miles per day, as the several stages made it necessary; and in the latter I trust they will give some indulgence for this neglect, for since our arrival in New York it has been the fate of this Corps to be generally stationed at advanced posts, and to act as a covering party, which must unavoidably expose troops to extraordinary duty and hazard, not to mention the extraordinary vigilance and attention in the commandant of such a party in disposing in the best manner, and having it regularly supplied; for here the commanders of regiments, exclusive of their military duty, are often obliged to exert themselves in the departments of Commissary and Quarter-Master General, and even directors of their regimental hospitals.

Perhaps it may not be improper to give a short detail of occurrences upon our march to Long Island and since that period. The enemy from the 21st to the 27th of August, were landing their troops on the lower part of Long Island, where they pitched a large encampment, and ours and their advanced parties were daily skirmishing at long shot, in which neither party suffered much. On the 26th the Maryland and Delaware troops, which composed part of Lord Stirling's Brigade, were ordered over. Col. Haslet and his Lieut.-Col. Bedford, of the Delaware Battalion, with Lieut.-Col. Ware and myself, were detained on the trial of Lieut.-Col. Ledwitz, and though I waited on General Washington and urged the necessity of attending our troops, yet he refused to discharge us, alleging there was a necessity for the trial's coming on, and that no other field-officers could be then had. After our dismission from the court-martial it was too late to get over, but pushing over early next morning, found our regiments engaged, Lord Stirling having marched them off before day to take possession of the woods and difficult passes between our lines and the enemy's encampment; but the enemy over night had stolen a march on our generals, having got through those passes, met and surrounded our troops on the plain grounds within two miles of our lines. Lord Stirling drew up his brigade on an advantageous rising ground, where he was attacked by two brigades in front, headed by the Generals Cornwallis and Grant, and in his rear the enemy's main body stood ready drawn up to support their own parties and intercept the retreat of ours. This excellent disposition and the superior numbers ought to have taught our Generals there was no time to be lost in securing their retreat, which might at least have been affected, had the troops formed into a heavy column and pushed their retreat; but the longer this was delayed it became the more dangerous, as they were then landing more troops in front from the ships. Our brigade kept their ground for several hours, and in general behaved well, having received some heavy fires from the artillery and musketry of the enemy, whom they repulsed several times; but their attacks were neither so lasting nor vigorous as was expected, owing, as it was imagined, to their being certain of making the whole brigade prisoners of war; for by this time they had so secured the passes on the road to our lines (seeing our parties were not supported from thence, which indeed our numbers would not admit of) that there was no possibility of retreating that way. Between the place of action and our lines there lay a large marsh and deep creek, not above 80 yards across at the mouth—(the place of action upon a direct line did not exceed a mile from a part of our lines), towards the head of which creek there was a mill and bridge, across which a certain Col. Ward from New England, who is charged with having acted a bashful part that day, passed over with his regiment, and then burnt them down, though under cover of our cannon, which would have *checked the enemy's* pursuit at any time; other ways, this bridge might have afforded a secure retreat. There then remained no other prospect but to surrender, or attempt to retreat over this marsh and creek at the mouth, where no person had ever been known to cross. In the interim I applied to Gen'l Washington for some regiments to march out to support and cover their retreat, which he urged would be attended with too great a risk to the party and the lines. He immediately afterwards sent for and ordered me to march down a New England regiment and Capt. Thomas's company, which had just come over from New York, to the mouth of the creek opposite where the brigade was drawn up, and ordered two field-pieces down, to support and cover their retreat should they make a push that way. Soon after our march they began to retreat, and for a small time the fire was very heavy on both sides, till our troops came to the marsh, where they were obliged to break their order and escape as quick as they could to the edge of the creek under a brisk fire, notwithstanding which they brought off 28 prisoners. The enemy taking advantage of a commanding ground, kept up a continued fire from four field-pieces, which were well served and directed, and a heavy column advancing on the marsh must have cut our people off, their guns being wet and muddy, not one of them would have fired, but having drawn up the musketry and disposed of some riflemen conveniently, with orders to fire on them when they came within shot; however, the latter began their fire rather too soon, being at 200 yards' distance, which notwithstanding had the desired effect, for the enemy immediately retreated to the fast land, where they continued parading within 800 yards till our troops were brought over. Most of those who swam over, and others who attempted to cross before the covering party got down, lost their arms and accoutrements in the mud and creek, and some poor fellows their lives, particularly two of the Maryland, two of the Delaware, one of Attley's Pennsylvania, and two Hessian prisoners were drowned. Thomas's men contributed much in bringing over this party. Have enclosed a list of the killed and wounded, amounting to 256, officers inclusive. It has been said the enemy during the action also attacked our lines; but this was a mistake. Not knowing the ground, one of the columns advanced within long shot without knowing they were so near, and upon our artillery and part of the musketry's firing on them they immediately fled. The 28th, during a very hard rain, there was an alarm that the enemy had advanced to attack our lines, which alarmed the troops very much, but was without foundation. The 29th it was found by a council of war that our fortifications were not tenable, and it was therefore judged expedient that the army should retreat from the Island that night, to effect which, notwithstanding the Maryland troops had but one day's respite, and many other troops had been many days clear of any detail of duty, they were ordered on the advanced post at Fort Putnam, within 250 yards of the enemy's approaches, and joined with two Pennsylvania reg'ts on the left, were to remain and cover the retreat of the army, which was happily completed under cover of a thick fog and a southwest wind, both of which favored our retreat; otherwise the fear, disorder and confusion of some of the Eastern troops must have retarded and discovered our retreat and subjected numbers to be cut off. After remaining two days in New York, our next station was at Harlaem, 9 miles above, at an advance post opposite Montresove's and Bohana's Islands, which in a few days the enemy got possession of without opposition; from the former of which we daily discoursed with them, being within two hundred yards, and only a small creek between. It being judged expedient to abandon New York and retreat to our lines below Fort Washington, the military stores, &c., had been removing some days, when on the 15th Sept. the enemy effected a landing on several parts of the Island below (and it is cutting to say without the least opposition). I have often read and heard of instances of cowardice, but hitherto have had but a faint idea of it till now. I never could have thought human nature subject to such baseness. I could wish the transactions of this day blotted out of the annals of America—nothing appeared but flight, disgrace and confusion. Let it suffice to say, that 60 light infantry upon the first fire put to flight two brigades of the Connecticut troops —wretches who, however strange it may appear, from the Briga-dier-General down to the private sentinel, were caned and whip'd by the Generals Washington, Putnam and Mifflin; but even this indignity had no weight—they could not be brought to stand one shot. General Washington expressly sent and drew our regiment from its brigade, to march down towards New York, to cover the retreat and to defend the baggage, with direction to take possession of an advantageous eminence near the enemy upon the main road, where we remained under arms the best part of the day, till Sergant's Brigade came in with their baggage, who were the last troops coming in, upon which the enemy divided their main body into two columns; one filing off on the North river endeavored to flank and surround us, the other advancing in good order slowly up the main road upon us; we had orders to retreat in good order, which was done, our Corps getting within the lines after dusk. The next day about 1000 of them made an attempt upon our lines, and were first attacked by the brave Col. Knolton of New England, who lost his life in the action, and the 3d Virginia regiment, who were immediately joined by three Independent Companies, under Major Price, and some part of the Maryland flying-camp, who drove them back to their lines, it is supposed with the loss of 400 men killed and wounded. Our party had about 100 killed and wounded, of the former only 15. Since which we have been viewing each other at a distance, and strongly entrenching till the 9th October, when three of their men-of-war passed up the North river above King's Bridge, under a very heavy cannonade from our Batteries, which has effectually cut off our communication by water with Albany. I must now break off abruptly, being ordered to march up above King's Bridge, the enemy having landed 6000 men from the Sound on Frog's Point. 50 ships are got up there, landing more troops—there is nothing left but to fight them. An engagement is generally expected and soon. Have enclosed a copy of a general return of the battalion and Veazy's company, being all the troops I marched from Maryland, with the accoutrements and camp equipage taken in Philadelphia, to be rendered the Congress, together with our general weekly return. The Independents are now about their returns of arms, accoutrements and camp equipage brought by them from Maryland, but not having time to finish, they must hereafter be returned to Council of Safety. We have upwards of three hundred officers and soldiers of the Maryland regulars very sick, which you will observe by the return; and

I am sorry to say, it's shocking to humanity to have so many of them; this must hurt the service upon the new enlistments. Major Price and Gist and Cap'n Stone are in the Jerseys very sick, and Col. Ware and myself are very unfit for duty, though we attend it; many more officers are very unwell. I am very respectfully,

Your obedient and very h'ble servant,

W. SMALLWOOD.[138]

The loss sustained by the Maryland troops in the battle of Long Island was unusually heavy. The killed and wounded numbered 256. Captain Veazy and Lieutenant Butlar were killed, and among the prisoners were Captain Daniel Bowie, Lieutenant William Steret, William Ridgely, Hatch Dent, Walter Muse, Samuel Wright, Joseph Butler, Edward Praul, Edward Decourcy and Ensigns James Fernandes and William Courts. The conduct of the battle of Long Island has called forth a great deal of unfavorable comment, taking in both officers and privates, but the Maryland troops taking part in it have received nothing but praise for their valor, in marked contrast to that of some of the New Englanders. McSherry says[139] "The people of Long Island point out to strangers the spot where half of the Maryland battalion stemmed the advance of the whole left wing of the British army when no other troops were left on the field," and Colonel Daniel Brodhead wrote:[140] "No troops could behave better than the Southern, for though they seldom engaged less than five to one, they frequently repulsed the Enemy with great Slaughter."

At White Plains the Marylanders sustained their reputation and were in the thickest of the fight, where their loss was over one hundred men. The Maryland battalion had

---

[138] Scharf's "Chronicles of Baltimore," p. 148 et seq.

[139] "History of Maryland," p. 166.

[140] Pennsylvania Archives, First Series, Vol. V., p. 22.

become veterans. In three months it had fought three battles, and it was the first organization to use the bayonet against the British regulars. At the defence of Fort Washington they held their own against a vastly superior force of Hessians. Washington had posted his army in three divisions, Colonel Rawlings with his Maryland regiment being stationed on a hill to the north of the lines. They were attacked by General Knyphausen with five thousand men.' At the same time another division of the enemy moved against Colonel Cadwallader, of the Pennsylvania troops, who commanded within the lines, and a third division crossed the East river in boats and landed within the lines. The superiority of the British force drove Cadwallader's men back into the fort, but the Marylanders, under Rawlings, bravely maintained their position. "Posted among the trees, his riflemen poured in upon the advancing column a murderous fire which they in vain endeavored to sustain. The Hessians broke and retired. Again they were brought to the attack and again repulsed with dreadful slaughter. The Maryland riflemen remembered the destruction of their brethren of the battalion by the Hessians at Yellow Mills and did not forget to avenge it. But what could a single battalion of riflemen, even of such matchless skill and courage, effect when opposed to five thousand men armed with the bayonet? Had every other post been defended as theirs was, victory would have crowned the American arms that day. But all the other troops were already in full retreat. The three divisions of the enemy were about to fall upon their rear while they contended with a force in front of them far greater than their own. At length, by sheer fighting and power of numbers, the Hessians reached the summit of the hill. Rawlings, perceiving the danger to his rear and learning of the retreat of the Pennsylvanians, abandoned his position, as no longer tenable, and retired under the guns of the fort."[141]

As Colonel Magaw was unable to hold the fort against such an overwhelming force he was compelled to surrender, and twenty-six hundred men became prisoners. The British lost nearly twelve hundred men, killed and wounded, more than half of this loss being sustained by the Hessians in their attack upon Rawlings' Maryland and Virginia riflemen.

A detailed account of all the battles in which the Maryland troops took part cannot be given here, but wherever they were called upon—at Trenton, at Princeton, at Monmouth, on the banks of the Brandywine, at Germantown— they were always to be found at the forefront, and acquitted themselves with glory. Many had been killed and many more were disabled on account of wounds and sickness. "In each succeeding action," says McSherry, "the Maryland troops had been further reduced until Smallwood's battalion and the seven independent companies, which had entered the campaign fourteen hundred strong, had been worn down to a mere captain's command." But new men filled up the ranks and until the end of the war the Marylanders continued to show their bravery on many a hard fought field, a bravery that had been bred in them through their arduous life on the frontiers of the province.

One of the matters which caused considerable trouble among the officers of the Maryland troops, as it did among those of other states, was the determination of the rank of the officers. When it became apparent that there would be a war between Great Britain and the colonies, military com-

141 McSherry's "History of Maryland," p. 171.

panies were formed in all parts of the country, officers were selected, and the companies were drilled in military tactics, so that by the time that hostilities actually broke out there were a number of these companies ready to march at a moment's notice, and many of them did so and took an active part in the early campaigns. Later on when the army was being reorganized under the authority of the Continental Congress, the officers of these companies naturally expected to be among the first ones promoted on account of their having been early in the field. In many instances these officers were disappointed in their expectation and saw promoted over them officers who had entered the service after they had. This naturally caused considerable resentment and protests were made to those in authority. Promises were made that the matter would be adjusted, but progress in this direction was slow and the feeling among those who felt that they were being slighted became so intense that something had to be done. Early in 1779 the legislature of Maryland adopted resolutions requesting General Washington to settle this question of rank. Upon receipt of these resolutions Washington wrote to Governor Johnson as follows.[142]

HEAD QUARTERS MIDDLE BROOK, 8th April 1779.

Sir

I have been honoured with yours of the 26th March inclosing a Resolve of the House of Delegates for the incorporation of parts of the German Battalion and Rifle Corps into a Regiment, and another for forwarding the recruiting service. I also at the same time received from the president of the Senate and the speaker of the House of Delegates two Resolves—one empowering me to fully settle the Rank of the Officers of the Maryland line, the other allowing half pay for life to such Officers as shall remain in the service during the war.

142 Archives of Maryland, Vol. XXI., p. 339.

By an allotment of the quota of troops to be raised by said State, made by Congress the 26ᵗʰ Febʳ 1778, the German Battalion was wholly attached to the State of Maryland and considered as her Regᵗ since which it hath done duty in that line. Had not this been the case, the incorporation of such parts of that Regiment and Rifle Corps as are deemed properly to belong to Maryland would still be attended with the greatest inconveniences particularly in regard to recruiting the Ranks of the Officers, Colᵒ Rawlins and most of his being elder than Colᵒ Weltner and those of the German would supersede them upon incorporation.

Indeed Colᵒ Weltner would not only be superseded, but he must be supernumerary. In short, the difficulties attending the measure recommended are more than can be conceived, and I am convinced by experience that it cannot be carried into execution without totally deranging the German Regiment.

In January last Congress, to make some provision for Colᵒ Rawlins and his Officers, resolved that he should increase his remaining men (who are not more than 70 or 80) to three Companies to be commanded by him as a separate Corps. The times of most of the old men are near expiring and whether they will reinlist I cannot say.

I entertain a very high opinion of Colᵒ Rawlins and his Officers, and have interested myself much in their behalf. It is to be regretted that they were not provided for in the States to which they belong, when the Army was new modelled in 1776, but as they were not, after a variety of plans had been thought of that above mentioned was esteemed the most eligible, and indeed the only one that could be accepted, as the introduction of those Gentlemen into the line would have been impracticable.

I have, agreeable to the powers invested in me, appointed a Board of General Officers to take into consideration and report to me the rank of the Maryland line. I do not imagine that it will be possible to give general satisfaction, but I am convinced that the Gentlemen who have the Business in hand will pay the strictest attention to the claims of all parties, and give the most disinterested decision.

Whatever the decision may be, I hope that it may be considered by the State as definitive, and that they will not in future pay any further regard to the importunities of those who may be discontented with the arrangemenet which is about to be made.

The matter was one that was not easily arranged and after several Boards of Officers had worked on it Washington wrote to Governor Johnson, on May 28, 1779, giving the rank of the different officers as it had finally been agreed upon. Instead of allaying the feeling of resentment among the officers the report determining their rank increased it, and a number of them promptly resigned. That their resignations were not due to any lack of patriotism, but to a feeling that they were not being treated properly, is shown by the actions of one Pennsylvania-German. Benjamin Spyker, Jr., a native of Berks county, Pennsylvania, who had been teaching school in Maryland, enlisted a company early in 1776, and upon the organization of the Maryland Line his company became a part of the Seventh Regiment. When the question of the rank of the officers had been finally settled he resigned his commission and went back to his home in Berks county, where he enlisted as a private in Captain John Anspach's company, in the Berks county militia.[143]

But the settlement of the question of the rank of the officers did not end the matter. On June 17, 1779, the principal officers of the Maryland regiments in the field addressed the following petition to the governor and the members of the Senate and House of Delegates:[144]

We beg leave, most respectfully, to represent to your Excellency and Honors that the several provisions hitherto made by the Legis-

[144] Scharf's "History of Maryland," Vol. II., p. 352.
[143] Pennsylvania Archives, Fifth Series, Vol. V., p. 185.

lature for the subsistence of her officers, though liberal at the time of being voted, have by no means been adequate to the exigent expenses of their respective stations.

That a zeal for the public cause, and an ardent desire to promote the happiness and interest of their country have, notwithstanding, induced them to continue in the service to the very great prejudice of their private fortunes; many of which being now entirely exhausted, we find ourselves under the painful and humiliating necessity of soliciting your Excellency and Honors for a further support, and the disposition of a generous and grateful people to reward the services of the faithful sons and servants of the State.

The very great depreciation of the Continental Currency renders it absolutely necessary that some further provision should be made for our support to enable us to continue a service in which nothing but a love of Liberty and the rights of mankind can retain us; and we trust that it will be such as will support with decency and dignity the respective ranks which our country has done us the honor to confer on us.

The inconveniences and difficulties we suffer are various and grievous, but we think it unnecessary to be particular or to point out a mode of redress as the examples of the State of Pennsylvania and others in providing for their officers and soldiers are the most eligible and ample we desire or expect.

We beg leave to assure your Excellency and Honors with the utmost candor and sincerity, that while we assiduously exert our best abilities in a hardy opposition to the enemies of our country, we earnestly wish the arrival of that period when our military services will be no longer requisite, and, being at liberty individually to procure a peaceful competence, we may again be numbered among the happy citizens of the Free and Independent State of Maryland.

We have the honor to be with great respect,

Your Excellency and Honors most obedient humble servants. Knowing the above representation to be a true state of the grievances of the officers in the Maryland line, on their behalf, and in justice to them, I have subscribed to it.　W. SMALLWOOD.

John Carvil Hall, colonel 4th regiment;

Otho H. Williams, colonel 6th regiment;

John Gunby, colonel;

R. Adams, lieutenant-colonel 7th regiment;

Thomas Wolford, lieutenant-colonel 2d regiment;

John E. Howard, lieutenant-colonel;

John Stewart, major;

John Dean, major;

Archibald Anderson, major;

Henry Hardman, captain;

A. Grosh, captain;

Thomas Lansdale, captain;

Harry Dobson, captain;

William D. Beale, captain;

Jonathan Sellman, captain;

Alexander Trueman, captain;

Joseph Marbury, captain;

Jacob Brice, captain;

John Smith, captain;

William Wilmott, captain;

Alexander Roxburgh, captain;

Henry Gaither, captain;

Edward Oldman, captain;

Richard Anderson, captain;

Edward Pratt, captain;

George Hamilton, captain;

Levin Handy, captain;

Walker Mun, captain;

John James,

John Carr,

Nicholas Gassaway,

Charles Smith,

R. N. Walker,

Lloyd Beall,

Richard McAlister,

James Brain,

Ed. Edgerly,

John J. Jacob,

James Ewing,

Wm. Lamar,

Wm. Woolford,

Charles Beaven,

John Hartshorn,

John M. Hamilton,

James Gould,

J. J. Skinner,

Richard Donovan,

John Gibson,

T. B. Hugan,

Gassaway Watkins,

W. Adams,

George Jacobs,

John Mitchell,

Philip Theid,

Edward Moran,

Thomas Price, engineer;

Henry Baldwin, quarter-master and engineer;

John Gassaway, lieutenant 2d Maryland regiment;

Samuel Hanson, ensign;

17*

James Woolford Gray, captain;
John Gale, captain;
John Sprigg Belt, captain;
John Smith, captain;
W. Beatty, captain;
J. C. Jones, captain;
John Davidson, captain;
John Jordan, captain;
James Somervell, captain-lieutenant;
Benjamin Price, captain-lieutenant;
Frederick Foird, captain-lieutenant;
George Armstrong, captain-lieutenant; and lieutenants;
Francis Reveley,
Nicholas Mamges,
Samuel Farmer,
Osborn Williams,
Isaac Duall,

Hezekiah Ford, ensign;
John Dorsey, surgeon 5th Maryland Regiment;
Thomas Parran, surgeon 6th regiment;
William Kiltz, assistant surgeon 5th regiment;
John Hamilton, paymaster and lieutenant, 4th Maryland regiment.
Richard Pindell, surgeon, 4th Maryland regiment;
Christopher Richmond, paymaster and lieutenant;
Benjamin Garnett, engineer;
James Woulds, adjutant;
W. Warfield, assistant surgeon, 6th regiment;
Robert Denny, engineer and paymaster, 7th regiment.

The legislature met on July 22, and after considering the address of the officers passed an act " relating to the officers and soldiers of this State in the American army." This measure provided that as the officers were bearing the heaviest burdens of the war with a pay that scarcely supplied them with the necessaries of life, and as most of them were now so reduced in means as to be dependent upon the gratuity of the state, each of the commissioned and staff officers of the Maryland Line and of the state troops in the Continental army was to be allowed every year during the war, at a fixed price, " four good shirts and a complete uniform, suitable to his station." They were also to be allowed tea, coffee, chocolate, sugar, rum, soap and tobacco, in certain portions, to be dealt out by the day and month. During that year, in lieu of these, they were to receive $2,000. The non-commissioned officers and privates were also to be given an allowance in rum and tobacco, which, for the year 1779, was commuted at £20 currency for each man. The act also provided that those who should enlist in a Maryland regiment to serve for three years, or during the war, should receive, in addition to the bounties provided by congress and the state, a hat, a pair of shoes, stockings and overalls.

CHAPTER XIX.

FORWARDING THE CAUSE AT HOME.

WHILE the Maryland troops were upholding the honor of the State in the field, those at home, the non-combatants, were doing their part to forward the patriotic cause. A feeling of patriotism was manifested everywhere among all classes, and in many instances those who could not very well afford it sacrificed the necessaries of life to contribute towards the support of the troops in the field. Everything that was possible was done to assist in the struggle and privations were endured by those at home as well as by those in camp. Patriotic sentiments were expressed on all sides. Scharf[145] gives a copy of a letter supposed to

[145] "History of Western Maryland," Vol. II., p. 1035. The letter is as follows:

To Capt. William Heyser, at the American Camp, Philadelphia. *Dear Father*

Through the mercies of almighty God, I my Mamma, my brother and

have been written to Captain William Heyser by his son, aged nine years. While the sentiments expressed in the letter were no doubt those entertained by almost everyone yet the letter itself is scarcely one such as would be written by a nine-year old boy.

Many of the German settlers in western Maryland had conscientious scruples against war and these people were averse to enlisting in the army and taking an active part in the war, but they contributed of their means, many of them liberally. Military stores, gunpowder, guns and cannon, were manufactured at a number of places, and supplies of various kinds also contributed. At a meeting of the Committee of Observation for that part of Frederick county which is now Washington county, held at Elizabeth Town (Hagerstown) on April 8, 1776, the following communication was received from the Council of Safety:

Sisters are well, in hopes these may find you enjoying these Felicities, which tend to happiness in life, and everlasting Happiness in Eternity your long absence and great distance is the only matter of our trouble, but our sincere Prayers, is for your Welfare and Prosperity, begging that God may prosper you, and your united Brethren, in your laudable undertaking, and in the end crown you with the laurels of a Complete victory, over the Enemies of the inestimable Rights, Liberties, and Privileges of distressed America, and hand them down inviolate, to the latest Posterity. My Dear father, my greatest Grief is, that I am incapable of the military Service, that I might enjoy the company of so loving a father, and serve my country in so glorious a cause, but tho' absent from you yet my constant prayer is for your Safety, in the Hour of danger, your complete victory, over the Enemies, of the united States of America, and your Safe Restoration to the government of your family. I and my brother Jacob Continue at School, and hope to give a full Satisfaction, to our parents, and friends in our regular conduct, and Progress in learning, my Mamma, my brother and Sister do join me in their Prayers and well wishes for you.

I am Dr. Father your most dutiful and obedt Son,

Hagers Town   WILLIAM HEYSER

October 12th

1776

In Council of Safety, Annapolis,
March 23, 1776.

Gentlemen:—The great difficulty we find in providing blankets for the regular forces raised for the defence of this province obliges us to apply to the committee of observation for the several counties and districts, earnestly requesting that they would use their endeavors to procure from the housekeepers in their respective counties and districts all the blankets or rugs that they can with any convenience spare, for which the council will pay such prices as the committees shall agree on, as well as any expense that may arise in collecting them together; and when you have procured any quantity, you will send them to Annapolis, to Col. Smallwood, or, in his absence, to the commanding officer on this station, who will receive the same, and give orders on the council for the payment thereof.

We hope that the friends to our cause in the county will contribute everything in their power to the comfortable subsistence of the soldiery in this respect; it will be an act of great humanity, and render an essential service to the public.

We are, Gentlemen, your most O^bt servants. By order.

DANIEL, of St. Thos., JENNIFER, P.

The proceedings of the Committee then go on to state[146]

In consequence of the preceding letter from the honorable the council of safety of this province, we have, agreeably to their request, furnished them with what quantity of blankets and rugs the inhabitants of this district can with any convenience spare, and a price estimated on them by this committee as follows:

	£ s. d.		£ s. d.
William Baird, 1 blanket...	0 17 6	John Ingram, 1 blanket....	0 15 0
John Parks, 1 rug.........	0 12 0	Adam Grimer, 2 blankets	1 18 0
Andrew Rench, 1 blanket...	0 12 6	Wm. Douglass, 1 blanket...	0 10 0
Simon Myer, " ...	0 15 0	Matthias Need, 1 blanket...	0 12 0

[146] Scharf's "History of Western Maryland," Vol. I., p. 134.

Philip Rymeby, 3 coverlets..	2 10 0	
Geo. Fry, 1 blanket........	0 7 6	
Felty Safety, 1 blanket.....	0 5 0	
Jacob Lazear, "	... 0 12 6	
Joseph Birely, 1 coverlet...	1 8 0	
" " 1 blanket...	0 5 0	
Richard Davis, "	... 0 10 0	
Thos. Prather, "	... 0 18 0	
Ch'n Rhorer, "	... 0 10 0	
Leonard Shryock, "	... 0 12 0	
Robert Guthrie, 1 coverlet..	1 10 0	
Christian Miller, "	... 1 10 0	
Jacob Prunk, 1 blanket....	0 14 0	
Jacob Rohrer, "	... 0 12 6	
Ellen Miller, "	... 0 9 0	
Chas. Swearingen, 1 blanket.	0 10 0	
Ch'n Eversole, "	... 0 9 0	
" " 1 quilt......	0 15 0	
" " 1 coverlet...	0 17 6	

Michael Ott, 1 blanket.....	0 5 0	
John Feagen, "	... 0 16 0	
" " "	... 0 16 0	
Jerentiah Wells, "	... 0 10 0	
Joseph Rench, "	... 0 11 0	
Zach'h Spires, "	... 0 10 0	
Matthias Nead, "	... 0 10 0	
Henry Startzman, "	... 0 12 0	
George Swingly, "	... 0 16 0	
George Hoffman, "	... 0 7 6	
Jacob Brumbaugh, "	...21 3 0	
Michael Miller, "	...42 17 0	
George Hartte, "	... 0 18 0	
John Roltrer, "	...20 10 0	
Christ'r Burgard, "	... 0 12 0	
Jacob Good, 1 rug........	0 16 0	
John Rench, 1 blanket.....	0 12 0	
John Stull, "	... 0 14 0	

Received of Conrad Sheitz forty-four blankets for the use of this province, which were delivered him by the committee of Observation of Elizabeth Town district.

Received by me this 12th day of April, 1776.

GEO. STRICKER.

While there were some of the inhabitants of Maryland who remained loyal to Great Britain, the majority of them, particularly among the Germans, were on the side of the patriots, and they were ever on the alert to detect any treasonable designs on the part of the Tories, and owing to their vigilance they were frequently able to frustrate well-laid plans which might have resulted seriously for the American cause. One of the most notable of these was that concocted by Dr. John Connolly, which was frustrated by some of the Germans of western Maryland. Connolly was a native of Lancaster county, Pennsylvania, where he became a physician. After taking part in the French and

Indian War, he spent some time with various Indian tribes, accompanying them on long marches into unexplored territory, and finally settled at Pittsburgh. When the Revolutionary War began he remained loyal to Great Britain. While at Pittsburgh he met Lord Dunmore, governor of Virginia, and when the latter was making strenuous efforts to help the royal cause he found an able ally in Connolly. A plan was formed by which Connolly, through his intimacy with the Indians, was to incite them to a war upon the frontiers, and to raise an army in Canada and the western settlements. Dunmore sent Connolly to General Gage, who commanded at Boston, with the following proposals:

Proposals for raising an Army to the Westward, and for effectually obstructing a Communication between the Southern and Northern Governments.

As I have, by direction from his Excellency Lord Dunmore, prepared the Ohio Indians to act in concert with me against his Majesty's enemies in that quarter, and have also dispatched intelligence to the different officers of the militia on the frontiers of Augusta County, in Virginia, giving them Lord Dunmore's assurances that such of them as shall hereafter evince their loyalty to his Majesty by putting themselves under my command, when I shall appear among them with proper authority for that purpose, of a confirmation of titles to their lands, and the quantity of three hundred acres to all who should take up arms in the support of the constitution, when the present rebellion subsided, I will undertake to penetrate through Virginia, and join his Excellency Lord Dunmore at Alexandria early next spring, on the following conditions and authority:

1st. That your Excellency will give me a commission to act as Major-commandant of such troops as I may raise and embody on the frontiers, with a power to command to the westward and employ such serviceable French and English partisans as I can employ by pecuniary rewards or otherwise.

2d. That your Excellency will give orders to Captain Lord on the Illinois to remove himself, with the garrison under his command, from Fort Gage to Detroit, by the Aubache, bringing with him all the artillery, stores, &c., &c., to facilitate which undertaking he is to have authority to hire boats, horses, Frenchmen, Indians, &c., &c., to proceed with all possible expedition on that route, as the weather may occasionally permit, and to put himself under my command on his arrival at Detroit.

3d. That the commissary at Detroit shall be empowered to furnish such provision as I may judge necessary for the good of the service, and that the commanding officer shall be instructed to give every possible assistance in encouraging the French and Indians of that settlement to join me.

4th. That an officer of artillery be immediately sent with me to pursue such route as I may find most expedient to gain Detroit, with orders to have such pieces of light ordnance as may be thought requisite for the demolishing of Fort Dunmore and Fort Fincastle, if resistance should be made by the rebels in possession of those garrisons.

5th. That your Excellency will empower me to make such reasonable presents to the Indian chiefs and others as may urge them to act with vigor in the execution of my orders.

6th. That your Excellency will send to Lord Dunmore such arms as may be spared, in order to equip such persons as may be willing to serve his Majesty at our junction, in the vicinity of Alexandria, &c., &c. If your Excellency judges it expedient for the good of the service to furnish me with the authority and other requisites I have mentioned, I shall embrace the earliest opportunity of setting off for Canada, and shall immediately dispatch Lord Dunmore's armed schooner, which now awaits my commands, with an account of what your Excellency has done, and that I shall be ready, if practicable, to join your Lordship by the twentieth of April, at Alexandria, where the troops under my command may fortify themselves under the cover of the men of war on that station.

If, on the contrary, your Excellency should not approve of what I propose, you will be good enough to immediately honor me with your dispatches to the Earl of Dunmore, that I may return as early as possible.

General Gage approved the plan, and in October, 1775, Connolly again joined Dunmore, who in accordance with instructions from General Gage, gave him a commission as lieutenant-colonel commandant of the Queen's Royal Rangers, to be raised "in the back parts and Canada." On November 13th Connolly left Dunmore and started for Detroit. He was accompanied by Dr. John Smith and Allan Cameron. The former was a Scotchman who lived on Port Tobacco creek, in Charles county, Maryland. Connolly had induced him to accept a commission as surgeon in the proposed expedition. Cameron was also a Scotchman who had left home on account of a duel and had come to Virginia with the intention of purchasing lands in that colony. He served for some time as deputy Indian agent in South Carolina, but having suffered much abuse there for his loyalty to the crown, and having gained some notoriety on account of a plan to incite the Creek and Cherokee Indians to fall on the colonists,[147] he readily engaged to join the party, being promised a commission as lieutenant.

The party set out in a flat-bottomed boat, intending to go up the Potomac and disembark near the home of Dr. Smith and from that point proceed on horseback. A storm drove them into the St. Mary's river and from that point they went forward on horseback. They had almost

---

[147] Steiner, "Western Maryland in the Revolution," p. 40.

passed the frontier when, on November 19, they stopped at a tavern about five miles from Hagerstown. Here Connolly was recognized and as information concerning his plans had been received a day or two before through a letter written by Connolly to a friend in Pittsburgh, the party was placed under arrest. They were taken to Hagerstown and the next day were brought before the Committee of Observation who ordered them sent to the Committee of Safety. They were taken to Frederick where their baggage was thoroughly examined and incriminating papers were found, although Connolly's commission and other important papers had been concealed in hollow pillion sticks and thus escaped detection and were later destroyed by Connolly's servant. Smith made his escape but was recaptured, and on the order of John Hancock, president of Congress, the three prisoners were sent to Philadelphia. Connolly, in a "Narrative of the Transactions, Imprisonment and sufferings of John Connolly, an American Loyalist and Lieutenant-Colonel in His Majesty's Service,"[148] has left an account of this expedition, while Smith tells of some of the incidents attending their capture.[149] He says that when they were taken to Frederick two musicians, with drum and fife, marched ahead of them playing the rogue's march. On reaching Frederick they were taken before "a committee which consisted of a tailor, a leather breeches maker, a shoemaker, a gingerbread maker, a butcher, and two tavern keepers. The majority were Germans and I was subjected to a very remarkable hearing, as follows:

"One said 'You infernal rascal, how darsht you make

[148] *Pennsylvania Magazine of History and Biography*, Vol. XII., pp. 310, 407; Vol. XIII., pp. 61, 153, 281.

[149] "A Tour through the U. S. of America," by J. D. F. Smyth.

an exshkape from this honorable committee?' 'Der fluchter Dyvel,' cried another, 'how can you shtand so shtyff for king Shorsh akainst dis koontry. 'Sacrament,' yelled another, 'dis committee will let Shorsh know how to behave himself,' and the butcher exclaimed, 'I would kill all the English tieves, as soon as ich would kill an ox or a cow.' "

While there were a number of Tories among the citizens of Maryland there were very few to be found among the German settlers. These, as a rule, were ardent patriots, and there were few instances where Germans were arrested as Tories. There was, however, one notable exception.

In 1781 another plan was formed by the British and Tories for dividing the northern colonies from the southern. According to this scheme Cornwallis was to march inland from the Chesapeake and meet the bands of Tories which were to be raised and armed in the interior. In maturing their plans it was arranged that a disguised British officer was to meet a Tory at a point in Frederick county to put him in possession of all the plans of the conspirators. But it so happened that an American officer was at the appointed place and the Tory's papers fell into his hands, revealing the plot and the names of the conspirators. The latter were arrested. Among them were a number of Germans: Peter Sueman, Nicholas Andrews, John George Graves, Yost Plecker, Adam Graves, Henry Shett, and Casper Fritchie. On July 25 these seven were placed on trial before a special court at Frederick, consisting of Alexander Contee Hanson, afterwards Chancellor of the State, Col. James Johnson and Upton Sheredine. The seven were found guilty of high treason in "enlisting men for the service of the king of Great Britain and administering an oath to them to bear true allegiance to the said king, and to obey his officers when called upon." Judge Hanson then sentenced the men as follows :[150]

Peter Sueman, Nicholas Andrews, John George Graves, Yost Plecker, Adam Graves, Henry Shett, Casper Fritchie, attend. It has been suggested to the court that notwithstanding your guilt has been ascertained by an impartial jury, you consider the proceedings against you nothing more than solemn mockery, and have adopted a vain idea, propagated by the enemies of this country, that she dare not punish her unnatural subjects for engaging in the service of Great Britain. From the strange insensibility you have heretofore discovered, I was indeed led to conclude that you were under a delusion, which might prove fatal to your prospects of happiness hereafter. I think it is my duty, therefore, to explain to you your real situation. The crime you have been convicted of, upon the fullest and clearest testimony, is of such a nature that you cannot, ought not, to look for a pardon. Had it pleased heaven to permit the full execution of your unnatural designs, the miseries to be experienced by your devoted country would have been dreadful even in the contemplation. The ends of public justice, the dictates of policy, and the feelings of humanity all require that you should exhibit an awful example to your fellow-subjects, and the dignity of the State, with everything that can interest the heart of man, calls aloud for your punishment. If the consideration of approaching fate can inspire proper sentiments, you will pour forth your thanks to that watchful Providence which has arrested you at an early date of your guilt. And you will employ the short time you have to live in endeavoring, by a sincere penitence, to obtain pardon from the Almighty Being, who is to sit in judgment upon you, upon me, and all mankind.

I must now perform the terrible task of denouncing the terrible punishment ordained for high treason.

You, Peter Sueman, Nicholas Andrews, Yost Plecker, Adam Graves, Henry Shett, John George Graves, and Casper Fritchie,

[150] Scharf's "History of Western Maryland," Vol. I., p. 143.

and each of you, attend to your sentence. You shall be carried to the gaol of Fredericktown, and be hanged therein; you shall be cut down to the earth alive, and your entrails shall be taken out and burnt while you are yet alive, your heads shall be cut off, your body shall be divided into four parts, and your heads and quarters shall be placed where his excellency the Governor shall appoint. So Lord have mercy upon your poor souls.

Four of these men were pardoned, the other three being executed in the court-house yard at Frederick. One of those executed was Casper Fritchie, the father of John Casper Fritchie, who was the husband of Barbara Fritchie, the heroine of Whittier's poem.[151]

With the close of the Revolutionary War the inhabitants of the western part of Maryland settled down to a peaceful life, turning all their energies to the development of the country. The population increased rapidly. Many of the Hessians who had come to fight the colonists took up land in that section and became their neighbors. Many emigrants came to Maryland from Germany without first stopping in Pennsylvania, so that the additions to the population lost the distinctively Pennsylvania-German type, but the influence of the first settlers was never lost.

Two hundred years have passed since the first Germans from Pennsylvania made their way through the trackless wilderness of Maryland: two hundred years which have seen that wilderness blossom into one of the fairest gardens

[151] Barbara Fritchie was a Pennsylvania-German. She was born in Lancaster, Pa., December 3, 1766, the daughter of Nicholas and Catherine Hauer. Although it has been conclusively shown that there is no foundation in fact for the incident given in Whittier's poem, yet, like the equally mythical story of Betsy Ross and the flag, the tale will no doubt continue to find believers in its authenticity.

on earth. Through the trials and sufferings of those early pioneers the foundations were laid upon which has arisen an empire, than which no more enduring monument to their memory could be erected. Their descendants have continued the work so well begun and have spread out and helped to conquer new fields and make them add to the wealth of the nation. To the south and west this stream of emigration made its way unceasingly. It would be impossible to particularize, but there is no part of the country, from the Atlantic to the Pacific, and from the Gulf to the frozen borders on the north, where the descendants of those early German settlers of Maryland cannot be found. Many of them have set their mark high in the record of the world's progress: in science, in art, in mechanics, in whatever makes for the betterment of mankind, and in reaching high honors themselves have honored the memory of those brave men and women who, leaving behind them all the comforts of civilization, and taking their lives in their hands, carved out a home in the forests of the western continent.

INDEX TO PROPER NAMES.

18*

Roemer, 99
Roessell, 93
Rogers, 149
Rohhbaugh, 237
Rohrbach, 237
Rohrback, 102
Rohrer, 118, 263
Roltrer, 263
Rolwagen, 225
Römer, 98
Rommelsem, 237
Romsburg, 188
Ronenberger, 227
Rorer, 175
Rosen, 61
Ross, 161, 211
Roth, 235
Rothe, 234
Rough, 174
Roullett, 102
Rout, 161
Roxburgh, 257
Row, 180, 206
Rowin, 218
Rowlands, 239
Rowlins, 217
Rudisiel, 93
Rudrieck, 216
Ruetenik, 103
Rumfell, 228
Rumfield, 237
Rummelson, 226
Runkel, 100
Ruppert, 228
Russ, 218
Rutlidge, 222
Rutt, 40
Ruttzn, 21
Ryan, 209
Ryley, 222
Rymeby, 263

Sachse, 27, 29

Sadler, 25
Safety, 263
Saffle, 211
Saftly, 221
Sahm, 61
Sailor, 234
Salmon, 213
Sam, 100, 101
Sands, 221
Sangar, 137
Sanglaer, 134
Sappor, 117
Sarjeant, 219
Saylor, 105, 236
Schaaf, 61, 188, 190
Schaefer, 93
Schaeffer, 225, 232
Schantz, 114
Scharf, 9, 54, 62, 87, 102, 104, 154, 167, 171, 179, 260
Schaub, 93
Schauffle, 93
Scherer, 41
Schesler, 232
Schilders, 22
Schippe, 25
Schister, 105
Schlatter, 51, 94, 95, 99, 115
Schleitz, 118
Schley, 56, 99, 114, 183, 188, 222
Schmauk, 92, 103
Schmidt, 61, 98
Schmit, 40
Schmucker, 104, 105
Schnebly, 105
Scholl, 40
Schorcht, 232
Schrawder, 225
Schreier, 232
Schreyer, 93
Schriver, 188, 190, 193
Schroder, 105

INDEX TO SUBJECTS

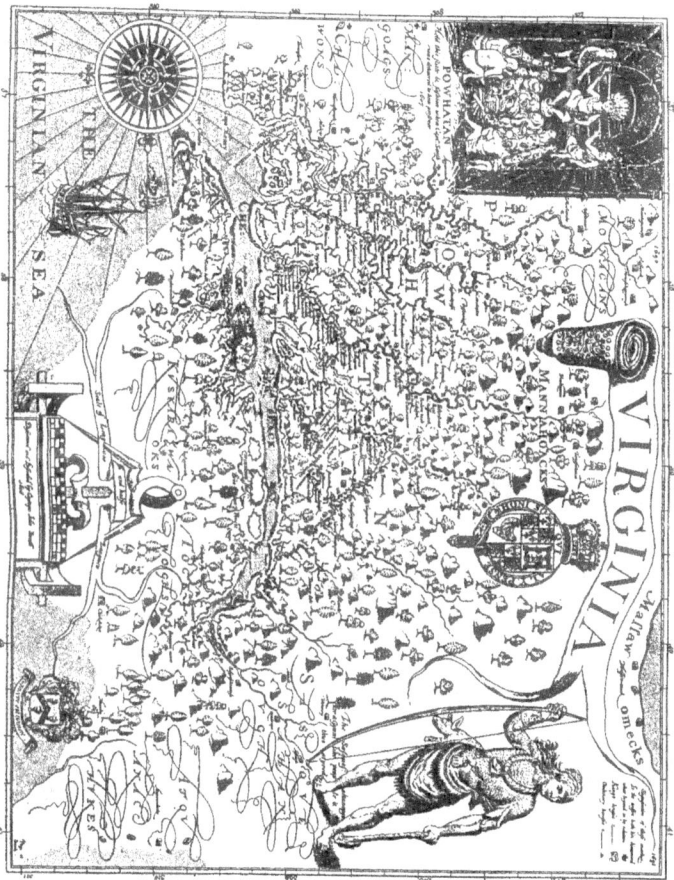

CAPTAIN JOHN SMITH'S MAP OF VIRGINIA, 1606.

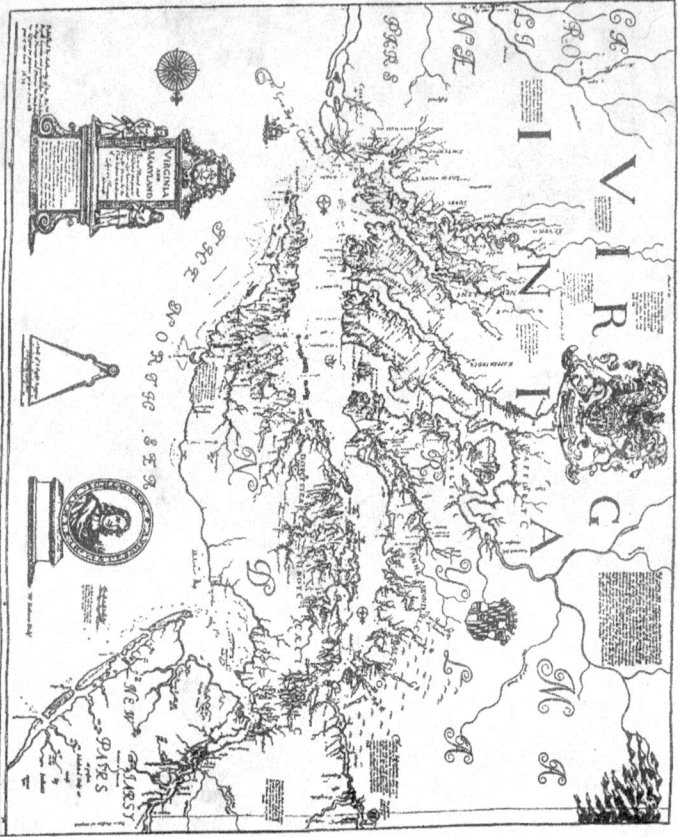

AUGUSTINE HERMAN'S MAP, 1670.

Other Heritage Books by Don Heinrich Tolzmann:

Amana: William Rufus Perkins' and Barthinius L. Wick's History of the Amana Society, or Community of True Inspiration

Americana Germanica: Paul Ben Baginsky's Bibliography of German Works Relating to America, 1493-1800

Biography of Baron Von Steuben, the Army of the American Revolution and Its Organizer: Rudolf Cronau's Biography of Baron von Steuben

CD: German-American Biographical Index (Midwest Families)

CD: Germans, Volume 2

CD: The German Colonial Era (four volumes)

Cincinnati's German Heritage

Covington's German Heritage

Custer: Frederick Whittaker's Complete Life of General George A. Custer, Major General of Volunteers, Brevet Major General U.S. Army and Lieutenant-Colonel Seventh U.S. Cavalry

Dayton's German Heritage: Karl Karstaedt's Golden Jubilee History of the German Pioneer Society of Dayton, Ohio

Early German-American Newspapers: Daniel Miller's History

German Americans in the Revolution

German Immigration to America: The First Wave

German Pioneer Life and Domestic Customs

German Pioneer Lifestyle

German Pioneers in Early California: Erwin G. Gudde's History

German-American Achievements: 400 Years of Contributions to America

German-Americana: A Bibliography

Germany and America, 1450-1700

Kentucky's German Pioneers: H.A. Rattermann's History

Lives and Exploits of the Daring Frank and Jesse James: Thaddeus Thorndike's Graphic and Realistic Description of Their Many Deeds of Unparalleled Daring in the Robbing of Banks and Railroad Trains

Louisiana's German Heritage: Louis Voss' Introductory History

Maryland's German Heritage: Daniel Wunderlich Nead's History

Memories of the Battle of New Ulm: Personal Accounts of the Sioux Uprising. L. A. Fritsche's History of Brown County, Minnesota (1916)

Michigan's German Heritage: John Andrew Russell's History of the German Influence in the Making of Michigan

Ohio's German Heritage

Outbreak and Massacre by the Dakota Indians in Minnesota in 1862: Marion P. Satterlee's Minute Account of the Outbreak, with Exact Locations, Names of All Victims, Prisoners at Camp Release, Refugees at Fort Ridgely, etc. Complete List of Indians Killed in Battle and Those Hung, and Those Pardoned at Rock Island, Iowa

The German Element in Virginia: Herrmann Schuricht's History

The German Immigrant in America

The Pennsylvania Germans: James Owen Knauss, Jr.'s Social History

The Pennsylvania Germans: Jesse Leonard Rosenberger's Sketch of Their History and Life